Myra Reynolds

The Treatment of Nature in English Poetry Between Pope and Wordsworth

Myra Reynolds

The Treatment of Nature in English Poetry Between Pope and Wordsworth

ISBN/EAN: 9783337033392

Printed in Europe, USA, Canada, Australia, Japan

Cover: Foto ©Thomas Meinert / pixelio.de

More available books at **www.hansebooks.com**

OF

NATURE IN ENGLISH POETRY

BETWEEN POPE AND WORDSWORTH

SUBMITTED TO THE FACULTY OF ARTS, LITERATURE, AND SCIENCE,
OF THE UNIVERSITY OF CHICAGO, IN CANDIDACY FOR
THE DEGREE OF DOCTOR OF PHILOSOPHY

BY

MYRA REYNOLDS

CHICAGO
The University of Chicago Press
1896

TABLE OF CONTENTS

INTRODUCTION.

The general theme of the treatment of nature in literature is not a new one. Schiller's essay entitled "Ueber die Naive und Sentimentale Dichtung" (1794), was the <u>first attempt</u> to state and explain the difference between the classical way of looking at nature and the modern way. The externality, the lack of heart, in the classical attitude towards nature, he attributed to the fact that the Greeks were in their thoughts and habits of life so a part of nature that they felt no impulse to seek her with the passionate longing of the modern poet, whose ardent and heartfelt love of nature is but the result of a mode of thought and life out of harmony with her. This essay, however inadequate as a presentation of the Greek attitude towards nature,[1] determined the lines on which much of succeeding study was made.

Introductory statement

Alexander von Humboldt in his *Kosmos* (1845–58), in the midst of his scientific generalizations and his encyclopædic accumulation of natural facts takes occasion to discuss the treatment of nature in poetry and landscape painting. The chapter on landscape painting is chiefly confined to such topographical, botanical, and other pictorial representations as serve to add to our knowledge of distant lands. The boundaries of the whole question are enlarged by a representation of the profound feeling for nature in Semitic and Indo-European races. There is a brief study of the mediæval feeling for nature as it appears in Dante, and finally of the treatment of nature in some prose writers of

[1] Humboldt was the first to attack Schiller's view. He said that after a full reading of Greek and Roman authors he found himself unable to accept Schiller's statement without many reservations. Later Biese spoke of Schiller's Essay as "*jener bahnbrechende Aufsatz*," but showed that the statement of the case was inadequate because it was based on the poetry of a single period and thus failed entirely to take account of many phases of nature presented in the poetry after the brief "*reflexionslose naive homerische Zeit.*"

the eighteenth century. The only English poets mentioned are Shakespeare, Thomson, and Byron, the whole subject of English poetry being disposed of in less than a page.

In Ruskin's *Modern Painters* (1843-60) are several most interesting chapters on Landscape in classical, mediæval, and modern times. "Of the Pathetic Fallacy" and "The Moral of Landscape" are also suggestive though misleading studies.

Victor de Laprade's *La Sentiment de la Nature* (1866, 1868) contains in full the theories already suggested in the preface to his *Les Symphones*. In the introductory chapters he outlines his conception of the development of art. He regards architecture as essentially the expression of man's interest in religion ; sculpture of his interest in the demi-god or hero ; painting of his interest in the complex and varied life of man as man ; while the characteristic art of the present age is music with which the love of nature is closely allied, since both affect the mind indirectly through indeterminate and vaguely suggestive harmonies, and both tend by their complexity and subtlety to rouse sweet reveries, luxurious emotion, nameless longings, ineffectual aspirations, but leave the conscience and the will untouched. No one can read these critical studies of Laprade or his earlier poems without feeling his enthusiastic joy in the presence of nature. But he feared this joy and counted it a part of the concupiscence of the flesh except as it became an avenue to communion with the divine spirit. His indictment against the passion for nature in modern music, painting, poetry, fiction, science, is that the material is everywhere exalted at the expense of the spiritual. To be of value the presentation of the external world in whatever realm of art must subordinate its appeal to the senses, and emphasize its appeal to man's inner life. Laprade's work is a plea for idealism as against realism. In all his brilliant presentation of the attitude towards external nature of different races in different epochs, this point of view must be taken into account. In his rapid survey of English poetry the poets to receive closest attention are Shakespeare, Spenser, and Milton. In later times the most significant of the poets who "*gravitent antour de Lord Byron*" are Wordsworth and Shelley, who, in their attitude towards nature, are respectively moralist and metaphysician. Byron's distinction is that he alone found " *le juste équilibre entre l'exubérance de la nature et celle du pur esprit.*" Thomson's *Seasons* are of value because of good *genre* pictures and vivid descriptions of English sports, but the initial force in the return to nature is Burns.

Unquestionably the most important of the books that treat of nature in the realm of art is Biese's *Die Entwickelung des Naturge-fühls im Mittelalter und in der Neuzeit* (1888).[1] The book is written with enthusiasm and is most stimulating and suggestive. The subject matter is well in hand, and so thoroughly organized that the great movements in the historical development of the love of nature are easily grasped. The plan is comprehensive, including not only poetry, but, in briefer outline, landscape painting and gardening, and, incidentally, even fiction and philosophy. The least satisfactory portion of the book is the treatment of the love of nature in English life and thought. There is some stress on the development of the English garden, but English landscape painting is not mentioned. In the casual mention of English fiction the emphasis is on Defoe. In poetry two epochs are recognized, that of Shakespeare and that of Byron. The chapter on Shakespeare is a close and valuable study. The work of Byron is estimated with justness and sympathy, as is also that of Shelley. But the study of Wordsworth as a poet of nature is singularly inadequate. His genius is considered as essentially of the pastoral-idyllic order, with now and then glimpses of an " *echte Liebe für die Natur,*" and an unmistakable Pantheism. He is chiefly important as having done for England what Scott did for Scotland and Moore for Ireland and as sounding certain notes which rang again in Byron " *in verstärkter Tonart.*" Thomson is the only eighteenth century poet studied. Here again is a failure to recognize the real importance of the poet's

[1] Biese has two earlier important books: *Die Entwickelung des Natur-gefühls bei den Griechen* (1882) and *Die Entwickelung des Naturgefühls bei den Römern* (1884). In *Zeitschrift für vergleichende Litteraturgeschichte, Neue Folge, Siebenter Band* (1894), p. 311, is a valuable annotated summary of recent (since 1882) German studies on *das antike und das deutsche Naturgefühl.*

work. Biese acknowledges the truth of Thomson's separate pictures of nature, and his genuine love of the country, but denies his importance as a "pathfinder," saying that he but followed where Pope's *Pastorals* and *Windsor Forest* had marked out the way.

In 1887 appeared John Veitch's *The Feeling for Nature in Scottish Poetry*. The first volume begins with the early romances and national epics, and takes up the chief poets down to James VI. The second volume is devoted to the modern period from Ramsay to David Gray. Most of the authors treated belong to the nineteenth century, but there are admirable brief studies of Ramsay, Thomson, Hamilton of Bangour, Bruce, Fergusson, and Burns. There is also a short but interesting chapter on the rise of landscape painting, with especial attention to its development in Scotland. Veitch's book is written out of a full knowledge and warm appreciation of Scottish poetry and of Scottish nature, and his critical dicta are usually trustworthy, though he shows, perhaps, a tendency to over-emphasize the influence of Scottish poetry on the love of nature in succeeding English poetry.

In John Campbell Shairp's *Poetic Interpretation of Nature* (1889) are studies of Homer, Lucretius, and Virgil; of Chaucer, Shakespeare, and Milton; and of Wordsworth. Two chapters are devoted to the eighteenth century. Ramsay is the poet to whom the reappearance of the feeling for natural beauty is traced. Thomson is praised for his minute faithfulness in description, and his genuine love of the country, but his tawdry diction and superficial conception of nature are heavy indictments against him. The chapter on Collins, Gray, Goldsmith, Burns, Cowper, Ossian, and the Ballads is interesting, but from its brevity is necessarily inadequate. The most suggestive chapter in the book is the one in which there is a classification of the ways in which poets deal with nature.[1] The whole subject of the treatment of nature in poetry is an attractive one to Mr. Shairp, and he fre-

---

[1] (*a*) They express childlike delight in the open-air world. (*b*) They use nature as the background or setting to human action or emotion. (*c*) They see nature through historic coloring. (*d*) They make nature sympathize with their

quently recurs to it in his *Studies in Poetry and Philosophy* and *Aspects of Poetry*.

In many books, also, not devoted exclusively to the treatment of nature in literature there are special studies and much running comment of a valuable sort. This is true of almost all essays on the early nineteenth century poets, and especially so of the various essays on Wordsworth. There is something to be found in Manuals of English Literature, as in Gosse's *Eighteenth Century* in the chapter, "The Dawn of Naturalism," in various notes in Perry's *English Literature of the Eighteenth Century*, Phelps's *The English Romantic Movement*, and others; also, in some histories, as in Lecky's *History of England in the Eighteenth Century;* in some philosophical studies, as in Leslie Stephen's *English Thought in the Eighteenth Century* ("The Literary Reaction"), and in Stopford Brooke's *Theology in the English Poets* (*passim*); in various literary studies, as in McLaughlin's *Studies in Mediæval Life and Literature* ("The Mediæval Feeling for Nature"), Vernon Lee's *Euphorion* ("The Outdoor Poetry"), Symonds's *Essays Speculative and Suggestive* ("Landscape") ("Nature Myths and Allegories"), Burroughs's *Fresh Fields* ("Birds and Poets") and Fischer's *Drei Studien zur Englischen Litteraturgeschichte* ("*Uber den Einfluss der See auf die Englische Litteratur*").

The books indicated show that there is much interest in the general theme of nature as an element of art. The literary periods that have been most studied are, however, the Greek and Roman, the mediæval, and the modern. The treatment of nature in so barren a time as the eighteenth century in England has naturally received little close attention. In my own work on this period I have endeavored to discover what indications there are that the attitude toward nature of the early nineteenth century is but the legitimate outcome of influences actively at work during the eighteenth century. This study is therefore one of origins.

I have divided my work into three parts. I have endeavored

own feelings. (*e*) They dwell upon the Inhuman or Infinite side of nature. (*f*) They give description for its own sake. (*g*) They interpret nature by imaginative sympathy. (*h*) They use nature as a symbol of spirit.

to give first a general statement of the chief characteristics that marked the treatment of nature under the dominance of the English classical poets. Then follows a detailed study of such eighteenth century poets as show some new conception of nature. The third division is made up of briefer studies of the landscape gardening, the fiction, the books of travel, and the painting of the eighteenth century, the purpose being to determine in how far the spirit found in the poetry reveals itself in other realms in which the love of nature might be expected to find expression.

CHAPTER I.

THE TREATMENT OF NATURE IN ENGLISH CLASSICAL POETRY.

The poetry of the English classical period falls naturally into four subdivisions.

Subdivisions of classical period

1. The period of inception may be reckoned as beginning with Waller's first couplets in 1621 and including the work of his followers, Denham, Davenant, and Cowley.[1]

2. The period of establishment includes the work between the Restoration and 1700. Dryden is the central figure.

3. The period of culmination is a brief period covering less than the first quarter of the eighteenth century. Pope is the central figure.

4. The period of decadence extends from about 1725 to the end of the century.

Any generalizations concerning the attitude of this classical period towards nature must be based on a large number of specific instances, but in collecting and using these specific instances certain cautions must be observed.

Purpose and method in this study

Chief among these is the necessity of keeping in mind the point of view from which the study should be made. It is not the purpose to discover all that has been said about nature by the classical poets between 1623 and 1798. It is the purpose, rather, to eliminate exceptions, and to dwell on the general, obvious qualities, the typical features, of the classical poet's conception of nature. This principle determines the relative importance of the periods noted above. Illustrations drawn from a large number of poems in the second and third periods would serve as the basis for a general statement. Illustrations from periods one and four would need to be

[1] Gosse: From Shakespeare to Pope.

1

scrutinized, for they might be purely classical, or they might be survivals of the Elizabethan romantic age or prophecies of the modern romantic age. Cowley, for instance, belongs to the first classical period because he wrote in couplets, but his diction, his conceits, and in some respects his attitude towards nature are post Elizabethan rather than classical. Illustrations from his poems are of value, therefore, for the present purpose, only when they are in accord with the spirit afterwards found in the time of Dryden and Pope. So, too. Milton and Marvell, though coming chronologically within the first and second periods, stand in the main quite aloof from any tendencies that can be called classical, and their poetry is referred to only when it seems to illustrate the dominant classical conception. Abundant and valuable illustration of the classical conception may be drawn from the fourth period, because tendencies are nowhere more clearly shown than in the inevitable exaggerations of a time of decadence, but the legitimacy of any illustration is determined by its likeness to the dominating traits of the preceding periods. While this study is confined in the main to the poets of the period, Journals, Letters, Travels, and Essays have been sparingly quoted where they serve as proof that the poetry fairly represents the spirit of the age in which it was written.

Pope called Wycherley an "obstinate lover of the town"[1] and the phrase may well be taken to mark one characteristic of the orthodox classicists. Poems, Letters, Journals, Biographies, and Essays bear witness to the reluctance with which the men and women of this age bade farewell to the "dear, damned, distracting town."[2] Charles Lamb's lifelong devotion to Fleet Street and the Strand, and the sentiment of the cockneys who, as Hazlitt said, preferred hanging in London to a natural death out of it,[3] have their true prototypes in the classical age. "When a man is tired of London he is tired of life," is Dr. Johnson's dictum. Gibbon said

Attitude towards nature shown by general preference for city life

---

[1] Pope: Letters, Vol. I, p. 73.
[2] Pope: A Farewell to London, Works, Vol. IV, p. 481.
[3] Hazlitt: On Londoners and Country People.

that when he visited the country it was to see his friends and not
the trees. Boswell's only justification of a hastily expressed lik-
ing for the country was that he had "appropriated the finest
descriptions in the ancient Classicks to certain scenes there."[1] But
not even the classics could reconcile most people to a country
life. It was dreary, monotonous, difficult. There was no
society, no news. The days went yawningly by with no vivid
interests, no stirring occurrences. "No person of sense,"
exclaimed Mr. Mallet's sister, "would live six miles out of Lon-
don."[2] To live in the country was to be buried. Lord Bath-
urst looked upon his sojourn in his country home as a "sound
nap"[3] preparatory to Parliament. "If you wish to know how I
live, or rather lose a life in the country," wrote Pope, "Martial
will inform you in one line :

> Prandeo, poto, cano, ludo, lego, caeno, quiesco."[4]

Pope found pure air and regular hours a physical necessity,
but he often rebelled at his banishment from town delights, as
did his "fond virgin" when compelled to seek wholesome coun-
try air.

> "She went to plain-work, and to purling brooks,
> Old-fashioned halls, dull aunts, and croaking rooks,
> She went from Opera, Park, Assembly, Play,
> To morning walks, and prayers three hours a day ;
> To part the time 'twixt reading and bohea,
> To muse, and spill her solitary tea,
> Or o'er cold coffee trifle with the spoon,
> Count the slow clock, and dine exact at noon."[5]

Isabella in Dryden's *The Wild Gallant* speaks the general senti-
ment : "He I marry must promise me to live at London. I
cannot abide to be in the country, like a wild beast in the wil-
derness :"[6] So, too, Harriet, in *The Man of Mode*, counted all
beyond Hyde Park a desert, and said that her love of the town

[1] Boswell : Life of Dr. Johnson, Vol. III. p. 178 and note.
[2] Pope : Letters, Vol. IV, p. 449.
[3] Pope : Letters, Vol. III, p. 346.
[4] Pope : Letters, Vol. I, p. 67.
[5] Pope : Works, Vol. III, p. 226.
[6] Dryden : Works, Vol. II, p. 74.

was so intense as to make her hate the country even in pictures and hangings.[1] In *Epsom Wells* the apostle of "a pretty innocent country life," is the boor Clodpate, but Lucia assures him that people really live nowhere but in London, for the "insipid dull being" of country folk cannot be called life.[2] It was in much the same spirit that Lady Mary Pierrepont responded to Lord Montagu's proposition that they should live at Wharnecliffe. "Very few people," she said, "that have settled entirely in the country but have grown at length weary of one another." Her preference for town life recurs in her poem, *The Bride in the Country*.

> "By the side of a half rotten wood
> Melantha sat silently down,
> Convinced that her scheme was not good,
> And vexed to be absent from Town.
>
> How simple was I to believe
> Delusive, poetical dreams!
> Or the flattering landscapes they give
> Of meadows and murmuring streams.
> Bleak mountains, and cold starving rocks,
> Are the wretched result of my pains;
> The swains greater brutes than their flocks,
> The nymphs as polite as the swains."[4]

When Shenstone's young squire went forth to London in search of a wife the desired lady declared that she "could breathe nowhere else but in town."[5] Lyttleton's fair maiden finds country life "supinely calm, and dully innocent," and affirms that

> "The town, the Court, is Beauty's proper sphere."[6]

Young's Fulvia had a similar passion for the town.

> "Green fields, and shady groves, and crystal springs,
> And larks, and nightingales, are odious things;

[1] Etherege: The Man of Mode, Act 3, Sc. 1; Act 5, Sc. 3.
[2] Shadwell: Epsom Wells, Act 2, Sc. 1.
[3] Montagu: Letters and Works, Vol. I, p. 72.
[4] Montagu: Letters and Works, Vol II, p. 505.
[5] Shenstone: A Ballad.
[6] Lyttleton: Soliloquy of a Beauty in the Country.

> And smoke, and dust, and noise, and crowds, delight,
> And to be pressed to death, transports her quite." [1]

In Aaron Hill's poems we find a characteristic contest over the respective merits of city and country. Philemon exclaims,

> " Let rustic sports engage the lab'ring hind,
> And cultivated acres plough his mind ;
> Let him to unfrequented woods repair,
> And snuff, unenvy'd, his lean mountain air."

Damon endeavors to defend

> " Th' unglorious preference of a country life "

by calling in evidence Cowley's retirement to the shades, but Philemon triumphantly shows that Cowley's dislike of the town was a clear case of sour grapes. In the end Damon recognizes that it is weak and unmanly to prefer the country.[2] Browne's Celia explains to Chloe that country life may become endurable if one does not give herself up to "dull landscape " but learns to think of the country as "the town in miniature."[3]

Such expressions as these are typical. They indicate the general dislike for any life away from the city. And even those who loved the country, or thought they did, were far enough from caring for any but the tamest of its possible delights. Pope's list of country pleasures, though half humorous, is nevertheless suggestive. In contrast to Mrs. M—'s devotion to " play-houses, parks, assemblies, London," he depicts his own " rapture" in the presence of "gardens, rookeries, fish-ponds, arbours."[4] When Bolingbroke "retired from the Court and glory to his country-seat and wife"[5] he bravely insisted that he liked the change. "Here," he wrote from Dawley, " I shoot strong and tenacious roots. I have caught hold of the earth and neither my enemies nor my friends will find it an easy matter to

[1] Young : Satire V ; On Women.

[2] Aaron Hill : Dialogue between Damon and Philemon.

[3] Isaac Hawkins Browne : From Celia to Chloe.

[4] Pope : Letters, Vol. IV, p. 476. Cf. From Soame Jenyns in the Country to the Lord Lovelace in Town.

[5] Pope : Letters, Vol. IV, p. 253.

transplant me again."[1]   But we must join Pope in the laugh against such a catching hold of the earth when we learn that Bolingbroke paid £200 to have his country halls painted with rakes, prongs, spades, and other insignia of husbandry in order to make it perfectly evident that he really did live on a farm.[2] The genuine lover of the country in the classical age expended his enthusiasm on the mild and easy pleasures of a well-kept country house easily accessible from the city.   That a sane man could choose to live as Wordsworth did in the Lake District would have passed belief.   In general the country was thought of but as a good place to recruit one's jaded energies, or as a refuge where disappointments might be hidden and disgrace forgotten.

According to Gay,

> "Whene'er a Courtier's out of place,
> The country shelters his disgrace."[3]

and his deserted, lovelorn Araminta felt that only the melancholy shades and croaking ravens of the country could suit her unhappy fate.[4]   Watts thought that none but "useless souls" should "to woods retreat."[5]   On the whole, the words of the city mouse to his country cousin expressed the prevailing sentiment.

> "Let savage beasts lodge in a country den ;
> You should see towns, and manners know, and men."[6]

The poet might sing the charms of the country if he chose, but he was, after all, as Denham said of Virgil and Cowley, only "gilding dirt."[7]

The attitude towards nature in the literature of any age may be tested in two ways, by what is said, and by what is left unsaid,

[1] Pope : Letters, Vol. II, p. 113.

[2] Pope : Letters, Vol. II, p. 133.

[3] Gay : Fable 33, First Series.

[4] Gay : Araminta.

[5] Watts : To David Polhill.   Cf. Shenstone : The Progress of Taste, 4 : 172 ; Lyttleton : To Mr. Poyntz.

[6] Cowley : The Country Mouse.

[7] Denham : On Mr. Abraham Cowley's Death, l. 79.

and of these the second is perhaps the more significant. Certainly in the poetry of the classical period the persistent ignor-

The grand and the terrible in nature ignored or disliked
ing of the grand and terrible in nature comes home to the mind as a most convincing proof of the prevailing distaste for wild scenery. And when we apply the other test and find that the conspiracy of silence is broken only by expressions indicative of positive dislike of such scenes, the case becomes a strong one. This point may be clearly illustrated by a somewhat detailed study of the poetical treatment of the mountains and the sea.

Rarely in the long period between Waller and Wordsworth do we find any trace of the modern feeling towards mountains. If
Mountains
they are spoken of at all it is to indicate the difficulty in surmounting them or to express the general distaste for anything so savagely and untameably wild. It is interesting to note that passages expressing the most active dislike of mountains show really some close observation and a good deal of picturesque energy of phrase They were evidently the outcome of a personal experience, the unpleasantness of which demanded forcible epithets. They show that when men were compelled by the exigencies of travel to go into a mountainous region there was not wanting a perception of certain characteristic mountain qualities, but that these qualities were only those exciting repulsion and terror. In no case does a sense of the sublimity and beauty of mountains find, or even apparently seek expression. This is true in travels. fiction, biography, and letters, as well as in poetry. A few typical illustrations may be given. Howell, who went abroad twice before 1622, strikes the keynote of the travelers who came later. He distinctly objected to the "monstrous abruptness" of the "Pyereny Hills" and he found the Alps even more "high and hideous." He was obliged to admit that the Welsh mountains were but mole-hills compared to the Alps, but he thought the scale more than turned by the fact that those "huge, monstrous excrescences of nature" were entirely useless, while Eppint' and

---

¹ James Howell: Epistolæ Ho Elianæ. Bk. 1. Sec. 1. Letters 23, 43.

Penminmaur at least furnished grass for the cattle. John Evelyn apparently regarded the Alps chiefly as an unpleasant barrier between the "sweete and delicious" gardens of France and the corresponding topiary paradises of Italy, and his final conception of them is as the place where nature swept up the rubbish of the earth to clear the Plains of Lombardy.[1] Addison was another of these early travelers, and he, too, found the journey over the Alps most trying. The "irregular, misshapen scenes" of a mountainous region gave him little pleasure.[2] He preferred the safe monotony of plains. Both Evelyn and Addison expended all the descriptive energy they had to spare for mountains on Vesuvius, but it was, of course, its character as a striking and curious natural phenomenon that attracted them.[3] Burnet of the Charter House, the tutor of Lady Mary Pierrepont, in his *Theory of the Earth* gives a theological reason for the existence of mountains. He conceives the present world as a gigantic ruin, the result of sin. Originally the earth was perfectly smooth. "It had the beauty of youth and blooming nature, fresh and fruitful, and not a wrinkle, scar, or fracture in all its body; no rocks nor mountains, no hollow caves, nor gaping channels, but even and uniform all over. And the smoothness of the earth made the face of the heavens so too; the air was calm and serene; none of those tumultuary motions and conflicts of vapours, which the winds cause in ours. 'Twas suited to a golden age, and to the first innocency of nature." But as a punishment for sin the interior fluid of the earth was allowed to break through the beautiful smooth crust, and in the ensuing chaos were piled up those "wild, vast, and indigested heaps of stone and earth," those "great ruins" that we call mountains.[4] In 1715 Pennecuik said that the swelling hills of Tweeddale were, for the most part, green, grassy, and pleasant, but he objected to the bordering mountains as being "black, craigie, and of a melancholy aspect, with deep and horrid precipices, a wearisome and

---

[1] John Evelyn: Diary (1641-1706) pp. 36, 185-9.
[2] Addison: Remarks on Italy. Geneva and the Lake.
[3] Evelyn: Diary, p. 126; Addison: Remarks on Italy.
[4] Thomas Burnet: Theory of the Earth. Ch. on "Mountains."

comfortless piece of way for travellers."[1]   In 1756 Thomas
Amory commented on the "dreadful northern fells," and called
Westmoreland a "frightful country," and spoke of "the ranges
and groups of mountains horrible to behold."[2]   So late as 1773
Dr. Johnson said of the Highlands of Scotland: "An eye
accustomed to flowery pastures and waving harvests is astonished
and repelled by this wide extent of hopeless sterility.   The
appearance is that of matter incapable of form or usefulness,
dismissed by nature from her care."[3]   In the same year Hutchin-
son deprecates the "dreary vicinage of mountains and inclement
skies" in the Lake District.   He describes Stainmore thus: "As
we proceeded Spittle presented its solitary edifice to view;
behind which Stainmore arises, whose heights feel the fury of both
eastern and western storms; . . . a dreary prospect extended to
the eye; the hills were clothed in heath, and all around a scene
of barrenness and deformity. . . . All was wilderness and horrid
waste over which the wearied eye travelled with anxiety. . . .
The wearied mind of the traveller endeavours to evade such
objects, and please itself with the fancied images of verdant
plains, purling streams and happy groves."[4]

The attitude towards mountains in the passages already
referred to appears in the poetry of the period with the same
general tone, though with less insistence.   Throughout Waller's
poetry the only epithets applied to mountains are "savage"[5] and
"craggy."[6]   Marvell, the most genuine lover of nature in this

[1] Pennecuik: Description of Tweeddale, p. 45.

[2] Thomas Amory: Life of John Buncle, Vol. I. p. 291; II, p. 97.

[3] Dr. Johnson: Works, Vol. IX, p. 35.   Cf. also Dr. Johnson's remark to
Boswell, "He said, he would not wish not to be disgusted in the Highlands;
for that would be to lose the power of distinguishing, and a man might then lie
down in the middle of them.   He wished only to conceal his disgust."   See
also his answer to the question, "How do you like the Highlands?"   "The
question seemed to irritate him, for he answered, 'How, Sir, can you ask me
what obliges me to speak unfavorably of a country where I have been hospit-
ably entertained?   Who *can* like the Highlands?   I like the inhabitants very
well.'"   Boswell's Life of Johnson, Vol. V. p. 317 and p. 377.

[4] Hutchinson: Excursion to the Lakes, pp. 11, 17.

[5] Waller: To my Lord Admiral.

[6] Waller: Story of Phœbus and Daphne.

age, was yet of the age in his feeling towards mountains, for he characterizes them as ill-designed excrescences that deform the earth and frighten heaven, and he calls upon them to learn beauty from the soft access and easy slopes of a well-rounded hill.[1] The unpleasant phrase, "high, huge-bellied mountains"[2] in one of Milton's youthful poems is hardly atoned for by the lines in *L'Allegro*,

> "Mountains on whose barren breast
> The labouring clouds do often rest,"[3]

and his poetry is, in general, marked by the absence of mountain scenery. Dryden's most famous mountains are "drowsy" and "seem to nod."[4] In Blackmore's summary of the charges made by Lucretius concerning the "unartful contrivance of the world," mountains are styled "the earth's dishonor and encumbering load." The only defence made by the poet is that these encumbrances do nevertheless restrain the tides, yield veins of ore, and bear forests of useful wood.[5] So John Philips defends his comfortable hypothesis that nothing is made in vain by the fact that even "that cloud-piercing hill Plinlimmon" is of some value since it furnishes "shrubby browze" for the goats.[6] And Yalden explains how erring Nature supplies her own defects by filling with mines the "vast excrescences of hills" that distort the surface of the earth.[7] Prior's only mountain is Lebanon with "craggy brow."[8] Pope has some "bright mountains" that serve to prop the incumbent sky,[9] and he occasionally mentions

---

[1] Marvell: Upon the Hill and Grove at Billbarrow.

[2] Milton: A Paraphrase on Psalm CXIV.

[3] Veitch calls attention to the fact that Shakspere with all his universality showed little if any delight in mountains, and that Milton with his directness of vision and sympathy went over Switzerland without bringing back an image of the Alps which he thought fit to preserve. Nature in Scottish Poetry. Vol. I. p. 107.

[4] Dryden: The Indian Emperor, Works, Vol. 2. p. 360.

[5] Blackmore: The Creation. Bk. 3:409.

[6] John Philips: Cyder 1:106.

[7] Yalden: To Sir Humphrey Mackworth.

[8] Prior: Solomon, Bk. 1., l. 52.

[9] Pope: The Temple of Fame.

mountains with such epithets as "hanging,"[1] "hollow,"[1] and "headlong."[2] Tickell showed his attitude towards mountains in his address to Lord Lonsdale whom he proposed to visit at Lowther Castle near Penrith, declaring that he did not dread the harsh climate and rude country, for the Earl's presence would be sufficient to "hush every wind and every mountain smooth."[3] Parnell instances in his catalogue of the horrors of Ireland her hills that with naked heads meet the tempests.[4] Dr. Akenside speaks of a "horrid pile of hills."[5] Along with this frank dis-approval of mountains is a similar dislike for their concomitants such as precipices, wildernesses, and even dense thickets.[6]

[1] Pope : On St. Cecilia's Day.
[2] Pope : Windsor Forest, l. 210.
[3] Tickell : Oxford : A Poem, l. 441.
[4] Parnell : To Mr. Pope, l. 83.
[5] Dr. Akenside : Pleasures of the Imagination, 2 : 274 (first version).

[6] This indifference to mountains or dislike of them was not a new thing. For further illustrations see Perry : Eng. Lit. of 18th Cent., pp. 144–148. Humboldt in Kosmos 2 : 16 says :

"Von dem ewigen Schnee der Alpen, wenn sie sich am Abend oder am frühen Morgen röthen, von der Schönheit des blauen Gletscher-Eises, von der grossartigen Natur der schweizerischen Landschaft ist keine Schilderung aus dem Alterthum auf uns gekommen : und doch gingen ununterbrochen Staats-männer, Heerführer, und in ihrem Gefolge Litteraten durch Helvetien nach Gallien. Alle diese Reisenden wissen nur über die unfahrbaren scheusslichen Wege zu klagen ; das Romantische der Naturscenen beschäftigte sie nie. . . . Silius Italicus. . . . beschreibt die Alpengegend als eine schrecken-erregende vegetationslose Einöde, während er mit Liebe alle Felsen-schluchten Italiens und die buschigen Ufer des Liris (Garigliano) besingt."

An interesting early exception to this general statement is Petrarch's description of his ascent of Mt. Ventoux. In a letter dated April 26, 1335, (Petrarca : Lettere Famigliari, Vol. I, p. 481) he tells how this mountain, ever before his eyes, had been from childhood a temptation to him, and how he was finally stimulated to make the ascent by an account of the wide view gained by Philip of Macedon from one of the highest mountains in Thessaly. The most significant passage in this letter is that in which are strangely mingled Petrarch's pleasure in the magnificent prospect and his ascetic fear of a consequent undue subordination of the soul of man.

"At last I turned to the occasion of my expedition. The sinking sun and lengthening shadows admonished me that the hour of departure was at hand, and, as if started from sleep, I turned around and looked to the west. The

One cause of this antipathetic attitude towards mountains and wild scenery is, doubtless, as has been often suggested, the hardships and perils of travel before good roads were built. Biese quotes several eighteenth century letters from German travelers to show how much "*die Schlechten Strassen*" had to do with the

Pyrenees — the eye could not reach so far, but I saw the mountains of Lyonnais distinctly, and the sea by Marseilles; the Rhone, too, was there before me. Observing these closely, now thinking on the things of earth, and again, as if I had done with the body, lifting my mind on high, it occurred to me to take out the copy of St. Augustine's Confessions that I always kept with me; a little volume but of unlimited value and charm. And I call God to witness that the first words on which I cast mine eyes were these: 'Men go to wonder at the heights of mountains, the ocean floods, rivers' long courses, ocean's immensity, the revolutions of the stars, — and of themselves they have no care!' My brother asked me what was the matter. I bade him not disturb me. I closed the book. angry with myself for not ceasing to admire things of earth, instead of remembering that the human soul is beyond comparison the subject for admiration. Once and again, as I descended, I gazed back, and the lofty summit of the mountain seemed to me scarcely a cubit high compared with the sublime dignity of man." [Translated and commented on by McLaughlin in The Mediæval Feeling for Nature.]

See also Biese: Die Entwickelung des Naturgefühls, p. 151.

"Und somit eröffnet uns dieser Brief, mit seiner Mischung reinen, modernen Naturgenusses und dogmatisch-asketischer Rückbesinnung, einen Blick in ein zwie-spältiges Herz eines an der Wende zweier Zeiten stehenden Menschen; es reagiert gleichsam der mittelalterliche Geist wider die aufkeimende moderne Empfindung."

Another significant utterance comes in 1541 in a letter by Gessner quoted by Biese, p. 328. It shows a recognition of the greatness and majesty of the Alps, and has something of the modern feeling:

"So lange mir Gott Leben schenken wird, habe ich beschlossen, jährlich einige Berge oder doch einen zu besteigen, teils um die Gebirgsflora kennen zu lernen, teils um den Körper zo kräftigen und den Geist zu erfrischen. Welchen Genuss gewährt es nicht die ungeheuren Bergmassen zu betrachten und das Haupt in die Wolken zu erheben! Wie stimmt es zur Andacht, wenn man umringt ist von den Schneedomen, die der grosse Weltbaumeister an dem einen langen Schöpfungstage geschaffen hat! Wie leer is doch das Leben, wie niedrig das Streben derer, die auf dem Erdboden umher kriechen, nur um zu erwerben und spiessbürgerlich zu geniessen! Ihnen bleibt das irdische Paradies verschlossen."

Biese thinks that Rousseau's Nouvelle Heloise (1761) "die Augen über die Herrlichkeiten der neu entdeckten Alpenwelt öffnete." It is interesting to note in this connection that the beginning of enthusiastic interest in the mountains

failure to appreciate the romantic beauty of the Alps.' He finds another partial explanation of the small interest in mountain travel in the fact that scientific study of natural phenomena such as glaciers, geological formations, mountain flora and fauna, was as yet in its infancy and that thus one whole class of motives for enduring fatigue and braving difficulties was wanting.[2] But these two reasons do not sufficiently account for the lack of mountain fervor. It is not merely good roads and scientific enthusiasm that bid men seek mountain solitudes today. Preoccupation with terror and fatigue were not the only nor the chief reason of this general dislike of wild scenery. The two charges even more persistently and definitely brought against mountains are that they are useless, and that they are a deformity on the surface of the earth. Now the first of these is but another expression of the dominant utilitarian standards of value, and the second is an outcome of the prevailing desire for orderly and systematic arrangement. Pronounced irregularity of outline was as irritating to the artistic consciousness as was exceptional license in verse forms. Mountains entered an inevitable protest against the spirit that found its highest pleasure in the petty symmetrical complexities of a typical eighteenth century garden. That this protest was on a great scale with accompanying suggestions of mystery and of a remote irresistible power, gives an added reason why the age turned thus decisively from forms of nature to which a romantic age yields fullest homage. Thus the attitude toward mountains finds its real explanation not so much in external conditions as in the spirit of the times.

The place of the ocean in the classical poetry is likewise significant. It awakened no sense of elation as in Byron, no

of the English Lake district found expression somewhat earlier in Dalton's poem (1755), Amory's novel (1756) and Brown's Letter and Rhapsody (before 1766 and probably before 1760). The earliest of the Ossian poems belong in 1760. Goethe's Briefe aus der Schweiz vom Jahre 1779 are according to Biese the first full and enthusiastic recognition by a German poet of the romantic charms of the Alps. Die Entwickelung, etc., p. 393.

[1] Biese: Die Entwickelung, etc., pp. 353–355; Lecky: History of England 6 : 180–183.

[2] Biese : Die Entwickelung, etc., pp. 324, 328.

sense of mysterious kinship as in Shelley.   It was simply a waste of waters, dangerous at times, and always wearisome.   Though more often mentioned than the mountains, it received **The ocean**   an even more narrow and conventional treatment. Except in some elaborate similes there are few descriptions of more than a line in length.   We find merely causal mention by means of stock epithets, or very short and unmeaning descriptive phrases.   To Waller the sea is "the world's great waste," " a watery field," a " watery wilderness," or a " main," liquid, or troubled, or angry as the case may be.[1] Dryden's epithets are hardly more felicitous.   He uses " watery "[2] with an insistence that finally becomes ludicrous.   He has one or two little ocean pictures written apparently for their own sake, but his best use of the ocean is in similitudes.[2]   In succeeding poets the treatment of the ocean is exceedingly commonplace and unimaginative.   Such small interest as the sea aroused was of a prosaic, utilitarian sort.   Young's *Sea Pieces* and *Ocean* may serve as examples, and they are little more than eulogies of England's commercial and naval prowess.   It is for Britain that "the servant Ocean " " both sinks and swells."   It is solely with reference to her prosperity that soft Zephyr, keen Eurus, Notus, and rough Boreas " urge their toil."

> " The main!   The main!
> Is Britain's reign ;
>
> . . . .
>
> The main ! the main !
> Be Briton's strain,"[3]

is the unvaried theme.   The few descriptive passages are of periods when "storms deface the fluid glass," and seem to have been composed in accordance with Pope's famous recipe for poetical tempests.[4]   The most popular sea poem of the eighteenth

---

[1] Waller: A Panegyric to my Lord Protector, st. 11 ; Instructions to a Painter, l. 228 ; On the Danger His Majesty Escaped, ll. 5, 63, 156.

[2] Dryden under " Similitudes," p. 28, and " Diction," p. 38.

[3] Young : The Merchant, strain 2, st. 15 ; strain 3, st. 9 ; strain 8, st. 13–17.

[4] " For a Tempest take Eurus, Zephyr, Auster and Boreas and cast them together in one verse; add to these rain and lightning, *quantum sufficit* : mix

century was Falconer's *Shipwreck* written in 1762. It is a suffi-
ciently remarkable production when thought of as the work of a
common sailor but it is difficult for the modern reader to under-
stand the extravagant praise bestowed upon it in its own day.[1]
Its tame and conventional love-story, its descriptions of the
sylvan scenes where Palemon and Anna gave pledges of undying
affection, its moralizings on the beneficial effect of poetry, the evils
of war, the corrupting lust of gold, its long digression on cities
and heroes "renowned in antiquity," its invocation to the Muses,
its mythology, its reverence for "sacred Maro's art," are all of
the commonplace, classical order. There is in the actual ship-
wreck scenes some vigorous writing, but it deals almost entirely
with the emotions of the sailors, and the management of the ship.
It would be difficult to find any really effective lines descriptive
of the storm itself. The following quotations may stand as fairly
representative of the best passages :

> "It comes resistless, and with foaming sweep
> Upturns the whitening surface of the deep."

> "But with redoubling force the tempests blow,
> And watery hills in dread succession flow."

> "A sea, upsurging with stupendous roll."[2]

One of the most striking characteristics of the descriptive
parts of the poem is the daring and novel use of technical sea
terms. Such lines as,

> "Reef top-sails, reef! the master calls again.
> The halyards and top-bow-lines soon are gone,
> To clue-lines and reef-tackles next they run.
>
> .   .   .   .
>
> Deep on her side, the reeling vessel lies :
> Brail up the mizzen quick! the master cries,
> Man the clue-garnets! let the main-sheet fly."[3]

your clouds and billows well together till they foam, and thicken your descrip-
tion here and there with a quicksand. Brew your tempest well in your head
before you set it a blowing." [Works, Vol. X, p. 403.]

[1] See Monthly Review, Vol. XXVII, p. 197, where Falconer's descriptions
are said to be equal to "anything in the Æneid."

[2] Falconer : The Shipwreck, Canto II, ll. 157, 268, 346.

[3] Falconer : Shipwreck, Canto II : 148–166.

are praised as minutely accurate but it certainly needs a specialist's training to understand them.[1] There is nothing new in Falconer's poem except his use of realism in describing the ship's manœuvres. The sea is, to be sure, more prominent than we have found it in preceding poems, but it is the same "desert waste," the same "faithless deep," the same "watery plain," and is deformed by the typical classical storm. Strange as it may seem, it is yet true that the poets of sea-girt England were very slow in making the discovery of the ocean.[2] The main points in the eighteenth century conception of the sea, were its usefulness as a commercial highway and its destructive power in storms. This impression of irresistible force is sometimes vivid enough to result in strong phrasing, but the changing beauty, the majesty, the mysterious suggestiveness of the sea found no expression in English classical poetry. Even in the poems that mark the transition spirit the adequate word for the sea is surprisingly slow to come.

In connection with the failure to understand or love the mountains or the sea we may note the avoidance of winter[3] or the conception of it as the "deformed wrong side of the year." Lyttleton thoroughly disliked "gloomy winter's unauspicious reign"[4] and Pope said that its bleak prospects set his very imagination a-shivering.[5] Lady Montagu called the glistening snows a painful sight, and said that the whole country was in winter "deform'd by rains and rough with blasting winds." The "icy, cold, depressing

Winter

---

[1] These descriptions rouse Dr. Clarke to a climax of admiration. "Homer has been admired by some for reducing a catalogue of ships into tolerably flowing verse; but who, except a poetical Sailor, the nursling of Apollo, educated by Neptune, would ever have thought of versifying his own sea-language? What other poet would even have dreamt of *reef-tackles, haliards, clue-garnets, buntlines, lashings, laniards,* and fifty other terms equally obnoxious to the soft sing-song of modern poetasters." Monthly Review, Vol. XXVII.

[2] Biese notes the same fact with regard to German poetry (Die Entwickelung, p. 320).

[3] Cf. Veitch : Feeling for Nature. Vol. I, 117.

[4] Lyttleton : An Epistle to Mr. Pope.

[5] Pope : Letters. Vol. I, 178.

hand" of winter, brought in a season of privations, discomfort, and dangers. Throughout the classical period the typical phrases are "shuddering winter," "winter's dreary gloom," "the sad, inverted year." Storms and blasts "deface the year." Hail-storms "deform the flowery spring." Clouds "sadden the inverted year." Winter's "joyless reign" is a season marked by "dusky horrors."

> "Fierce winter desolates the year,
> Deserts of snow fatigue the eye,
> Successive tempests bloat the sky
> And gloomy damps oppress the soul,"

is a typical description.[1] Another indication of the dislike of this season is found in a curious *Pastoral* by Washbourne in which hell is represented as a place where it is "alwaies winter."[2] It will be observed later that a sense of joy in winter scenes is one of the very early indications of a reviving interest in the out-door world.

Correspondent with the dislike and neglect of the grand and the terrible in nature is a similar feeling towards such aspects of the external world as especially suggest mystery, **Dislike of the remote and the mysterious in nature** remoteness, unseen forces. That this is true may be seen by a study of the sky phenomena that appear, or fail to appear, in this classical poetry. The day-time sky is but briefly and vaguely mentioned or it passes unobserved. A phrase so imaginative as Blackmore's "blue gulph of interposing sky"[3] is rare. In general

[1] For illustrative passages, see Montagu : Letters and Works 2:464 ; Congreve : Tears of Amaryllis, l. 50 ; Broome : Daphnis and Lycidas, l. 47 ; Shenstone : Upon a Visit in Winter ; Pitt : Hymn to Apollo ; Hughes : Myra ; Savage : Wanderer, 1 : 42, 52 ; John Scott : Elegy on Winter ; Akenside : On the Winter Solstice.

[2] For a similar dislike of winter in mediæval poetry, see McLaughlin's Studies in Mediæval Life and Literature, p. 20. He quotes as typical the following from a Latin student song : "The cold icy harshness of winter, its fierceness, and dull, miserable inactivity."

[3] Blackmore : Creation 2:393. Cf. Wordsworth's

> " The chasm of sky above my head
> Is heaven's profoundest azure . . . . an abyss
> In which the everlasting stars abide."   Excursion 3:94-98.

it is only the more striking aspects of the sky that are noticed, such aspects as would catch the attention of a **Day-time sky** child or of a mere casual observer. Fleeting, delicate effects are unheeded. Clouds receive little attention except as they portend or accompany a storm, and even then their chief use is in similitudes. Apparently the best known appearance of the day-time sky is the rainbow. But though it is often mentioned there is singularly little variety in the phrases used to describe it. A brief summary of those phrases most frequently used is interesting: "Painted clouds;" "the clouds' gaudy bow;" "the gaudy heavenly bow;" "the watery bow;" "the painted bow;" "painted tears;" "the gaudy drapery of heaven's fair bow;" "the showery arch;" the bow "painted by Iris;" the bow "deck'd like a gaudy bride;" "the painted arch of summer skies,"[1] and so on through a wearisome list of kaleidoscopic combinations of the same words. The constant repetition of adjectives so unmeaning as "watery" and "showery," or so external and artificial as "gaudy" and "painted" is as characteristic of the general attitude toward nature as is the fact that the attention of poets should have been concentrated on the obvious beauties of the rainbow rather than on the finer, more subtle charms of the sky. In the same way sunrise, and especially sunset, are often mentioned and occasionally described. But there is practically no discriminating and appreciative study of what was actually to be seen in the heavens. It was more natural to sit at home and read the classics, and then announce that the golden god of day "drives down his flaming chariot to the sea."[2]

Cf. also Dryden's

"The abyss of heaven, the court of stars." (Works, 4: 276).

[1] For illustrative passages, see Waller: Of the Lady; Cowley: Davideis, 2:440, Hymn to Light, and Shortness of Life, st. 11; Young: Ocean, st. 23; Broome: Paraphrase of Ecclesiastes; Yalden: Hymn to Morning; John Philips: Cyder, 2:293; Tickell: Prospect of Peace; Gay: The Espousal; Rowe: The Queen's Success; Watts: Disappointment; Pitt: Verses, etc., etc.

[2] For descriptions of this sort, see Hughes: Court of Neptune; Prior: Solomon, 3:557; Broome: Poem on Death, l. 151; Gay: Rural Sports, 2:323; Gay: Wine, l. 141; Beattie: The Minstrel, 1:17; etc., etc.

Twilight had, as might be expected, little charm or suggestiveness. Moonlight also plays a most subordinate part in this

Twilight and moonlight
poetry.[1] We seldom find anything more direct or vivid than the time-honored statement that "fair" or "pale" Cynthia "mounts the vaulted sky," and "adorns the night" with her silver beams.[2]

The night sky was counted beautiful because of its stars. The recurrent conception is that the azure heavens are gilded or adorned with these orbs of gold. The favorite

The night sky
words are "spangled" and "gilded."[3] In Young's *Night Thoughts* we might expect to find some faithful and sympathetic study of the nocturnal heavens, but in the first eight books not seventy-five lines refer even remotely to external nature, and in the ninth book the stress is laid on "the moral emanations of the skies." In his efforts to find a sufficiently varied star vocabulary, Young was driven to the invention of some new phrases, but in no case do they show imagina-

---

[1] Cf. Biese : Die Entwickelung, etc., p. 307.

[2] The following are illustrative phrases :

"Silver Cynthia lights the world," Garth : Claremont, l. 284 ; "Pale Cynthia mounts the vaulted sky," Shenstone : Elegy VI ; "Cynthia came, riding on her silver car," Beattie : Minstrel, 2:12 ; "Cynthia's silver white," Hughes : The Picture ; "Cynthia, fair regent of the night," Gay : Trivia, 3:3 ; "Cynthia's silver ray," Addison : Imitation of Milton ; "Cynthia, great Queen of Night," Garth : Disp., 5:282 ; "Pale Cynthia's melancholy light," Falconer : Shipwreck, 1:311.

[3] The following are illustrative phrases :

"Rich Spangles," Waller : Of the Queen ; "Spangled nights," Cowley : Davideis, 1:94 ; "Spangled sphere," Cowley : The Extasy ; "Burning spangles of sidereal gold," Broome : Paraphrase of Eccl.; "Freezing spangles," Tickell : On the Prospect of Peace ; "The sky spangled with a thousand eyes," Gay : Fables, Part I:11 ; "Spangled pole," Pitt : On the death of Mr. Stanhope ; "Heaven's gilded troops," Cowley : Davideis, 1:183 ; "Stars that gild the gloomy night," Parnell : Hymn to Contentment ; "Twinkling stars who gild the skies," Watts : Sun, Moon, etc.; "Shooting star that gilds the night," Somerville : Hobbinol, 3:261 ; "Stars that gild the northern skies," Pitt : Congress of Cambray ; "Meteor that gilds the night," Somerville : Field Sports, 1:139 ; "Globes of light in fields of azure shine," Watts : God's Dominion ; "Orbs of gold in fields of azure lie," Parnell : Queen Anne's Peace, l. 38 ; "Yon blue tract enriched with orbs of light," Parnell : David, l. 358.

tive power. They are perfunctory and stiff and indicate that his mind was on the "system of divinity" he meant his stars to teach rather than on the stars themselves.[1] In Burnet's *Theory of the Earth*, a work already quoted from, we find a striking, because an exaggerated, example of the way an undue love of order could modify one's æsthetic perception. Burnet enjoyed the night sky but he felt that the stars might have been more artistically arranged. "They lie carelessly scattered as if they had been sown in the heaven like seed, by handfuls, and not by a skilful hand neither. What a beautiful hemisphere they would have made if they had been placed in rank and order; if they had all been disposed into regular figures, and the little ones set with due regard to the greater, and then all finished and made up into one fair piece or great composition according to the rules of art and symmetry. What a surprising beauty this would have been to the inhabitants of the earth ? What a lovely roof to our little world ? This indeed might have given us some temptation to have thought that they had been all made for us; but lest any such vain imagination should now enter into our thoughts Providence (besides more important reasons) seems on purpose to have left them under that negligence or disorder which they appear unto us."[2] The final impression from the study of these passages that refer to stars or moonlight is that the poets of this period were not unlike Peter Bell into whose heart "nature ne'er could find the way :"

> " Nor for the moon cared he a tittle,
> And for the stars he cared as little." [3]

Night itself, aside from its starry glories, was thought of but to be feared for its brown horrors and melancholy shades. The

[1] Some of Young's phrases are "rolling spheres," "tuneful spheres," "revolving spheres," "unnumbered lustres," "sparks of night," "lucid orbs," "radiant choir," "etherial fires," "mathematic glories," "aërial racers," "midnight counselors," "nocturnal suns," "etherial armies," "radiant lamps," "splendours," "ambient orbs," "nocturnal sparks," "night's radiant scale," etc.

[2] Burnet : Theory of the Earth, Chapter on Stars. Cf. Prior : Solomon, 1: 502–511.

[3] Wordsworth : Peter Bell.

conception of daylight as useful and safe was a part of classical good sense. The earliest poem in which we find the beauty and something of the spiritual power of night repre-
Night　sented is by Lady Winchelsea.　Later we find the characteristic sentimental melancholy of the poets involved in a tissue of moonlight and mystery, while the faint colors and pearly dews of the dawn, and the gentle sadness of evening shades, or in extreme cases, even midnight glooms, seem to be the only fit setting for struggling emotions and vague aspirations.　There are also, as we shall see, throughout the romantic revival, not infrequent studies of the sky, especially of sunrise and sunset, from what we may call the artist's point of view.　But all this belongs to the new spirit and is a very evident break from classical traditions.　Poetry in which the classical note is dominant shows the utmost coldness and barrenness in all that has to do with the beauty and significance of the sky whether by night or by day.[1]

In contrast to the general turning away from the grand or the mysterious in nature we find a certain friendly feeling
Pleasure in the gentler aspects of nature　towards the gentler forms of out-door life.　Spring and summer, blue skies, gently sloping hills, flowery valleys, cool springs, and shady groves appear in the poetry with a frequency indicative of some real delight in

---

[1] Ruskin (Mod. Painters, 3: 248) comments on Dante's "intense detestation of all mist, rack of cloud or dimness of rain."

McLaughlin says of clouds, moonlight, etc.:

" Let any reader of mediæval poetry recall how imperceptible a part they play in it, even as plain facts of description.　A line in one of the Latin songs expresses the feeling : their thought of clouds is how delightful not to see them. Moonlight, too, is seldom dwelt on as poetical ; the most romantic touch that comes to my mind with it, is in Chrestien de Troyes where it shines over the reconciliation of estranged lovers.　Just as we find little notice of sunrise, sunset, clouds, and moon, we find little feeling for the stars.　They are mentioned occasionally in a facile way, thought scarcely ever with manifest sentiment."-- Studies in Mediæval Life and Literature, p. 21.

Mr. Symonds says of the same period :

" The earth is felt chiefly through the delightfulness of healthy sensations. The stars and clouds, and tempests of the heavens, the ever-recurring miracle of sunrise, the solemn pageant of sunsetting are almost as though they were

them.[1]   But real affection for nature even in her idyllic forms, an affection the evident outgrowth of personal experience, is the exception rather than the rule.   When such regard for nature is apparent, however narrow in scope, it is rightly to be regarded as an indication of a new feeling towards the external world, for in general these so-called idyllic descriptions are to the last degree artificial and unreal.   They show that what the poet really enjoyed was not so much nature itself, as the creation of fanciful pictures of nature, the flowing combination of attractive details into such scenes as he would like to find in the country in case he should go there.   Garth's description of the Fortunate Islands is typical. There

> " No blasts e'er discompose the peaceful sky,
> The springs but murmur, and the winds but sigh.
> The tuneful swans on gliding rivers float
> And warbling dirges die on every note.
> Where Flora treads, her Zephyr garlands flings,
> And scatters odors from his purple wings ;
> Whilst birds from woodbine bowers and jasmine groves
> Chant their glad nuptials and unenvy'd loves.
> Mild seasons, rising hills, and silent dales,
> Cool grottoes, silver brooks, and flowery vales,
> Groves filled with palmy shrubs, in pomp appear,
> And scent with gales of sweet the circling year."[2]

The details of this listless, luxurious description are such as are combined and recombined in many a picture of supposedly English scenes.   The poet found his pleasure in the vague,

not in this literature."—J. A. Symonds, Essays Speculative and Suggestive, p. 300.

[1] In commenting on mediæval out-door poetry Vernon Lee says (Euphorion p. 120):

"Spring, spring, endless spring—for three long centuries throughout the world a dreary green monotony of spring. . . . Moreover this mediæval spring is the spring neither of the shepherd, nor of the farmer, nor of any man to whom spring brings work and anxiety and hope of gain ; it is a mere vague spring of gentle-folk, or at all events of well-to-do burgesses, taking their pleasure on the lawns of castle parks."   •

[2] Garth : Dispensary 4 : 309.

highly generalized representation of such scenery as might exist in some imagined Elysium or Garden of Eden. The final effect on the mind of the reader is never one of reality. All is traditional and bookish. Perhaps there is no more effective way of showing the general characteristics of these poetical descriptions than by an accumulation of examples. Since there is no danger of spoiling the poetry, it may be permissible for purposes of emphasis, to print in italics such phrases as belong to the common poetical stock. The first passage is Rosamond's description of Woodstock Park :

Description traditional and bookish in character

> " *Flowery mountains,*
> *Mossy fountains,*
> *Shady woods,*
> *Crystal floods.*" [1]

Here the union of phrases, all conventional in their character, is entirely fortuitous and undiscriminating. It is impossible not to feel that Addison picked up his items at random, according to the scheme of his verse. Take next this invocation by Broome :

> " Hail ye soft seats! ye *limpid springs* and *floods* !
> Ye *flowery meads,* ye *vales* and *woods.*
> Ye *limpid floods* that ever murmuring flow !
> Ye *verdant meads,* where flowers eternal blow !
> Ye *shady vales,* where *zephyrs* ever play !
> Ye woods where little *warblers* tune their lay." [2]

Or Shenstone's description of the place of his birth :

> " Romantic scenes of *pendent hills*
> And *verdant vales,* and *falling rills*
> And *mossy banks,* the fields *adorn,*
> Where Damon, *simple swain,* was born." [3]

Or Lyttleton's lines:

[1] Addison: Rosamond, Act I, Sc. 1. Cf. A longer description in the same poem beginning,
> " O the soft, delicious view."   Act II., Sc. 3.

[2] Broome :   On the Seat of War in Flanders.

[3] Shenstone: The Progress of Taste 3:7.

> " Here *limpid fountains* roll through *flowery meads*,
> Here *rising forests* lift their *verdant heads*." [1]

Or Congreve's description of the scenery along the Thames:

> " And soft and still the *silver surface glides*,
> The *zephyrs fan the field*, the *whispering breeze*
> With fragrant *breath remurmurs through the trees*." [2]

Or Parnell's

> " High sunny summits, *deeply shaded dales*,
> Thick *mossy banks*, and *flowery winding vales*." [3]

Or Prior's

> " The *verdant rising* of the *flowery hill*,
> The *vale enamelled* and the *crystal rill*." [4]

Or Pope's

> " Her fate is *whispered* by the *gentle breeze*,
> And told in *sighs* to all the *trembling trees;*
> The *trembling trees* in every plain and wood,
> Her fate *remurmur* to the *silver flood*." [5]

Or Marriott's

> " The mimic voice repeats the *gales*,
> That *sigh along* the *flowery vales;*
> The *flowery vales*, the *falling floods*,
> The *rising rocks*, and *waving woods*,
> To the *sighing gales* reply
> Redoubling all the harmony." [6]

Further quotation is useless. It is easy to see that these passages have no individuality. They might be transposed from poet to poet without injustice either to poem or poet. They are like ready-made clothing, cut out by the quantity to fit the average figure, and never having any niceness or perfection of fit for any individual form. They are not specific. They have no local color. They are, furthermore, absolutely superficial. There is no

[1] Lyttleton: Eclogue IV.
[2] Congreve: The Birth of the Muse.
[3] Parnell: Health: An Eclogue.
[4] Prior: Solomon, 3: 158
[5] Pope : Winter.
[6] Marriott: Rinaldo and Armida.

hint of anything deeper than the conventional external details mentioned.

Throughout the classical age the most genuine interest in nature had to do with parks and gardens. The formal garden,

Gardens however, which held its own in England till early in the eighteenth century, makes but a small figure in the poetry of the period. Its affinities were rather with prose. In later poetry we find many references to the classical garden, but they are of the nature of a scornful retrospect, and they belong to the new spirit. The whole subject of gardening will be presented in a separate section.

In the study of the evolution of the love of nature from Waller to Wordsworth we may perhaps mark out three stages in the atti-

Nature as a storehouse of similitudes tude towards the external world. The last of these stages is the one based on the cosmic sense, or the recognition of the essential unity between man and nature. Of this Wordsworth stands as the first adequate representative. The second stage is marked by the recognition of the world about us as beautiful and worthy of close study, but this study is detailed and external rather than penetrating and suggestive. Very much of the work of the transition period is of this sort. In the first stage nature is counted of value chiefly as a storehouse of similitudes illustrative of human actions and passions. This first stage represents the use of nature most characteristic of the classical poetry.

A study of the abundant similitudes of this period indicates that they were drawn from a very narrow range of natural facts. The lily, the rose, the lark, the nightingale, the wren, bees, stars, drops of dew, the sea in a storm, the oak and the ivy, leaves, the milky way—these are the most important sources of similitudes. The poet chose his similes from facts already canonized by long literary service, or from the obvious facts of the park or the town garden. There is, in the second place, little apparent effort to secure accuracy or picturesque effect in the statement of the illustrative side of the simile. The entire emphasis is on the human fact to to be illustrated. There is, therefore, in the third place, a failure to perceive subtle or delicately true analogies. In most com-

parisons the likeness is superficial or it is far fetched. The sim-
iles from nature were not the literary expression of inner congrui-
ties. They were consciously sought for as a part of the necessary
adornment of poetry. Sheridan says:

> "I often try'd in vain to find,
> A *simile* for womankind,
> A *simile* I mean to fit 'em,
> In every circumstance to hit 'em.
> Through every beast and bird I went,
> I ransack'd every element;
> And after peeping through all nature,
> To find so whimsical a creature,
> A *cloud* presented to my view,
> And strait this parable I drew."[1]

It is this elaborate desire for similitudes together with the small
knowledge of nature that led not only to wearisome iteration of
the same similes but also to the still more wearisome iteration of
the same points of comparison. A rose, for instance, is a perenni-
ally beautiful source of comparisons,[2] but in the eighteenth century
poetry it is used almost exclusively either with the lily in matters
of the complexion, or by itself as representative of a young
maiden. If she is overtaken by misfortune the rose is easily
blasted by northern winds. If she is neglected the rose withers
on its stalk. If she weeps the rose bends its head surcharged
with dew. If she dies young, the rosebud is blasted before it is
blown. The words of the "Angry Rose" to the poet gently satir-
ize this prevalence of rose similes.

> "Of all mankind you should not flout us;
> What can the Poet do without us?
> In every love-song Roses bloom;
> We lend you color and perfume."[3]

The nightingale has also a conventional use. He gener-
ally represents the poet and is either singing with a thorn against

[1] Sheridan: New Simile for the Ladies. Dr. Johnson's Eng. Poets. Swift.

[2] For an interesting study of the rose in literature from Ausonius to Waller
see "The Pathos of the Rose in Poetry," in Symonds: Essays. p. 368.

Gay: Fables, Part 1:45.

his breast, or is engaged in a musical contest with other birds, in which contest he quickly silences all competitors, or is himself driven away by the clamorous noise of a crowd of common birds. The lark has his own established set of applications. Dryden, Waller, and Savage represent the poet as a lark singing when the sun shines, and Waller suits the figure to the times by making the Queen the Sun.[1] Tickell called himself an artless lark.[2] Cowley professed himself emulous of the lark.[3] Somerville is a morning lark.[4] Wycherley compares both Virgil and Pope to larks.[5] Any Fair One has a voice like a lark, and to Dyer's delighted ear the maidens who spun English yarn sang like a whole choir of larks.[6] Not infrequently comparisons are drawn from the old custom of daring larks by mirrors or objects that would excite terror.[7] The wren carried aloft on the eagle's back serves a variety of poetical purposes, but is especially apt when representing a needy poet and some powerful patron.[8] Bees are by far the most prolific source of similitude. Their number, their activity, their stings, their honey-making are all recognized means of illustration.[9]

To express great numbers the most useful similes are drawn from stars, pearly drops of dew, and, most frequently, leaves in

[1] Dryden : Works 11:13.　Waller "To the Queen."　Savage "To Bessy."

[2] Tickell : To Mr. Addison.

[3] Cowley: The Shortness of Life.

[4] Somerville: Field Sports.

[5] Wycherley: To Mr. Pope.

[6] Dyer: The Fleece.

[7] Dryden: Works 4:202, 9:162.

[8] Dryden : Works. 4:214, 5:365. Congreve:　"On His taking of Namur;" st. 2.

[9] See as illustrative of the bee similtudes :　Waller: Battle of the Summer Island, Canto 3, l. 24; Cowley: The Inconstant, st. 6; Milton: Paradise Lost, 1:768; Dryden: Works, 9:145, 172; 2:463; Hughes: The Triumph of Peace, l. 118; Prior: Alma, 3:171; Pope: Dunciad, 4:79; Pope: Temple of Fame; Gay: Trivia, 2:555; Congreve: Ovid's Art of Love Imitated, l. 200; A. Philips: To James Craggs, l. 151; Stepney: To the Earl of Carlisle, l. 26; Buckingham: Essay on Poetry, l. 255; Young: Night Thoughts, 2:462; 6:516; Akenside: Odes, 1:1, st. 2; Dyer: Fleece; 2:496; 3:413; 4:317; Somerville: To Allan Ramsay, l. 24; Watts: Divine Songs, XX; etc.

autumn.[1] An exceedingly popular simile is that of the oak and ivy, or the elm and the vine.[2] Its use is obvious. The rising and the setting sun represent various forms of prosperity and adversity.[3] From Waller on, the Milky Way typifies virtues so numerous that they shine in one undistinguished blaze.[4] A large class of similitudes is drawn from water in some form. In this respect Dryden is typical. It is surprising to observe how many of his metaphors and similes are based on seas, streams, and storms,[5] and his most excellent use of nature is in these similitudes, though after going over many of them one comes to feel that they are all made upon much the same pattern. After Dryden conventional comparisons based on floods and angry seas are frequent.

The customary form of the river simile of this period is the comparison of some man's character, or actions, or literary style to some historic rivers with marked features. Prior uses the rapid Volga to represent the impetuous "young Muscovite," while

[1] See as illustrative: Cowley: Davideis, 4:728; Isaiah, ch. 34, st. 2; Plagues of Egypt, st. 9; Milton: Paradise Lost, 1:302; Dryden: Works, Vol. 3, p. 422, p. 354; Prior: The Turtle and the Sparrow, l. 206; King: Art of Love, l. 1700; Pope: Essay on Criticism, 2:109; Temple of Fame, l. 430; Young: Night Thoughts, 5:336; The Last Day, 2:183; Blair: The Grave, l. 469; etc.

[2] See as illustrative : Waller: On Repairing St. Paul's, l. 25; Cowley: Davideis, 2:58; Milton: Paradise Lost, 5:215; Yalden: To his perjured Mistress, l. 11; Parnell: The Hermit, l. 41; Young: Satire IV. l. 1; Dyer: The Fleece, 2:648; Halifax: On the Death of Charles II, l. 77.

[3] See as illustrative Dryden's use of the sun in Works, 4:276; 2:148, 185, 215, 454, etc.

[4] See as illustrative: Waller: To Amoret; Addison: An Account of the Greatest English Poets; Spratt: On the Death of the Lord Protector; Dryden: Works, 11:132; Cowley: Clad all in White.

[5] As illustrative of Dryden's use of similitudes drawn from water note the following: Revenge and rage are sudden floods; joys are torrents that overflow all banks; contending passions are tides that flow against currents; fame is a swelling current; anger is a dammed up stream that gets new force by opposition; a ruined life, destroyed fortunes, are shipwrecks; love is like springtides, full and high, or like a flood that bursts through all dams, or like a stream that cannot return to its fountain, or like tides that do turn; the disappointed lover dies like an unfed stream; the mind of a capricious tyrant is like a vast sea

he compares his own king to the gentle Thames;[1] and he com-
pares the Romans to the Tyber.[2]   Pope scornfully likens Curll to
the Uridanus.[3]   Cowley compares Jonathan to the fair Jordan.[4]
Halifax compares the reign of Charles II. to the Thames.[5]   Arm-
strong wishes his own style to combine the qualities of the Tweed
and the Severn.[6] Hughes likened his Muse to the wanton Thames.[7]
Roscommon thought a dull style was like the passive Soane.[8]
Somerville compared Allan Ramsay's poetry to Avona's silver
tide.[9]   Thomson said that De La Cour's numbers went gliding
along in "trickling cadence" and were like the flow of the
Euphrates.[10]   Chief among similes of this sort is Denham's well-
known apostrophe to the Thames.[11]   There is also frequent use of
open to every wind that blows; the army of the enemy comes like the wind
broke loose upon the main; an obdurate foe is as deaf to supplication as seas
and wind to sinking mariners; an open mind is a crystal brook; grief under-
mines the soul as banks are sapped away by streams; the voice of a mob is like
winds that roar in pursuit of flying waves; unspeakable anger is like water
choking up the narrow vent of the vessel from which it is poured; and so on
through a long list.

[1] Prior: Carmen Seculare, st. 22.
[2] Prior: Carmen Seculare, st. 4.
[3] Pope: Dunciad, Bk. II, 182.
[4] Cowley: Davideis, 2:20.
[5] Halifax: On the Death of Charles II, l. 125.
[6] Armstrong: Benevolence, l. 152.
[7] Hughes: Greenwich Park.
[8] Roscommon: Essay on Translated Verse, l. 316.
[9] Somerville: An Epistle to Allan Ramsay, l. 5.
[10] Thomson: To De La Cour.

[11] Denham : Cooper's Hill.—The echoes of Denham's oratorical antitheses
are frequent enough to justify Swift's prohibition.   Denham's lines are,

> " O could I flow like thee, and make thy stream
> My great example, as it is my theme !
> Though deep, yet clear; though gentle yet not dull :
> Strong without rage, without o'erflowing full !"

Pope's lines (Dunciad 3: 169), beginning,

> " Flow, Welsted, flow ! like thine inspirer, Beer,
> Tho' stale, not ripe ; tho' thin, yet never clear,
> .   .   .   .
> Heady, not strong ; o'erflowing, tho' not full."

rivers in a more general way, as when Parnell compares the strains of the Psalmist to a rolling river,[1] and Stanhope compares Pope's style to a gliding river,[2] and Addison compares Milton's poems to a clean current showing an odious bottom,[3] and Dryden compares Sir Robert Howard's style to a mighty river.[4] The use of a river as a simile for life is not infrequent. For various purposes the Nile was often used. Its annual overflow and its unknown fountain-head are the chief characteristics drawn upon. The river similes seem as a whole to be more effectively worked out and more gracefully managed than most of the other similes of the period, although they have in no case the beauty and profound symbolism characteristic of the river similes of Wordsworth, Matthew Arnold, and Lowell.

are a parody rather than an imitation. The same cannot be said of the line (Temple of Fame, l. 374.)

> "So soft, though high, so loud, and yet so clear."

Prior has these lines (C. S. st. 22),

> "But her own king she likens to the Thames,
> With gentle course devolving fruitful streams;
> Serene yet strong, majestic yet sedate,
> Swift without violence, without terror great."

Fr. Knapp addresses the sea on the Irish coast in the following lines (To M Pope.)

> "Let me ne'er flow like thee! nor make thy stream
> My sad example, or my wretched theme."

Mallet has the lines (cf. Verbal Criticism, l. 228)

> "Great without swelling, without meanness plain;
> Serious, not silly; sportive, but not vain;
> On trifles slight, on things of use profound,
> In quoting sober, and in judging sound."

n Dyer we have a fainter echo (The Country Walk, l. 69),

> "Methinks her lays I hear,
> So smooth! so sweet! so deep! so clear!"

[1] Parnell: David, l. 49.

[2] Stanhope: Progress of Dullness.

[3] Addison: An Account of the Greatest English Poets.

[4] Dryden: Works, Vol. II, p. 7.

Another common form of comparison is that in which the seasons or the various aspects of the day are used to describe **The seasons in similitude** some person. One of the happiest examples is from Marvell.

> "She summ'd her life up ev'ry day,
> Modest as morn, as midday bright,
> Gentle as ev'ning, calm as night."[1]

Later similes are less graceful, but they usually have the antithetical form of expression.[2]

Fairly numerous similes are drawn from trees. Dryden gives typical examples, as,

> "And lofty cedars as far upward shoot
> As to the nether heavens they drive their root."[3]

This equal spread of roots and branches, the heavy fall of a great tree, and the superior height of some tall pine or cedar, are the . chief sources of similitudes.

The abundant commonplaces, the fluent ineptitudes of these eighteenth century similitudes did not escape satire in their own day. Now and then a critic looked with scorn upon the ingenious and exhausting attempts of the poet lovers to devise comparisons adequately expressive of the beauty, the fascination, the cruelty, the coldness, the inconstancy, of their Cynthias of the' minute. Butler thus notes the tendency of poor and unmeaning metaphors to advance in a mob when female charms were to be depicted:

> "In praising Chloris, moons, and stars, and skies,
> Are quickly made to match her face and eyes—
> And gold and rubies, with as little care,
> To fit the colour of her lips and hair;
> And, mixing suns, and flowers, and pearl, and stones,
> Make them serve all complexions at once."[4]

---

[1] Marvell: An Epitaph upon ——.
[2] Cf. Cowley: Davideis, 3: 553, and Pope: Spring, l. 81.
[3] Dryden: Works, 11:131; 3:390; 2:451.
[4] Butler: Satire to a Bad Poet.

This easy method of praising a mistress is also humorously described by Ambrose Philips:

> "To blooming Phyllis I a song compose,
> And, for a rhyme, compare her to the Rose;
> Then, while my Fancy works, I write down Morn,
> To paint the blush that does her check adorn,
> And, when the whiteness of her skin I show;
> With extasy bethink myself of Snow.
> Thus, without pains, I tinkle in the close,
> And sweeten into Verse insipid Prose."[1]

And Swift in his *Apollo's Edict*, 1720, specifically prohibits the use of some of the more wearisomely frequent similitudes. Some of the laws he imposes on the poets of his realm are:

> "No simile shall be begun
> With *rising* or with *setting* sun."

> "No son of mine shall e'er dare say,
> *Aurora ushered-in the day*,
> Or even name the *Milky-Way*."

> "The bird of Jove shall toil no more
> To teach that humble wren to soar."

> "Nor let my votaries show their skill
> By aping lines from Cooper's Hill;
> For know, I can not bear to hear
> The mimicry of 'deep, yet clear.'"

In general we may say of the similitudes of this period that in no other literary form was nature so widely used, and in no other form with so little beauty and spirit; that they were based on an insufficient and inexact knowledge of nature; and that they were used without any sympathetic sense of inner fitness.

A further characteristic of the use of nature in the classical period is a personification of natural objects with the ulterior purpose of making them conscious of the charms or emotions of some person. When such personification arises out of an intimate identification of man with nature, a subjective recognition of the

Artificial subordination of nature to man

---

[1] Ambrose Philips: Epistle to a Friend.

unity of all existence, or when it is the outgrowth of a supreme passion compelling the phenomena of nature into apparent sympathy with its own joy or grief, the expression is sure to bear the mark of inner conviction or strong emotion. But when the personification is manifestly a laborious artistic device, when it is based on neither belief nor passion, it must then be considered the mark of an age slightly touched by real feeling for nature. And such, in general, were the personifications so freely used in the English classical poetry. There is an artificiality, even a grotesqueness about some of them that forbids even temporary poetic credence on the part of the reader. A good example is in Waller's *At Pens-hurst* where the susceptible deer and beeches and clouds mourn with Waller over the ·cruelty of his stony-hearted Sacharissa.[1] At the death of any illustrious man or fair lady all nature was convulsed with grief. When Cælestia died the rivulets were flooded by the tears of the water-gods, the brows of the hills were furrowed by new streams, the heavens wept, sudden damps overspread the plains, the lily hung its head, and birds drooped their wings.[1] When Amaryllis had informed nature of the death of Amyntas all creation "began to roar and howl with horrid yell."[2] When Thomas Gunston died just before he had finished his seat at Newington, Watts declared that the curling vines would in grief untwine their amorous arms, the stately elms would drop leaves for tears, and that even the unfinished gates and buildings would weep.[3] In love-poetry nature is frequently represented as abashed and discomfited before the superior charms of some fair nymph. Aurora blushes when she sees cheeks more beauteous than her own. Lilies wax pale with envy at a maiden's fairness.[4] When bright Ophelia comes lilies droop

[1] Congreve: The Mourning Muse of Alexis, 1. 89. Cf. also Fenton: Florelia.

[2] Congreve: The Tears of Amaryllis for Amyntas, 1. 143.

[3] Watts: A Funeral Poem on Thomas Gunston. 1. 252, and 1. 308.
Compare the indifference of nature to the death of Lucy whose body is
"Rolled round in earth's diurnal course
With rocks, and stones and trees."
Wordsworth: Lucy.

[4] Cowley: Constantia and Philetus, st. 5 and st. 10.

and roses die before their lofty rival.[1]   So the sun, when he sees
the beautiful ladies in Hyde Park.

> "Sets in blushes and conveys his fires
> To distant lands."[2]

And when that modest luminary is aware of the presence of the
fair Maria he

> "Seems to descend with greater care;
> And, lest she see him go to bed,
> In blushing clouds conceales his head."[3]

Nature is thus constantly compelled into admiring submission to
some Delia or Phyllis or Chloris.   Even further than this do the
poets go.   They make all the beauty of nature a direct outcome
of the lady's charms.   In the gardens at Pens-hurst the peace and
glory of the alleys was given by Dorothea's more than human
grace.[4]   No spot could resist the civilizing effect of her beauty. ·
The most charming example of this sort of fanciful exaggeration
is in Marvell's verses on Maria and the Nunappleton gardens.

> "'Tis she, that to these gardens gave
> That wondrous beauty which they have;
> She straightness on the woods bestows;
> To her the meadow sweetness owes;
> Nothing could make the river be
> So crystal pure, but only she,
> She yet more pure, and straight, and fair
> Than gardens, woods, meads, rivers, are."[5]

If later examples of the subordination of nature to man were
so graceful and quaintly tender as this poem of Marvell's we might
simply regard them as permissible instances of pathetic fallacy.
But even taken at its best we cannot fail to see that this concep-
tion of nature in its relation to man is quite unlike the dominant

---

[1] Shenstone: Roxana. For an interesting variation of this theme see
Cowley: The Spring.

[2] Hughes: Cupid's Review, l. 17.

[3] Marvell: Upon Appleton House, l. 661.

[4] Waller: At Pens-hurst.

[5] Marvell: Upon Appleton House, l. 689.

conception in the romantic school. In the one case we have
the subordination of nature; in the other the ministry of nature.
A significant comparison might be made between Marvell's
Maria, and Wordsworth's Lucy.[1] The one is the typical fair
maiden ruling over her flower world and inspiring to beautiful
life all the gentle nature forms about her. The other is
"Nature's Lady." Her whole being is moulded by her sus-
ceptibility to the deeper influences of nature untouched by art.
Maria gives to the external world the charm that it has. Lucy
is graced by the spirit of nature with all lovely qualities. But
Marvell's poem is really no fair criterion of the use of nature
in the classical love and elegiac poetry, for in most of that poetry
the emotion, the passion, that would justify extravagant or even
impossible conceptions is conspicuously absent. The extrava-
gance of speech stood as the sign of an intensity of feeling that
did not exist. The poet was not swept away by overwhelming
passion. He worked out his verses with conscious delibera-
tion. A lady-love was one of the necessary poetical stage prop-
erties, so the poet cast about him for a Phyllis or an Amoret,
and then cast about him for something to say to her. Such
lines as Waller's on Dorothea, who is so much admired by the
plants that

> " If she sit down, with tops all tow'rds her bow'd,
> They round about her into arbours crowd :
> Or if she walks, in even ranks they stand,
> Like some well-marshal'd and obsequious band" [2]

are at once felt to be merely cold, tasteless hyperbole. The
lines do not win a second's suspension of disbelief. Modes
of speech, a conception of nature, such that high-wrought emo-
tion might justify it, or that might be natural and inevitable
when the poet's thought was ruled by a living mythology,
became mere frigid conventionalities when there was no passion,
and when the spirits of stream and wood no longer won even
poetic faith.

[1] Wordsworth : Lucy.

[2] Waller : At Pens-hurst.

To speak of the poetic diction of the classical poetry has become a commonplace of criticism. By universal consent certain **Poetic diction** words and phrases seem to have been stamped as reputable, national, and present, and to have formed the authorized storehouse of poetical supplies. If one writer hit out a good word or phrase, it became common property like air or sunshine, and other writers did not waste their time beating the bush for a different form of words. Frequently words in the accepted diction may be traced to some Latin author, but the point to be noted here is that, whatever the origin of the word, its use is incessant. The fatal grip with which certain words clung to the poetical mind in the classical period receives interesting exemplification from a comparison of Chapman's and Pope's translations of Homer. It will be observed that in frequent passages Pope uses the words "purple," "deck," "adorn," and "paint," chief words in the classical poetic diction. But in the corresponding passages in Chapman some other form of words is used. And in most cases Pope's use of these terms has no warrant in the original. Likewise, in Dryden's translation of Virgil the stock diction is used when there is no idea or picture in the Latin to call for it, and when the use of the stock phraseology results in distinct loss of force or beauty. Compare for instance, Virgil's vivid *flavescet* and Dryden's tame "the fields adorn,"[1] used with reference to harvests of ripened grain. Or compare *novis rubeant quam prata coloribus* and "painted meads:"[2] *noctem ducentibus astris*, and "stars adorn the skies."[3] We find the same spirit illustrated in Dryden's modernization of Chaucer. The fresh, spontaneous simplicity of a poet like Chaucer serves exceptionally well to show the comparatively insipid and feeble treatment of nature on the part of those poets who were content to take their expressions, as well as their facts, at second hand. "The briddes" becomes "the painted birds:" "a goldfinch" is amplified into "a goldfinch with gaudy pride of painted plumes." "At the sun upriste" becomes

---

[1] Virgil: Eclogue IV, l. 28. Dryden: Pastoral IV, l. 33.

[2] Virgil: Georgics 4 : 306. Dryden: Georgics 4 : 433.

[3] Virgil: Georgics 3 : 156. Dryden: Georgics 3 : 250.

> "Aurora had but newly chased the night
> And purpled o'er the sky with blushing light."[1]

The same point is well exemplified in some of the changes made by Percy in the Ballads. For instance,

> "As itt befell in Midsummer time
> When burds singe sweetlye on every tree"

was modernized to,

> "When Flora with her fragrant flowers
>   Bedeckt the earth so trim and gaye,
> And Neptune with his daintye showers
>   Came to present the monthe of Maye."[2]

Full illustration would require much more space than is here at command, but the point to be made is clear, namely, that even when the poet had his natural facts furnished for him, he instinctively put them into the moulds of an accepted poetic diction.

By all odds the most frequent and significant words in this stock poetic diction, so far as it has to do with the presentation of nature, are indicative of dress or adornment in some form. The word "paint" is everywhere. Snakes and lizards and birds; morning and evening; gardens, meadows, and fields; prospects, scenes, and landscapes; hills and valleys; clouds and skies; sunbeams and rainbows; rivers and waves; and flowers from tulips to white lilies—nothing escapes. It is little wonder that Somerville called God "the Almighty Painter."[3] The word "paint" is really an Elizabethan survival, and as such came into the possession of Cowley whose use of it is absolutely vicious. A rainbow is "painted tears." The wings of birds are "painted oars." David after the fight with the giant is "painted gay with blood," and the blood of the Egyptians lost in the Red Sea "new paints the waters' name."[4] "Gaudy" is another word of frequent occurrence. In general the meaning was as now, "ostentatiously

---

[1] Dryden: Works 12 : 5 ; 11: 221.

[2] Percy: Reliques 2 : 190.

[3] Somerville: To Anne Coventry, l. 25.

[4] Cowley: The Shortness of Life, st. 11; The Muse; Davideis. 2 : 29: The Plagues of Egypt, st. 17.

fine" as we see in Shakespeare's phrase "rich but not gaudy," and in Dryden's "gaudy pride of painted plumes." In that sense it was fitly applied to peacocks, and perhaps even to rainbows, but such phrases as "a gaudy fly,"[1] the "gaudy plumage"[2] of falcons; the "gaudy axles of the fixed stars,"[3] the "gaudy month" of May,[4] the "gaudy opening dawn,"[5] the "gaudy milky soil"[6] and the "gaudy Tagus"[7] seem to have no exact meaning. "Bright" might often serve as a synonym, but not in the application of the word to flies and falcons. The word "adorn" is likewise eminently serviceable. Fruit adorns the trees, fleecy flocks adorn the hills, flowers adorn the green, rainbows adorn clouds, blades of grass adorn fields, vegetables adorn gardens, Phœbus adorns the west and is himself adorned with all his light, and Emma's eyes adorn the fields she looks on. "Deck" is another favorite. Flora's rich gifts deck the field, herbs deck the spring, and corals deck the deep. Vales, meadows, fields, mountains, rivers, shores, plains, paths, turf, gardens—all are profusely "damasked" or "enamell'd" or "embroider'd." The wings of butterflies and linnets are "gilded." The rising sun gilds the morn; the gaudy bow gilds the sky; gaudy light gilds the heavens: lightning gilds the storm; meteors and stars gild the night; and a Duchess gilds the rural sphere when she condescends to visit the country.

These milliner-like words were not, however, the only ones that the poet could claim as lawful heritage. He knew, for instance, that he could always call honey "a dewy harvest," or "balmy dew," or "ambrosial spoils," and have his hearers know what he meant. His birds, though almost necessarily a "choir" could be "feathered" or "tuneful" or "plumy" or "warbling" according to his taste. His fish were easily labeled as "finny,"

<hr>

[1] Blackmore: Creation, 6:170; 5:101; Yalden: The Insect.

[2] Somerville: Field Sports, l. 161.

[3] Pitt: Earl Stanhope; Psalm 144.

[4] Tickell: Kensington Garden; Somerville: Rural Games, 1:94.

[5] Dyer: Gronger Hill, l. 65.

[6] Dryden: Works, Vol. VI, 228.

[7] Cowley: Ode 2.

"scaly," or "watery." Breezes were "whispering," "balmy," "ambrosial"; zephyrs were "gentle," "soft," and "bland"; gales were "odoriferous," "wanton," "Elysian"; and no other kinds of winds blew except in storm similes. "Vernal" and "verdant" come in at every turn. From Waller on the epithet "watery" seems eminently satisfactory to the poetic mind. Dryden may be taken as illustrative. To him the ocean is a "watery desert," a "watery deep," a "watery plain," a "watery way," a "watery reign." The shore is a "watery brink," or a "watery strand." Fish are a "watery line" or a "watery race." Sea-birds are "watery fowl." The launching of ships is a "watery war." Streams are "watery floods." Waves are "watery ranks."[1]   The word occurs with wearisome iteration in succeeding poets. It is applied not only to the sea, but to rivers clouds, and rain, to glades, meads, and flowers, to landscapes, to mists, to the sky, to the sun, and to the rainbow. The set phrases for the sky are such as "azure sky," "heaven's azure," "concave azure," "azure vault," "azure waste," "blue sky," "blue arch," "blue expanse," "blue vault," "blue vacant," "blue serene," "aërial concave," "ætherial vault," "aërial vault," "vaulted sky," "vaulted azure," with such other changes as may be rung on these words. The chief words applied to stars, "spangle" and "twinkle,"[2] have been already noted.   The usual adjectives for streams and brooks are pleasant, easy words like "liquid," "lucid," "limpid," "purling," "murmuring," and "bubbling." "Rural," "rustic" and "sylvan" are epithets applied to anything belonging to the country, whether to the hours spent there, the songs of the birds, the charming country-maidens and their loves, their bowers, their bliss, their toil. "Flowery" is so constantly used as descriptive of brooks, borders, banks, vales, hills, paths, plains, and meads, that it really has not much more meaning than the definite article prefixed to ·

---

[1] Many of these words occur in the translations by Dryden but in none of the instances quoted is there any justification in the Latin phrase for the adjective "watery."   For instance, "watery way"=spumantibus undis; "watery reign"=altum; "watery deep"= pelago, and so on through the list."

[2] See p. 19.

a noun. "Vocal" is applied to vales, shades, hills, shores, mountains, grots, and woodlands. "Pendent" and "hanging" belong to cliffs, precipices, mountains, shades, and woods. "Headlong" and "umbrageous" are favorite adjectives for groves or shades of any sort. "Mossy" applies to grottos, fountains, streams, caves, turf, banks, and so on. "Gray" is the usual descriptive word for twilight, and "brown" for night. "Lawns" are usually "dewy."

Some words in this poetic diction are no longer much used. "Breathing," is an example. It usually referred to the air in gentle motion, as "breathing gales," but we also find "breathing earth," referring to mists, and "breathing sweets," and "breathing flowers" or "breathing roses," where the reference is to perfume. "Maze" and "mazy" are also much used. The Thames and other streams lead along "mazy trains." The track of the hare is an "airy maze." Paths meet in narrow mazes and stars unite in a mazy, complicated dance. Milton's stream flows with "mazy error." This word "error" is frequently used in its exact derived meaning. In another place Milton speaks of streams that wander with "serpent error."[1] Blair has a stream that slides along in "grateful errors."[2] In Falconer the light strays through the forest with "gay romantic error."[3] In Gay the fly floats about with "wanton errors."[4] Dyer winds along a mazy path with "error sweet."[5] Armstrong's "error" leads him through endless labyrinths.[6] Addison's waves roll in "restless errors,"[7] and Thomson treads the "maze of autumn with cheerful error."[8] "Amusive" is a word applied by Pitt[9] to the ocean,

[1] Milton, Paradise Lost, 4:239; 7:302.

[2] Blair: The Grave.

[3] Falconer: The Shipwreck, 1:359.

[4] Gay: Rural Sports, 1:226.

[5] Dyer: Ruins of Rome, l. 86.

[6] Armstrong: Art of Preserving Health, 2:7.

[7] Addison: To the King, l. 115.

[8] Thomson: Autumn, 626; cf. also Summer, l. 1574; Autumn, l. 628.

[9] Pitt: Ode to John Pitt, st. 5; Mallet: Amyntor and Theodora, 1:153; Shenstone: To a Lady; Rural Elegance, st. 17.

and by Mallet to clouds; Shenstone says that country joys "amuse securely." It seems to be half apologetic in tone in some cases; in others it merely means pleasing. Thomson used the word as verb or adjective several times.[1] We also find it in Parnell.[2] Another word of unusual application is "towering." When used of the Alps it is easily understood, but it seems a heavy word to apply to the flight of hawks, falcons, and eagles, though more appropriate there than when applied to swans, and larks, and even to spiders. It probably meant simply "ascending." "Lawn" is used in the sense of an open glade in the woods. Even so late as Wordsworth this meaning persists.[3] One unpleasant but not uncommon word is "sweat." It may be a survival from the metaphysical conceits, for we find in Dr. Donne a reference to the "sweet sweat of roses," and Cowley has flowery Hermon "sweat" beneath the dews of night. Dryden has flowers sweat at night.[4] Fenton's flowers

> "All pale and blighted lie,
> And in cold sweats of sickly mildew die."[5]

Even Gray talks about the "sickly dews"[6] of night, and Thomson has caverns "sweat."[7] Garth, as a physician, may possibly be excused for having the "sickening flowers" drink up the silver dew, and the grass tainted with "sickly sweats of dew," but when he has the fair oak adorned with "luscious . sweats,"[8] he has gone into the realm of æsthetics, and no excuse can prevail.

The power of fashion in words in a conventional age is further shown by the prevalence of adjectives ending in "y." They are favorites with Dryden, and hold their own steadily through the century that followed. Beamy, bloomy, forky, branchy, flamy,

---

[1] See Thomson, p. 87.
[2] Parnell: Hymn to Contentment.
[3] Wordsworth: Three Years She Grew.
[4] Dryden: Works, 2:360; 9:104.
[5] Fenton: Florelio, l. 43.
[6] Gray: Progress of Poetry.
[7] Thomson: Autumn, l. 843.
[8] Garth: Dispensary, 2:3; 2:14; 4:260.

purply, steepy, spumy, surgy, foamy, blady, dampy, chinky, sweepy, sheltry, moony, paly, tusky, heapy, miny, saggy, and many more occur where at present there would be no ending or the ending "ing."

The stock poetic diction may serve also to illustrate the indebtedness of the English classical poets to their Latin masters in the matter of phraseology. Compare, for instance, the use of the word *cavus* in its application to *montes*, *cavernæ*, *trunci*, *saxa*, *umbra* and *flumina*, and the English word "hollow," as applied to caves, rocks, mountains, shores, valleys, and even to the dark. Or compare the Latin use of *horridus*, meaning rough, rugged, wild, with "horrid," in its application to mountains, rocks, and thickets. "Savage mountains" and "shaggy mountains" sound like an echo from Virgil's *montes feri* and *intonsi montes*. The fundamental conception is certainly the same. Milton's "hairy thickets" and bushes with "frizzled hair" and Dryden's "hairy honours of the vine" are suggestive of the Latin use of *comae* as a trope for foliage. The word "honours," as applied to foliage or fruits, is also of Latin origin. The *tristis* or *dura hiems* of Virgil finds its echo in the general epithets applied to winter in English poetry. "Deform'd" and "inverted" seem to be mere Latin transcripts. Dryden was fond of the word "nodding." He used it twice in translations in places where some other word would more accurately represent the original.[1] In its application to mountains the word may, perhaps, be traced to Virgil's *nutantem mundum*. Its further use by Dryden, Pope, Akenside, Shenstone, and others, with reference to forests, rocks, and precipices, is apparently a later outgrowth from its application to mountains. "Sylvan Muse" and *silvestris musa;* "flowery plains" and *florea rura;* "liquid fountains" and *liquidi fontes;* "mossy springs" and *muscosi fontes* are

---

[1] Virgil: Georgics, 1:329, quo maxuma motu Terra tremit; Dryden: Georgics, 1:430, the mountains nod and earth's entrails tremble; Virgil: Pastoral 6, rigidas motare cacumina quercus; Dryden: Pastoral 6, nodding forests to the numbers danced; Cf. Pope: Messiah, nodding forests on the mountain dance, and Milton: Comus, l. 38, nodding horror of the wood.

but a few of the many exact parallels between the English
and Latin phrases descriptive of scenery. So, too, the super-
ficial conception of the various beauties of nature as "adorn-
ments" of the earth finds its prototype in such expressions as
lucidum caeli decus, applied to the moon, or *pulla ficus, ornat
arborem,* or *vitis ut arboribus decori est, ut vitibus uvae.* An
instructive example of the way in which borrowed epithets
lose their significance and become merely conventional is
the word "painted" in its application to birds. In Virgil
pictaeque volucrae[1] meant birds of many colors, or of bright
colors. Milton uses the phrase "painted wings,"[2] referring
apparently to brilliant birds in the Garden of Eden. But by
Pope's time the word "painted" had become a stock epithet
with its connotation so vaguely widened that it would be difficult
to give its exact meaning. It was simply indefinitely associated
with birds, hence Pope applied it to the brown wings of a
pheasant.[3] Shenstone uses it of the wings of a fly,[4] and Parnell
applies it to the eye of a peacock,[5] and Waller to the peacock's
nest.[6] In the same way "painted," in its application to flowers,
might easily be a picturesque descriptive adjective for bright
blossoms of any sort, but being gradually more and more closely
associated with flowers, it would lose its first meaning and come
to be applied to white lilies as well as tulips. "Purple" is
another borrowed word. It brought with it its whole train of
Latin meanings. In ordinary English speech "purple" had a
fairly definite reference to a specific color composed of red and
blue, but in the English classical poetry it was used in exactly
the Latin sense. The fundamental idea of *purpureus* was color,
but a secondary meaning was brightness; in its twofold applica-
tion it was a descriptive epithet applicable to light,[7] to flowers in

[1] Virgil: Georgics, 3:243. Æneid, 4:525.

[2] Milton: Paradise Lost, 7:434.

[3] Pope: Windsor Forest, l. 118. Cf. Note in Courthope edition.

[4] Shenstone: Virtuoso.

[5] Parnell: Anacreontic.

[6] Waller: On a Brede of Divers Colors.

[7] Hugo Blümner: Die Farbenbezeichnungen bei den Römischen Dichtern;

general, to roses, spring, or morning. The English phrases, "morning's purple wings," "the purple day," "the purple east," "the purpled air," "ground empurpled with roses," "the purple spring," "purple daffodils," are such as would serve the purpose of a modern impressionist painter, but in eighteenth century poetry they chiefly indicate a knowledge of the classics. They were clearly imitative phrases.

In individual cases the charge of imitation is a hazardous one to make because so difficult to prove. However close the parallelism it is always possible to believe that two persons thought of the same thing independently. Where a whole literary period is under consideration as here, all that can be said is that the similarities between the English and the Latin forms of expression are numerous and striking, that the phrases are frequently such as would not naturally occur to an English poet, that the English poets had little first-hand knowledge of nature, and that they knew their Virgil and Horace by heart. But after all, the inner conviction of imitation with which one turns from a consecutive reading of the two literatures is a more legitimate proof, perhaps, than even a liberal assemblage of debatable specific cases.

The imitation is not confined to diction. Many of the favorite similes, especially those drawn from trees, bees, leaves in autumn, the oak and vine, angry seas, and streams, have a Latin cast. They seem to be worked out on Virgilian models. As one reads, it is impossible not to feel that the English poet owed more to his classical library than to his knowledge of nature. One striking mark of imitation is the prevalence of the artificial cumulative simile so common in Virgil.

The details in the Latin pastoral poetry are also freely transferred to descriptions of English scenes. The poet could not describe English meadows without a desire to transplant therein some fairer blooms from "the unenvious fields of Greece and

pp. 184–198. Blümner shows that πορφύρεος was used by the Greeks with widely varying meanings, and adds, "Ganz ähnlich ist der Gebrauch, den die römischen Dichter von purpureus machen nur zweifellos in viel weniger ursprünglicher Weise." He says further that the Latin poetical use of purpureus did not follow the speech of daily life.

Rome." English rivers, skies, seas, plains, hills, and valleys were presided over by classic deities. Ceres, Pomona, and Bacchus, Dryads and Naiads, were as omnipotent as if they were still believed in. The hardy English shepherd was transformed into a languid swain eternally seeking mossy caves as a refuge against burning heats. His chief occupation was to lie beside some murmuring rill, or beneath some spreading beech, or under some myrtle hedge, and charm the listening vale with love ditties played on his pipe: or, for variety, to enter into some amoebean contest with a neighboring swain concerning the rival beauty of their respective nymphs. His chief troubles were the coyness, fickleness, and desertion of this same much-praised Phyllis or Chloris,[1] and the occasional incursion of nightly predatory wolves among his fleecy flocks. And all this calmly in the face of the fact that there were no predatory animals in English forests, that the chief enemies of the English shepherd were cold and storm, and that he would be much more likely to seek a sunny bank than a cooling grot. The classical English poets not only knew nothing of the genuine English shepherd such as Wordsworth's Michael, but they did not wish to know of him. It was their ambition to follow in the path marked out by the Mantuan swain. If they could write so that every line would "confess Virgil"[2] they

[1] This constant use of Latin and Greek names for English peasants was frequently satirized. Dryden makes Limberham say to Brainsick,

"But why, of all names, would you choose a Phyllis? There have been so many Phyllises in song I thought there was not another to be had for love or money."—Works, Vol. 6, p. 62.

Cf. Watts: Meditation in a Grove.

"No Phyllis shall infect the air
With her unhallow'd name."

[2] Compare Ridley's characteristic commendation of Christopher Pitt's poems.

"In every line, in every word you speak
I read the Roman and confess the Greek,"

and Pitt's precept in Vida's Art of Poetry, 1:102,

"Explore the antients with a watchful eye,
Lay all their charms and elegancies by,
Then to their use the precious spoils apply."

were satisfied.   Pope said that it was the poet's office to repre-
sent shepherds not as they are but as they may be conceived to
have been in some past golden age.[1]   That golden age existed
apparently in the Italy of Virgil and the Greece of Theocritus.
Dryden gave the acceptable advice,

> " For guides take Virgil and read Theocrite.
>   By them alone you'll easily comprehend
>   How poets, without shame, may condescend
>   To sing of gardens, fields, of flowers, and fruit,
>   To stir up shepherds, and to tune the flute."[2]

Except in burlesque no poet of that day cared to change
"Strephon and Phyllis" into "Tom and Bess."   The great effort
was to dignify humble themes by constant reference to the great
poems of the past.

The general structure of many English poems was evidently
conformed to Latin models.   A comparison of the *Pastorals* of
Pope, Gay, and Ambrose Philips would sufficiently establish this
point.[3]

Throughout the classical poetry of nature there is little reli-
ance on first-hand observation.   There was safety and dignity in
following Dick Minim's advice, "When you sit down to write
think what your favorite author would say under such and such
circumstances," and the favorite authors were sure to be Virgil,
and Horace, and Ovid.

The imitations were not, however, exclusively from the Latin
authors.   Often the Latin borrowings came at second-hand from
other English poets, and English poets borrowed freely from
each other.   A single instance may be cited to show how an
insipid and almost unmeaning collocation of words could hold
its own and be re-echoed from poet to poet.   Addison's couplet,

> " My humble verse demands a softer theme,
>   A painted meadow, or a purling stream,"[4]

[1] Pope: Discourse on Pastoral Poetry.

[2] Dryden: Works, 15:231.

[3] Compare especially Gay's Monday, Pope's Spring, and Virgil's Third
Eclogue.   Also Gay's Thursday and Virgil's Eighth Eclogue.

[4] Addison: Letter from Italy (1701).

was imitated by Tickell in,

> " By Nature fitted for an humble theme
>   A painted prospect, or a murmuring stream," [1]

and twice by Pope in,

> " Enough to shame the gentlest bard that sings
>   Of painted meadows and of purling springs," [2]

and

> " Like gentle Fanny's was my flowery theme,
>   A painted mistress or a purling stream." [3]

Compare also,

> " Most of our poets choose their early theme
>   A flowery meadow or a purling stream." [4]

But one other sort of imitation can be noticed here, and that is a natural outcome from the use of the rhymed couplet. It is what Pope calls " the sure return of still expected rhymes." The common rhyme of "stream" and "theme" has already been noted. Pope calls attention to others :

> " Whene'er you find the ' cooling western breeze '
> In the next line it ' whispers through the trees.'
> If crystal streams ' with pleasing murmurs creep '
> The reader's threatened, not in vain, with ' sleep.' " [5]

The last reference is an ungracious hit at one of Wycherley's poems recommendatory of Pope's *Pastorals*, but the rhyme of " breeze " and " trees " is certainly of a bewildering, dizzying frequency. There is a stanza in point in one of the doubtful poems attributed to Gray.

> " First when Pastorals I read,
>   Purling streams and cooling breezes

---

[1] Tickell: Oxford (1707).

[2] Pope: January and May, l. 454.

[3] Pope: Epistle to Dr. Arbuthnot, l. 149.

[4] William Thompson: To the Author of Leonidas.

[5] Pope : Essay on Criticism, 1 : 350.

> I only wrote of; and my head
> Rhimed on, reclined beneath the Tree-zes."[1]

One cause of the artificial and forced effect of the classical poetry of nature is undoubtedly the sameness of impression producted by this frequent recurrence of the same rhymes.

In the foregoing study of the attitude of the classical poets towards nature certain dominant characteristics have beeen indicated, all of them pointing to a lack of interest in nature. The attention of the age was concentrated elsewhere. Not nature, but man was the supreme interest. And the limitations must be drawn even more closely for the interest was not in man as man according to the democratic spirit of the succeeding romantic age, nor in man as a creature of daring, of wild passions, of lawless enthusiasms, of boundless energies, as in the preceding Elizabethan age, but man as part of a well-organized social system. Man in London was the central thought of the age. This supremacy of the interest in man accounts for the acknowledged preference for city life. In the country bad roads and poor conveyances effectually separated men from each other. In the city the wits of the coffee-house and the beaux and belles of the drawing-room were able to gain the social converse and mutual admiration necessary to their happiness. What they had to say to each other was incomparably more interesting than any revelation from nature's solitary places. Men feared and disliked mountains and the sea because these natural features stood as obstacles to the easy pursuit of many pleasures, and because in the presence of forces so vast and elemental men felt themselves overawed and threatened. What they could not understand and conquer was their foe. They turned uneasily from all forms of nature that suggest mysterious, unseen forces over which man has no control. The limitless spaces of the sky, the "solemn midnight's tingling silentness," the magical charm of moonlight, whatever is infinite in its suggestiveness, drawing the spirit of man into the vast, shadowy realms of the unknown, filled them with dismay. In nature as

Man the supreme interest of the age

---

[1] Gray: Ode.

in everything else they instinctively confined themselves to such portions of truth as they could clearly state and use. The kind of nature they loved was that in which man was easily supreme. Their delight in cultivated rural England was largely based on its power of ministering to man's ease and physical well-being.[1] Their delight in the formal garden grew out of their pleasure in seeing the triumphal expenditure of human effort. There nature

[1] In this connection see the following passages from Ruskin, Humboldt, and Veitch on nature in the poetry of the ancients:

"Thus, as far as I recollect, without a single exception, every Homeric landscape, intended to be beautiful, is composed of a fountain, a meadow, and a shady grove. This ideal is very interestingly marked, as intended for a perfect one, in the fifth book of the Odyssey; when Mercury himself stops for a moment, though on a message, to look on a landscape 'which even an immortal might be gladdened to behold'. . . . Now the notable things in this description are, first, the evident subservience of the whole landscape to human comfort, to the foot, the taste, or the smell; and, secondly, that throughout the passage there is not a single figurative word expressive of the things being in any wise other than plain grass, fruit or flower. . . . If we glance through the references to pleasant landscape which occur in other parts of the Odyssey, we shall always be struck by this quiet subjection of their every feature to human service, and by the excessive similarity in the scenes. Perhaps the spot intended, after this, to be most perfect, may be the garden of Alcinous, where the principal ideas are, still more definitely, order, symmetry, and fruitfulness."
—Ruskin: Modern Painters, Chapter on "Classical Landscape."

"Homer looks on nature as it affects man — its power of sustaining life, its subserviency to our physical wants. Hence the side of nature which is lovingly regarded by him is not mountain, or rock, or wild sea — all fruitless and barren —but flat soft meadow-land, diversified, it may be, with tree and fountain, filled with waving grass — good pasture-land for nourishing the useful ox, or cow, or sheep." "In Theocritus . . . we do not go beyond the softer side . . . the accessories of the shepherd's life faithfully noted." "The aspect of nature which Virgil loved was the soft and pastoral side of Italian scenery. In so far as he has depicted free nature, it is seen almost wholly from the human side, and in its relation to man's works, life and action."—Veitch: The Feeling for Nature in Scottish Poetry, Vol. I, pp. 88–91.

"Es is oftmals ausgesprochen worden, dass die Freude an der Natur, wenn auch dem Alterthume nicht fremd, doch in ihm als Ausdruck des Gefühls sparsamer und minder lebhaft gewesen sei denn in der neueren Zeit. . . . In dem hellenischen Alterthum, . . . das eigentlich Naturbeschreibende zeigt sich dann nur als ein Beiwerk, weil in der griechischen Kunstbildung sich alles gleichsam im Kreise der Menscheit bewegt.

was "rhymed and twisted and harmonized" at pleasure. Man's supremacy was nowhere else more effectually acknowledged. Not art concealed but art manifest was the ideal. Evelyn's enjoyment of French and Italian gardens is almost always based on his pleasure in some mechanical device whereby man had conquered nature.[1] What Cowley most enjoyed in the country was the sense of his own skill and mastery. The "best natured" satisfaction of all is, he says, the husbandman's delight in "looking round about him and seeing nothing but the effects and improvements of his own art."[2] The supremacy of the interest in man is further explanatory of the facts already sufficiently commented upon that the most abundant use of nature was in simil-

"Beschreibung der Natur in ihrer gestaltenreichen Mannigfaltigkeit, Naturdichtung als ein abgesonderter Zweig der Litteratur, war den Griechen völlig fremd. Auch die Landschaft erscheint bei ihnen nur als Hintergrund eines Gemäldes, vor dem menschliche Gestalten sich bewegen. Leidenschaften in Thaten ausbrechend fesselten fast allein den Sinn. Ein bewegtes öffentliches Volksleben zog ab von der dumpfen, schwärmerischen Versenkung in das stille Treiben der Natur; ja den physischen Erscheinungen wurde immer eine Beziehung auf die Menschheit beigelegt, sei es in den Verhältnissen der äusseren Gestaltung oder der inneren anregenden Thatkraft. Fast nur solche Beziehungen machten die Naturbetrachtung würdig, unter der sinnigen Form des Gleichnisses, als abgesonderte kleine Gemälde voll objectiver Lebendigkeit in das Gebiet der Dichtung gezogen zu werden."—Kosmos. Vol. 2, pp. 5, 6.

[1] In this connection compare the following significant passage from Taine: " Rien ne m'a plus intéressé dans les villas romaines que leurs anciens maitres. Les naturalistes le savent, on comprend très-bien l'animal d'après la coquille. L'endroit où j'ai commencé à le comprendre est la villa Albani. . . . Cette villa est un débris, comme le squellette fossile d'une vie qui a duré deux siècles, et dont le principal plaisir consistait dans la conversation, dans la belle représentation, dans les habitudes de salon, et d'antichambre. L'homme ne s'intéressait pas aux objets inanimés, il ne leur reconnaissait pas une âme et une beauté propre; ils ne servaient que de fond au tableau, fond vague et d' importance moins qu' accessoire. Toute l'attention était occupée par le tableau lui-même, c'est-à-dire par l'intrigue et le drame humain. Pour reporter quelque partie de cette attention sur les arbres, les eaux, le paysage, il fallait les humaniser, leur ôter, leur form et leur disposition naturelle, leur air 'sauvage,' l'apparance du désordre et du désert, leur donner autant que possible l'aspect d'un salon, d'un galerie à colonnades, d'une grande cour de palais."—Taine: Voyage en Itálie, Tome I, pp. 231, 232. (Paris. Librairie Hatchette et Cie, 1893.)

[2] Cowley: Of Agriculture.

itudes for human qualities and passions, that these similitudes were drawn from a surprisingly small number of natural phenomena, and that the nature side of the similitudes was often carelessly and ignorantly handled. The dominance of man is also back of the conception of nature as stirred by man's joys and woes, and plunged into despair by his death. Nature is, at the utmost, but the comparatively unimportant background against which man acts his part, and there is seldom any effort to suit the background to the picture. There is likewise significance in the twofold fact that in the set poetic diction there are many words and phrases relating to nature and comparatively few relating to man. Where there was a concentration of interest the vividness of the conception demanded new and original forms of speech, while the stock diction, like cant in religious expression, showed the absence of genuine feeling. It is in Pope's *Pastorals* not in *The Dunciad* that we find stock words, conventional phrases, and hereditary similes.

In summary we may note that the characteristic attitude
Summary   towards nature in the classical period is marked by,

a. Prevailing dislike or neglect of the grand or the terrible in nature as mountains, the ocean, storms, and winter.

b. A similar dislike or neglect of the mysterious or the remote, as the various phenomena of the sky.

c. A certain apparent friendliness towards the gentle, pleasant, serviceable forms of nature as in rural cultivated England, in spring and summer, in good weather, in various forms of horticulture.

d. An especial pleasure in nature ordered and made symmetrical by art, as in formal gardens and parks.

e. Descriptions of a highly generalized sort with almost no touches of local color.

f. Full but conventional and superficial use of nature in similitudes for human passions and actions.

g. Narrow, uninterested, and hence frequently inaccurate observation of natural facts.

h. Cold and lifeless imitation of the forms and details without the spirit of Latin models.

i. A vocabulary restricted and imitative in character.

j. An underlying conception of nature as entirely apart from man, and to be reckoned with merely as his servant or his foe.

CHAPTER II.

In this chapter the method of work is quite unlike that in the
preceding study.   The typical and the dominant are not regarded.
Attention is rather converged upon the significant exception.
We are led into nooks and corners and byways.   The most famous
author is not necessarily the one on whom emphasis is placed.   In
searching for legitimate proof of a tendency we may safely turn to
the work of men of unoriginal genius and moderate power.[1]   A
study of this sort would certainly give a distorted view if it were
for a moment thought to represent the period as a whole.   But
if it is held in mind that the attitude towards nature was in general
through the eighteenth century marked by indifference and arti-
ficiality, we may throw as high lights as we please on the excep-
tions.   This study will serve its purpose if, in its following out
of the complexities and inconsistencies that make a transition
period interesting, it shall succeed in showing that, along with
the classical feeling towards nature, there was also a real and
vital love for the out-door world, and that this new attitude
towards nature is marked by first-hand observation, by artistic
sensitiveness to beauty, by personal enthusiasm for nature, by a
recognition of the effect of nature on man, and, occasionally,
by an imaginative conception of nature somewhat in the Words-
worthian sense.

The new attitude towards nature, of which Thomson is the
first adequate exponent, finds occasional and not
ineffective expression during the two decades before
The poets between 1706 and 1726 the publication of *Winter* in 1726.   In the works
of John Philips, Ambrose Philips, Lady Winchelsea,
John Gay, Thomas Parnell, Samuel Croxall, William Pattison,

[1] See Gosse : Seventeenth Century Studies.   Introduction.

Allan Ramsay, Riccaltoun, and Armstrong, we become more or less definitely aware of a new outlook on the external world.

Dr. Johnson praised Philips's poem *Cyder*[1] because it had the "peculiar merit" of being "grounded in truth." On the whole this poem is of the didactic classical order, but here and there among the minutely accurate horticultural precepts we come upon indications that the poet was not insensible to the charms of nature in other than its utilitarian aspects. His delight in color may be seen from his specific descriptions of apples. The pippin is "burnish'd o'er with gold;" the red-streak "with gold irradiate and vermilion shines." "Plumbs" are "sky-dyed." He notes the "Ore, Azure, Gules," and the blending of colors in the rainbow. He observes the contrast between fields yellow with grain, and green pasture land. And he sees the colored edges of clouds when the sun breaks through. There is also apparent a sensitiveness to odors. He speaks of cowslip-posies "faintly sweet," of odorous herbs, of the fragrance of apples on a dewy autumn morning, and of "the perfuming flowery bean." Mr. Shairp credits Thomson with being the first poet to mention the fragrance of the bean fields,[2] but Philips is at least twenty years ahead of Thomson in noting this fact.

John Philips
(1676-1708)

We see further indication of Philips's enjoyment of nature in a few lines.

> " Nor are the hills unamiable, whose tops
> To heaven aspire, affording prospect sweet
> To human ken,"[3]

which were perhaps the earliest expression in the eighteenth century of that pleasure in high hills and wide prospects that was so marked a characteristic of later poetry. Philips's explanation of the satisfaction he found in an early morning walk, namely, that the mind perplexed with irksome thought is calmed by the influence of nature,[4] seems like a prophecy of the thought afterwards dominant concerning man's indebtedness to nature.

[1] Cyder, 1:248.
[2] Shairp: The Poetic Interpretation of Nature, p. 199.
[3] Cyder, 1:563.   [4] Cyder: 2:65.

In Ambrose Philips's *Pastorals* we find a mingling of first-hand observation and classical imitation. His references to the
Ambrose Phil-ips (1675-1749) ancients, his amœbean contests, the supposed effect of the death of Albino on the external world, the emphasis on dangers from heat and the nightly wolf, the frequent use of cumulative comparisons,[1] and, in general, the form of his *Pastorals*, show how closely he was held by conventional ideas. Furthermore, his facile use of nature is always determined by his attitude towards some pastoral nymph or swain. He rejoices to paint an idyllic background for some Rosalind. He heaps up images from nature to express the amorous praises of some Colinet. He has no conception of a relation between man and nature more intimate than the highly artificial one of his *Pastorals*. What is of importance in his poetry is the fact that in the midst of his imitations and conventionalities are many true and charming observations drawn entirely from English country life and not found in earlier eighteenth century poetry. His work is, to be sure, rendered weak and childish by two unpleasant mannerisms in diction; his use of adjectives ending in "y," as bloomy, dampy, bluey, steepy, purply, and so on, and his use of diminutives such as kidlings, lamb-kins, younglings, firstlings, and steerlings. But on the whole we find in his poems a more full and accurate knowledge of nature than is at all common in the poetry of the time. He notes the fleeting, dusky shadows cast by moving clouds, the glossiness of plums, the blue color of mists, the sweet odors of morning, the moaning of the night wind in the grove, the sportive chase of swallows, the loud note of the cuckoo, the speckled breast of the thrush, and the song of the backbird "fluting through his yellow bill." He usually calls flowers, trees, birds, and other animals by their specific names, and he seldom extends his list beyond his own probable observation. That Philips had a genuine love for nature in her milder forms is further seen from the preface to his *Pastorals*. "As in Painting," he says, "so in Poetry, the country affords not only the most delightful scenes and prospects, but

[1] Pastorals. 1:6; 3:1; 6; 3:41-44; 3:69-74; 1:10; 4:154; 5:8; 1:27; 2:59; 2:125-128; 3; 65-68; 4:153-160.

likewise the most pleasing images of life." He loved the songs of birds because the "sedate and quiet harmony" of their simple strains gives "a sweet and gentle composure to the mind." And he was conscious of an "unspeakable sort of satisfaction" when he saw "a little country-dwelling, advantageously situated amidst a beautiful variety of hills, meadows, fields, woods and rivulets."

Lady Winchelsea is, in the study of the poetry of nature, one of the most significant of the minor poets before Thomson. She was a friend of Rowe and Pope, and was honored **Lady Winchel-** by complimentary verses from them.[1] She is **sea (1660?-1720)** known now chiefly because of Wordsworth's reference to her,[2] and through the poems published in Ward's *English Poets.* Three of the poems there given, *The Nightingale, The Tree, A Nocturnal Revery,* have to do with nature. With these exceptions the eighty-one poems in the collection of 1713[3] are thoroughly classical in their form and spirit, though unmarked by any preponderance of artificial fancies. But these three short poems are remarkable productions when thought of in connection with their author's poetical environment. They are the earliest eighteenth century poems in which nature is frankly chosen as the theme, and they show a personal knowledge that must have been the accumulated result of many experiences.

The observation in *The Nightingale* is especially truthful and sympathetic. That there is no attempt to describe the bird is an omission justified by the fact that the nightingale is seldom seen.[4] The two characteristics noted in the bird's song are its exceeding sweetness and its sadness, or rather, its sense of pain.[5]

[1] Rowe : An Epistle to Flavia ; Pope : An Impromptu to Lady Winchelsea.

[2] Wordsworth : Essay, Supplementary to the Prefaces.

[3] Miscellany Poems on Several Occasions, Written by a Lady. 1713.

[4] In the references to the nightingale by Chaucer, Milton, Cowper, Wordsworth, Keats, Shelley, Matthew Arnold, and Mrs. Browning, the only approaches to description of the appearance of the bird are Matthew Arnold's "tawny-throated," Keats's "full-throated," and Coleridge's "bright, bright eyes, their eyes both bright and full."

Cf. Milton's, "sweetest, saddest plight ;" or "most musical, most melancholy ;" and Shelley's, "melodious pain ;" and Keats's, "plaintive anthem ;" and Matthew Arnold's, "Wild, unquenched, deep-sunken, old-world pain."

A comparison of the phrases in the notes will show that Lady Winchelsea listened with the hearing ear of a true poet. But we cannot fail to notice as well that the song is not fully heard or reported. In the other poets we find represented a richness, a fullness, an ecstasy, a tumult, not even hinted at in Lady Winchelsea's poem.[1] Nor does she mention the passion most poets have heard in the song.[2] But however incomplete the impression received may have been, the poetical record of what was perceived is both truthful and vivid. She seems to write as she listens and the reader follows the variations of the song through their effect on her own mind.

In the fifty-two lines of the poem on night twenty-two natural facts are recorded. Some of these would not escape the most careless, but only close observation would discover such details as the sleepy cowslip, the grass standing upright, the unusual strength of odors, the clearer sound of falling waters, the horse's audible cropping of the grass, the waving moon seen in the stream, and the distant call of the curlew. Lady Winchelsea's love of nature was of the most unambitious sort. To have seen the stately tree, to have heard the nightingale, to know all she did about night, would not have called her beyond the gates of her own park. But her joy in nature needed no strong or novel stimulus. It is her distinction that she had fixed an "exquisite regard" on the commonest facts of the

Coleridge speaks once of "pity-pleading strains," but in another poem contends for the "merry nightingale," and refuses to hear anything but "love and joyance" in the song.

[1] Cf. Matthew Arnold's,
    "How thick the bursts come crowding through the leaves;"
and Chaucer's "lusty nightingale" whose voice made a "loud rioting;" and Shelley's "storm of sound;" and Wordsworth's "tumultuous harmony;" and Keats's "pouring forth thy soul abroad in such an ecstasy;" and Coleridge's

        "The merry nightingale
    That crowds and hurries and precipitates
    With fast thick warble his delicious notes."

[2] Cf. Arnold's "Eternal passion!" Milton's "amorous power;" Shelley's "voluptuous nightingale;" Coleridge's "wanton song;" and all of Mrs. Browning's Bianca Among the Nightingales.

external world. and that she spoke quite clearly and simply from her own life. Hence her knowledge had the new quality of being specific and local and accurately defined.

Still more noteworthy is Lady Winchelsea's spiritual sensitiveness to nature. Such a phrase as "the mysterious face of heaven" marks a new conception of the sky. Night is no longer "the parent of fears" but a time whose solemn quiet suggests a strange and subtle sense of something too high for syllables to speak. Nature is to her no mere background for human life. Man is influenced by nature. His rage is disarmed. His spirit is led to feel a sedate content. And sometimes in moments of especial insight there is revealed to him in the inferior world an existence "like his own." Not often before Wordsworth is there so distinct a prevision of his way of looking at nature.[1]

In the slow turning of English poetry from the artificial to the natural John Gay was distinctly helpful, yet the reader of *Trivia, The Fan, The Epistles*, the *Fables*, and even the *Eclogues* would hardly suspect their author of knowing, in any close way, any life outside the city. It is only in *Rural Sports*, written when he was twenty-eight, and *The Shepherd's Week*, when he was twenty-nine, that we find any real study of nature. In *Rural Sports* hunting and especially fishing are described with the enthusiasm and technical accuracy of an expert. There is no hint of the feeling towards animals that made Thomson and Cowper abhor hunting. There is simply a thoroughly sportsmanlike knowledge of details, a sense of pleasurable excitement in the chase, and joy in victory. This delight in open air pursuits is often far enough removed from any real love of nature, and is here of much less significance than casual passages showing Gay's love of the world about him. He tells us that it was his habit to take morning walks through the fields,[2] that at sunset he often strayed out to the cliffs near Barnstaple. and lingered to watch the glowing colors of the sunset, and the later beauty of an "unclouded sky"

John Gay
(1685-1732)

---

[1] Cf. Gosse : Gossip in a Library, p. 123. Eighteenth Century, p. 35.

[2] Rural Sports, 1 : 35.

bright with stars and a silver moon that marked a glittering path along the sea.[1] This passage is interesting as being the first poetical record in this period of a walk purely to observe the beauties of nature. It is also one of the earliest appreciative mentions of the ocean. Gay's love of nature was largely confined to the milder aspects, but he seems not to have been entirely indifferent to hills. In speaking of Colton Hill in North Devonshire he said,

> " When its summit I climb, I then seem to be
> Just as if I approached nearer heaven !
> When with spirits depress'd to this hill I repair
> My spirits then instantly rally ;
> It was near this bless'd spot, I first drew vital air,
> So—a hill I prefer to a valley." [2]

In six or seven unimportant passages Gay speaks of hills or mountains, apparently using the words interchangeably, but not in a manner indicating much knowledge of them. Yet such little pictures as that of the dawn when the sun "strikes the distant eastern hills with light," or that of "the evening star shining above the western hill," show some recognition of hills as an attractive part of a landscape. Gay has also frequent mention of moonlight and starry skies. He knows flowers and birds and trees with some definiteness. He speaks of many domestic animals. He notes colors and odors.[3] He observes the lengthened shadows stretched across the meadows in the late afternoon, the long flight of crows seeking the wood at sunset, the streams "wrinkled" by a fresh breeze, the yellow showers of leaves in autumn. Abundant and varied as is this use of nature, it is not marked by especial delicacy of feeling or accuracy of observation. But for all that *The Shepherd's Week* is a notable piece of work, and it is in these pastorals that we find Gay's real service. Whether meant as a friendly aid in Pope's castigation of Ambrose Philips or not, these poems were unquestionably

[1] Rural Sports, I : 99.

[2] See Life of John Gay in Fables, Warne & Co., 1889.

[3] See Coquette Mother and Daughter for a second reference to the fragrant bean-flower before Thomson.

meant as a good-humored satire on pastorals that ventured to deal truthfully with English rustic life. The Latin form was counted the ideal one for pastoral. To this form Gay held, evidently with the conscious purpose of suggesting the Latin at every turn. Then he filled in this mould with the homeliest, most realistic details of English country life.[1] The plain, practical truth of these details is simply amazing as will be seen from the passages indicated in the note. See also the flowers brought in, the primrose, kingcup, clover, daisie, gilliflower, mary-gold, butter-flowers, cowslip, and others; and the animals, the witless lamb, frisking kid, udder'd cow, clucking hen, waddling goose, squeaking pigs, worrying cur, whining swine, paddling ducks, guzzling hogs, and others; and the country sports, as romping in the fields, blindman's buff, hot cockles, swinging, and others.[2] In *Pastoral IV* is an assemblage of curious country superstitions; in *Pastoral I* are given signs of rain; in *Pastoral V* are funeral customs; and in *Pastoral VI* an account of the favorite country songs. These poems are a veritable treasure-house for the student of folk-lore. They might also serve as a diary of country occupations. Take for example Bumkinet's reminiscences of Blouselinda's life in *Pastoral V.* In such a wood, he remembers, they gathered fagots. There he drew down hazel boughs and stuffed her apron with brown nuts. In another place he had helped her hunt for her strayed hogs, and as they drove the untoward creatures to the stye had seized the opportunity to tell his love. At the dairy he had often seen her making butter pats, or feeding with floods of whey the hogs that crowded to the door. In the barn as he plied the flail, he had watched her sift out food for the hens. In the field she had ranged the sheaves as he pitched them on the growing mow. The object of these

---

[1] As illustrative of this point compare, Virgil, Eclogue VIII, 27, 28, and Gay, Pastoral III, 59–62; Virgil, Eclogue I, 59-63, and Gay, Pastoral III, 67–72; Virgil, Eclogue V, 36–39, and Gay, Pastoral V, 83–87; Virgil, Eclogue V, 76–78, and Gay, Pastoral V, 153–158; Virgil, Eclogue IV, 1–3, and Gay, Pastoral VI, 1–3; Virgil, Eclogue VI, and Gay, Pastoral VI; Virgil, Eclogue VIII, and Gay, Pastoral IV.

[2] Pastoral I.

pastorals was to show the absurd incongruity between the Latin form with its suggestions of Arcadian days, and the roughness of English country life. The result was unexpected. Readers in general, indifferent to scholarly congruities, were delighted with the novelty, the air of freshness and truth in the pictures scattered through the *Pastorals*. Poetry had suddenly and without meaning to do it, gone from the city and the park to the very plainest and most matter of fact sort of country people and country occupations, and had somehow made them attractive. Blouzelinda and Buxoma are not in the same order of beings as the traditional Phyllis and Chloris, and they are equally far removed from the vulgar repulsive country wenches in Swift's coarse satires. They are real beings with a charm of their own, and the love they inspire in Lobbin Clout and Cuddy is an everyday, quite comprehensible affair.

The dirge for Blouzelinda indicates well the covert laugh with which Gay wrote these descriptions of country life. The clergyman said

> "that Heaven would take her soul, no doubt,
> And spoke the hour-glass in her praise—quite out."

After the funeral the men trudged

> "homeward to her mother's farm,
> To drink new cyder mull'd, with ginger warm,
> For gaffer Tread-well told us, by the by,
> ' Excessive sorrow is exceeding dry.' "

This sense of fun is everywhere apparent, and shows how unwittingly Gay broke a lance in a new cause. Yet some parts of his *Preface* are startlingly modern in their plea for truth to nature. Here is a passage which, so far as its spirit is concerned, might have been said by either Crabbe or Wordsworth.

" Thou wilt not find my shepherdesses idly piping on oaten reeds, but milking the kine, tying up the sheaves, or, if the hogs are astray, driving them to the styes. My shepherd gathereth none other nosegays but what are the growth of our own fields ; he sleepeth not under myrtle shades, but under a hedge ; nor doth he vigilantly defend his flock from wolves for there are none."

Whatever Gay meant to do, he really did accomplish what his Preface states as his aim. He turned poetry away from the "insipid delicacy" of the conventional pastoral, and truthfully represented the "plain downright hearty cleanly folk" of rustic England. And external nature, though nowhere dwelt upon for its own sake, is everywhere present and so vividly portrayed, that the reader had what was certainly a poetic novelty at that day, "a lively landscape of his own country, just as he might have seen it, if he had taken a walk in the fields at the proper season."

The use of external nature in Parnell's poems has narrow limits. There is no mention of winter, autumn, or summer.

Thomas Parnell (1679–1718) Mountains are merely noted in passing as disagreeable features in the poet's dreary surroundings in Ireland. There is but one line about the sea. Wild scenery of whatever sort is ignored. The only storm is described in some conventional lines in *The Hermit*. There is almost no record of specific knowledge of trees, or flowers, or birds. There are few indications of openness to sensuous impressions from specific forms, colors, odors, sounds. But in spite of these widely inclusive negations, Parnell is of distinct importance as a poet of nature. He has, to begin with, some accurate first-hand observation. He speaks once of the "differing green" of trees in spring. He describes a fern with some minuteness. There are two charming descriptions of banks and skies reflected in clear water.[1] Other fresh observations are,

> "Now early shepherds o'er the meadow pass
> And print long footsteps in the glittering grass."[2]

> "When in the river cows for coolness stand
> And sheep for breezes seek the lofty land."[3]

Or this of the close of a storm,

> "But now the clouds in airy tumult fly;
> The sun emerging opes an azure sky;

[1] Night Piece on Death. The Hermit.

[2] Health.   [3] The Flies.

> A fresher green the smelling leaves display,
> And, glittering as they tremble, cheer the day."[1]

Such lines are of value for they indicate, though they are few in number, some power of direct vision and of restrained, simple expression.

Parnell's distinctive excellence is, however, along different lines. He records not facts but impressions. He is essentially a poet of the spring; he felt intensely all the glad, abundant life of the early year. But there is not a description of spring in his poems. He gives instead curiously happy descriptive touches that suggest far more than they say. Note such lines as,

> " When spring came on with fresh delight,"[2]

or

> " Green was her robe, and green her wreath,
> Wher-e'er she trod 'twas green beneath."[2]

or

> " The planted lanes rejoice with dancing leaves."[3]

There is a lilt in such lines, a joyousness, an off-hand certainty of touch, not in keeping with the customary cold and labored descriptions of spring.

Of still greater significance is Parnell's literary use of nature. In the *Night Piece* the external scene serves as an appropriate background for the thought presented. The few natural facts are so well chosen and so delicately touched that all the moral reflections seem permeated with an appropriate out-of-doors atmosphere. The calm, perfect beauty of the picture of night with its closing suggestions of mystery and sadness, the fading of the pale moon, and the sounds that come over the long lake, fit exactly the course of the poet's melancholy meditation and contribute to it. The gay light pictures in the *Hymn to Contentment* are equally well suited to the spirit of joyous praise with which that poem concludes.

Bishop Jebb has pointed out for the enjoyment of the "classical and pious reader" the similarity between the moral reflections in this poem and those in Cardinal Bona's *Divina*

---

[1] The Hermit.   [2] Anacreontic.   [3] Health.

Psalmodia.[1] Parnell's close adherence to the thought of the
Cardinal in the didactic part of the poem, and the fact that the
last forty-two lines, the ones that deal with nature, are entirely
Parnell's own, give striking proof of the originality of his thought
concerning the external world and its power over the human
heart. It is in these lines that we find his most subtly suggestive
conception of nature. He represents himself as sad at heart.
He seeks contentment in earthly pomp, in the paths of knowledge,
in solitary search after diverting scenes in nature, but in vain.
At last he goes to a wood, and as he yields himself to the influ-
ence of the place becomes suddenly aware that in this quiet spot
the true spirit of contentment is speaking to him wise lessons of
self-control and communion with God. In gratitude for the joy
that has come to him through nature he utters a song of praise
to the "source of all nature," but as he looks about him on the
glad world, he feels that his song is merely an expression in
words of the great chorus of thanksgiving going always silently
up from sun and moon and stars, from seas, woods, and streams.

Such work as this is indeed remarkable before 1713; and
for spirituality and insight, for what has well been called "a
sense of the thing behind the thing," it was many years before
it was paralleled.

The Morning Contemplation is the only one of Pattison's poems
that has much to do with nature. It was written, his friend tells us,
on the banks of a river where the young poet used
to wander, endeavoring to attune his verses to the
smoothness and harmony of the stream. He was
especially sensitive to the "sadly pleasing melan-
choly" of moonlight nights and solitary walks, and he was one
of the first poets to express a longing for solitude with nature.
Gilded rooms of state, the purple slavery of towns, rob him of
the bliss he finds in the living forest. When alone in the spacious
fields he thinks himself almost a god. Even little scrubby thorns
are to him more pleasing objects than courts can show. Nature
charms his senses and soothes his soul; she is his best teacher,
and he trusts her plain instructions.

**William
Pattison
(1706-1727)**

[1] Parnell: Poetical Works, p. 77.

> " Tell me, all ye mighty wise,
>   Ye governors of colleges ;
>   What deeper wisdom can you know
>   Than easy nature's works here show,"

reads like a crude prevision of Wordsworth's *The Tables Turned.*
The "excellent morality" of *The Morning Contemplation* is much
in the vein of Dyer's *Grongar Hill.* Every fact in nature arouses
some thought or some emotion. By contrast or analogy it sug-
gests human life, as in the lines,

> " See this river as it goes,
>   With what eloquence it flows?
>
>   .   .   .   .
>
>   Believe me, life's the very same,
>   The very image of this stream."

Pattison's poem is of real importance, because its early date[1]
ranks it as probably the first of the eighteenth century poems
that treat of nature in the romantic, sentimental, fervid fashion
afterwards brought to its culmination by the Wartons.

Allan Ramsay's education was of the most limited sort, so
that, in early life at least, the development of his genius was
Allan Ramsay (1685-1758) unbiased by a knowledge of Latin and Greek or
even English models. After he was fifteen he lived
in Edinburgh and there began to be infected by
the pseudo-classicism of his day. The poems in which country
scenes and people were most fully represented were, however,
pretty clear and unadulterated records of his early experiences in
the secluded mountainous district of Lanarkshire where he was
brought up. The best poems of this sort are the pastoral dia-
logues, *Patie and Roger,* 1721, and *Jenny and Meggy,* 1723, or
rather, *The Gentle Shepherd,* 1725, which is a combination of the
two pastorals thrown into completer dramatic form. A second
edition of *The Gentle Shepherd* appeared in the same year as
Thomson's *Winter.*[2] It is worthy of note that the service ren-

---

[1] Pattison died in 1727, and he was in college during the four preceding
years. The records of his life are scanty, but he probably wrote this poem
before 1723, when he left the region of his dear Ituna, that being the stream on
whose banks he was accustomed to murmur out his verses.

[2] See Ramsay's Poems, I, p. xxvii.

dered by Gay to English poetry is in many respects paralleled by
Allan Ramsay's contributions to Scottish song. There are in
Ramsay's pastorals similar closely studied scenes from peasant
life, wherein are minutely described the superstitions,[1] the house-
hold customs,[2] the out-door occupations,[3] the trials,[4] and the
pleasures,[5] of the homely folk among the hills of Scotland. But
there are important differences. What Gay did lightly and with-
out serious intent was with Ramsay a service of love. He was
not laughing in his sleeve at the very truth he so capitally por-
trayed. Throughout his work there is, in general, an air of sin-
cerity. It is as if Gay wrote from the point of view of an out-
sider with an unfailingly keen eye, and a quick sense of humor.
But Ramsay wrote from a life that he had known and loved,
and that he thoroughly respected.[6] There are occasional false
notes in his pastorals. He gives his shepherds flutes and
reeds; his comparisons, especially his cumulative similes, are
conventional; he makes rather stiff use of personification; and
his desire to make his hero and heroine well born interferes with
the pastoral simplicity of the drama. But these are extraneous
and hardly affect the real texture of the work.

We find in Ramsay's poems occasional hints that his presen-
tation of homely Scottish scenes and people was not merely
instinctive, but that it was in some measure a deliberate choice.
In *Tartana*, written in 1721, he said that his chosen muses were
those that wandered through the clover meadows and the groves
along the smooth meandering Tweed, or by the gentle Tay, or
where the haughty Clyde roar'd over lofty cataracts.

[1] Cf. Richy and Sandy, l. 8; Robert, Richy, and Sandy, II. 31–34; Gentle
Shepherd, I, 1, 89; I, 1, 148; II, 2, 17–40; II, 3, 27–47; V, 1. 19–43.

[2] Cf. Gentle Shepherd, I, 2, 190–193, 207; I, 2, 200–204; II, 1, 76–86; II,
2, Prologue; II, 1, Prologue; III, 3, 111–116; V, 2, Prologue.

[3] Cf. Gentle Shepherd, I, 1, 205; I, 2, 1–4.

[4] Cf. Richy and Sandy, II. 49, 50; Gentle Shepherd, I, 1, 43, 44, 67–70, 156;
I, 2, 131–137; Song VIII.

[5] Gentle Shepherd, I, 2, 138–147; II, 4, 43–66; IV, 2, 148–158.

[6] In the copious notes to the 1815 edition of Pennecnik's *Tweeddale* is a
full account of the country about New-Hall, accompanied by quotations from
Ramsay's poem, to show the accuracy of his descriptions.

> " Phœbus, and his imaginary nine
> With me have lost the title of divine;
> To no such shadows will I homage pay,
> These to my real muses shall give way."

And again, protesting against the narrowness of poetic rules and customs, he said,

> " With more of Nature than of art
> From stated rules I often start,—
> Rules never studied yet by me.
> My muse is British, bold and free,
> And loves at large to frisk and bound," [1]

and he called a wide, wild garden where all sorts of plants grew in wanton confusion, a paradise made by nature herself. Even more emphatic is his Preface to *The Evergreen* in 1724. In commendation of the poems he had collected he said, "The morning rises as she does in the *Scottish* horizon. We are not carried to *Greece* or *Italy* for a shade, a Stream, or a Breeze. : . . I find not Fault with these Things, as they are in *Greece* or *Italy*: But with a Northern Poet for fetching his Materials from these Places, in a Poem, of which his own Country is the Scene; as our *Hymners* to the *Spring* and *Makers of Pastorals* frequently do."

Ramsay's use of external nature is more charming than Gay's. Scottish poetry had never, in its attitude towards the out-door world, passed through so barren and arid a period as that of the pseudo-classicism in England, nor had the Scottish people ever

---

[1] *Answer to the Foregoing* (To Somerville).

In the poems addressed to Allan Ramsay on the publication of his works in 1721 we find significant critical approval based on Ramsay's avoidance of tame nature, and his turning from the authority of the schools. The simile of a garden recurs in a poem by " C. T." He planted trees in equal rows and arranged flowers in a parterre, but found his labor in vain. The narrow scene became daily more distasteful to him, and finally he went back to the fields where "Nature wantoned in her prime." Here he found space, variety, surprise, and was content. Ja. Arbuckle praises Ramsay for roaming over hill and dale and leaving "carpet-ground " to "tender-footed beasts," and for choosing to subsist on his native stock while other poets pilfered fame by picking the locks of their predecessors. Poems of Allan Ramsay. I. p. 4–7.

lost their sense of the beauty and especially of the mysterious power of glens and braes and burns. So Ramsay's love of nature was not without a considerable background in the way of national poetic spirit. He spoke out in fresh, true words what everybody knew, and described scenes familiar to every eye. There are, however, distinct limitations in Ramsay's knowledge of nature and his power of sympathetic representation. His recognition of colors is fresh and charming, but elementary, like that shown in ballads. " Caledonian hills are green," " beneath a green shade," " the simmer green," " a green meadow," " my native green plains," are characteristic phrases.

> " When corn-riggs wav'd yellow, and blue heather bells,"[1]

and

> " To pu' the rashes green with roots sae white."[2]

are almost the only instances of any other color than green. Such phrases as "scented meadows," "sweet scented rucks," "new blown scents," "sweetest briar," "blooming fragrance," show the same simple, undifferentiated recognition of odors. A few lines as,

> " How fast the westlin winds sough through the reeds "[3]

are more specific representations of sounds, but we do not often find words so discriminating. His references to trees, flowers, and birds are of the same general, limited sort. There are "bonny haughs" and "bonny woods;" there are rising plants, primroses, daisies, and gowans; there are "quiristers on high," the merle, the mavis, and the lark. But there is no subtle, detailed observation. It is the open, frank, spontaneous joy of a child happy in the glad world about him. Ramsay's best lines are descriptive of shining days, clear heavens, dancing streams. "The sun shines sweetly, a' the lift looks blue,"[4] "ae shining day," "ae clear morn of May," "the morning shines," "the lift's unclouded blue," "fair simmer mornings" indicate the general

---

[1] The Gentle Shepherd, 2 : 4, 62.

[2] The Gentle Shepherd, 2 : 4, 50.

[3] The Gentle Shepherd, 2 : 4, 10.

[4] To Mr. William Starrat, 46.

atmosphere of the scenery introduced. Occasional closer touches
are seen in such lines as,

> " I've seen with shining fair the morning rise,
>   And soon the fleecy clouds mirk a' the skies." [1]

> " For yet the sun was wading thro' the mist." [2]

Best of all are the lines about streams.

> " A trotting burnie wimpling through the ground
>   Its channel pebbles, shining, smooth and round," [3]

> "A little fount
>   Where water poplin springs." [4]

> " I've seen the silver spring a while rin clear,
>   And soon the mossy puddles disappear." [5]

> " Between twa birks out o'er a little lin
>   The water fa's and makes a singan din,
>   A pool breast-deep, beneath, as clear as glass,
>   Kisses with easy whirles the bord'ring grass," [6]

are descriptions almost perfect of their kind. In their beauty
and freshness they show that the eye was on the object. Mr.
Shairp says of Habbie's How, "A pool in a burn among the
Lowland Hills could hardly be more naturally described," and
one need not be a Scotchman to feel sure that the same is true
of the minor descriptive touches.

Though Ramsay was brought up in a rugged part of Scot-
land, he seems to have had none of the modern feeling for
mountains. But he speaks of " black, heathery mountains," of
" northern mountains clad with snow," of " mountains clad with
purple bloom," and of hills that " smile with purple heather."
Once he exclaims,

> " Look up to Pentland's tow'ring top.
>   Buried beneath great wreaths of snaw,

[1] The Gentle Shepherd, 3 : 3, 41.
[2] The Gentle Shepherd, 1 : 1, 137.
[3] The Gentle Shepherd, Prologue, 1 : 2.
[4] The Gentle Shepherd, Prologue, 2 : 3.
[5] The Gentle Shepherd, 3 : 3, 43.
[6] The Gentle Shepherd, 1 : 2, 7.

> O'er ilka cleugh, ilk scar, and slap,
> As high as any Roman wa,' " [1]

and he notes that

> " Speats aft roar frae mountains heigh." [2]

Such passages, though they show no love for the mountains, are yet sufficiently picturesque and exact to save Ramsay from the imputation of never having seen the wild country around him. To the ocean he gives but a single line,

> " Along wild shores, where tumbling billows break." [3]

It is interesting to note that in Ramsay as in Gay nature is made subordinate to man, in the sense that the pictures from nature are nowhere elaborated or dwelt upon ostensibly for their own sake. The main interest is in the study of the characters.

The chief contribution of Gay and Ramsay to the growing love of nature in poetry had to do with the natural man in natural scenes, rather than with the natural scene itself. Gay's service in the way of external nature was largely the outcome of his fidelity to the fact. Ramsay did more. He not only gave separate pictures both beautiful and true, but he somehow fused them with the human elements of his pastoral in such a way that we cannot think of the racy love-scenes apart from their fresh and lovely surroundings.

In 1725, or shortly before, were written three poems on Winter.[4] They are important as marking the first real turning, from the softer to the sterner aspects of nature.

Dr. Armstrong (1709-1779) Dr. Armstrong's poem was inspired by a winter spent among the wild romantic scenes about the river Esk. His later poetry is not important so far as the use of nature is concerned. He became a great admirer of Thomson whose style he imitated with some success, but he shows little of Thomson's sensitiveness to natural beauty.

---

[1] An ode to the Ph − − −, 1721, st. I.

[2] Answer to the foregoing (To Somerville).

[3] Prospect of Plenty.

[4] (a) Dr. Armstrong's Winter in Imitations of Shakespeare, written in 1725, though not published till 1770.

His point of view is that of the physician. His hatred of the town is based on his objection to smoke and bad air.[1] His summons to the mountains rests on the value of exercise and oxygen.[2] One of the most effective passages is his apostrophe to the Liddal, that stream "unknown to song, where he played when life was young."[3] The only poem on which we need to dwell is the *Winter*, which, though often absolutely unintelligible from its inflated and periphrastic form of expression, has yet a rugged vigor and originality. It shows occasionally a homely realism suggestive of Crabbe, as in the description of the shivering clown. The observation is most of it first-hand. The description of the birds that, when the storm comes on,

> "With domestic tameness, hop and flutter
> Within the roofs of persecuting man,"

suggest Thomson's famous red-breast. Note also the truth of lines such as these :

> "when the murk clouds
> Roll'd up in heavy wreaths, low-bellying, seem
> To kiss the ground, and all the waste of snow
> Looks blue beneath them;"

or these:

> "huge sheets of loosen'd ice
> Float on their bosoms to the deep, and jar
> And clatter as they pass."

Or, to strike a lovelier note, this closing hint of the coming spring:

> "Hark ! how loud
> The cuckoo wakes the solitary wood !"

The whole poem is characterized by a delight in the wildest phases of winter weather and it shows an originality of concep-

(b) Riccaltoun's A Winter's Day, written before 1725, published in Savage's Miscellany in 1726, and in Gentleman's Magazine, 1740.

(c) Thomson's Winter, written in fragments before 1725, but fused into one poem at Mallet's suggestion in 1726.

[1] The Art of Preserving Health, 1 : 64-96.
[2] The Art of Preserving Health, 1 : 97-102; 3 : 39-52.
[3] The Art of Preserving Health, 3 : 71-96.

tion, a fullness of observation, and an occasional strength of expression remarkable in a boy not yet sixteen.

Riccaltoun's poem is chiefly remarkable because its author was a friend of Thomson in his boyhood and doubtless helped to cultivate his taste for nature; because it was this **Robert Riccaltoun (1691–1769)** poem that suggested Thomson's descriptions of winter; and because winter was at that time a new poetic theme. The "masterly touches" of which Thomson speaks are hard to find unless he referred merely to the rough truth in the catalogue-like summaries of natural facts. A discussion of Thomson's *Winter* will come more naturally in the next section.

In this study of the period preceding Thomson we have still to notice the indications that even Pope and Addison were not left untouched by the new spirit. Such indica- **Pope (1688– 1744) and Addison (1672–1719)** tions, however, show but faintly in their poetry. Addison's *Cursus Glacialis* (1699) was written in Latin, and the few descriptive lines are purely conventional. It is simply an attempt to show that the vigorous sports of winter

> "New brace the nerves, and active life supply."

Pope's *Pastorals* appeared in Tonson's Miscellany in 1709. They were enthusiastically received, and apparently considered a charmingly natural presentation of country life. Wycherley called Pope's Muse "a sprightly lass of the plains," and said, that "in her modest and natural dress she outshone all Apollo's court ladies in their more artful, laboured, and costly finery."[1] But no assemblage of such contemporary judgments could convince a modern reader that these poems show any real traces of a conception of the outer world unlike that of the classicists. *Windsor Forest* must be more carefully noted, both because of Wordsworth's implied commendation[2] in his reference to the "passage or two" that contain new images of external nature, but chiefly because it is, as Courthope observes, the first

[1] Pope: Works, VI, pp. 36, 37.

[2] Wordsworth: Essay Supplementary to the Preface, 1815.

"professed composition on local scenery" since Denham, and Marvell.[1] The poem was written at two different times. The first 290 lines have to do with the country. They were written in 1704, at about the same time as the *Pastorals*. Although this part of the poem purported to be the outcome of daily rides in Windsor Forest, the descriptions are so vague and general that most of them would fit any other spot as well. The lines that show personal observation are certainly few. What passages Wordsworth meant can only be surmised. He may have had in mind the description of the pheasants. But more exact observation is shown in the references to the doves flocking on the naked, frosty trees, the flight of the clamorous lapwing, the trembling of trees reflected in a stream, and the purple heather.[2] That Pope had some desire to conform to the truth in representing English scenery is indicated by his doubt as to the advisability of referring to the vintage in describing an English autumn.[3] And when he revised his poems he omitted "blushing," as not being applicable to violets,[4] and "wolves," as not belonging to England.[5] Warton points out, also, that in adapting a Latin description of the Eurotas to serve him in a description of the Thames, he changed "laurels" to "willows."[6]

In spite of these indications of a desire to be true to nature, it is to Pope's prose rather than his poetry that we must turn for any real influence in favor of simplicity and truth in the presentation of natural facts. Though in reading Pope's letters every statement is instinctively taken *cum grano. salis*, because of his known insincerity and striving after effect, we now and then

---

[1] Pope : Works, I, p. 322.

Denham : Cooper's Hill.

Marvell : Upon the Hill and Grove at Billbarrow, and Upon Appleton House.

[2] Veitch in Feeling for Nature in Scottish Poetry, II, p. 52, credits Thomson with being the first poet to mention purple heather, but this mention by Pope is more than twenty years earlier.

[3] Pope : Works, I, p. 346, n. 3. (But compare Autumn, l. 74.)

[4] Pope : Works, I, p. 269, n. 1.

[5] Pope ; Works, I, p. 283, n. 3 : p. 296, n. 9.

[6] Pope : Works, I, 293. Cf. Warton : Essay on Pope, I, p. 6. '

strike passages that have a genuine tone of pleasure in such mild forms of nature as his physical condition enabled him to know.[1] Addison's *Essays* also show real delight in the milder forms of the external world. "A beautiful prospect," he says, "delights the soul as much as a demonstration." "A man of polite imagination often feels a greater satisfaction in the prospect of fields and meadows than another does in the possession."[2] We note, too, his pleasure in wide views,[3] in sunset,[4] and in spring.[5] He also deprecated the use of pagan mythology as meaningless in the poetry of a Christian nation,[6] and he heartily praised Ambrose Philips's attempts to confine English pastorals to English scenes.[7] And finally, both Pope and Addison were strong influences in bringing about the change from the formal to the natural school of gardening.[8]

SUMMARY.

In a statement of the influences in this period that make for a new spirit towards nature we must not forget that it was in reality a classical period, most of its tendencies and all of its best work being classical. The indications of the new spirit are fugitive, occasional, and usually unconscious. With this proviso, we may sum up the new tendencies. The change from the formal to the natural school of gardening was begun in this period, and

---

[1] *a.* Description of moonshine walk. (This letter, perhaps a sincere expression when first written (1713), was a favorite of Pope's. When he published his Letters he made an amusing blunder by transferring this passage to a letter dated February 10, 1715, at which time the park where he was supposed to have watched the moonshine and reflected on mortality, was under water from the great flood of February 9th. See Letters, I, p. 367.)

b. Pleasure in birds, etc., I, p. 338.

c. Twickenham in spring, IV, pp. 72, 74.

d. Autumn, IV, p. 89.

[2] Spectator, June 21, 1712 (No. 411).

[3] Spectator, June 23, 1712 (No. 412); June 25, 1712 (No. 414).

[4] Spectator, June 23, 1712 (No. 412).

[5] Spectator, May 31 (No. 393).

[6] Spectator, October 30, 1712 (No. 523).

[7] Spectator, October 30, 1712 (No. 523). Cf. Guardian, Nos. 22, 23, 28, 30, 32, 40.

[8] See further discussion under "Gardening."

' owed much to Pope and Addison.   The artificial shepherds and shepherdesses of the conventional pastoral were supplanted by real English and Scottish peasants, as in Ambrose Philips, Gay, and Ramsay.   There was a growing sense of the beauty and charm of the external world, as in Lady Winchelsea, Parnell, and Ramsay.   In most of the poets mentioned in this period, there was a new quickness and minuteness of observation leading to a wider knowledge of natural facts.   There was appreciative recognition of new aspects of nature, as night and winter. There was not lacking a hint of the romantic note of melancholy which later became one characteristic of the poetry of nature. And there was a dawning consciousness of the spiritual potencies in the external world.   There was also an occasional self-conscious statement of new principles, as humorously in Gay, seriously in Ramsay, and casually in Pope and Addison.

THE POETS BETWEEN 1726 AND 1730.

Thomson is confessedly the most important figure in the early history of Romanticism.   He foreshadowed the new spirit in various ways, as in his strong love of liberty, his constant plea for the poor as against the rich, his preference for blank verse, his imitation of older models, especially Spenser, and in his tendency towards comprehensive schemes; but his chief importance is in his attitude towards external nature.   If, however, we take into consideration all his work, we shall find in more than three-fourths of it the utmost apparent indifference to nature.   In the five tragedies written between 1738 and 1748 there is no hint that their author knew more of the world about him than the veriest classicist of them all.   In *Alfred* (1740), written by Thomson and Mallet, there are occasional descriptive touches, but these are almost too slight to mention when we think what effects might have been produced in a play the action of which occurs on a beautiful wooded island inhabited only by a few peasants.   In the other tragedies nature is drawn upon merely for conventional similitudes, as in *Edward and Elenora* (1739), where five of the eleven similitudes are the comparison of rage

**James
Thomson
(1700-1748)**

or fierce passions to tempests; or in *Sophonisba*, an earlier play (1728). where there is not a fresher or more forceful comparison than that of an army to a torrent, passion to a whirlwind, the hero to a lion, and the heroine to a blooming morn. In the 3300 lines of the tedious poem, *Liberty* (1734–1736), not more than fifty refer to external nature, and of these the only passages that suggest, even remotely, the author of *The Seasons* are the descriptions of the sullen land of Sarmatia[1] and the shaggy mountain charms of the Swiss Alps.[2] *The Castle of Indolence*, written in 1733, is the only one of the poems written after 1730 that indicates any genuine love of nature. The charm of this poem for modern readers is perhaps largely due to its use of external nature, for, though there is little of the rich, elaborate description characteristic of *The Seasons*, what there is is so exquisitely appropriate that all the listless, luxurious life of this land of soft delights is seen through a romantic and picturesque setting of waving, shadowy woods, sunny glades, and silver streams. Yet a closer study of the descriptive stanzas shows little more than a musically felicitous combination of the attributes conventionally recognized as belonging to a pleasing landscape. The only lines really indicative of a love of nature such as the classicists had not known are the following from the second Canto :

> " I care not, Fortune, what you me deny :
> You can not rob me of free Nature's grace ;
> You can not shut the windows of the sky,
> Through which Aurora shows her brightening face ;
> You can not bar my constant feet to trace
> The woods and lawns, by living stream, at eve."[3]

It is to *The Seasons* that we must go if we wish to understand Thomson's work as a poet of nature. A brief analysis of the study of external nature in these poems will serve to show both in what respects Thomson's work was the outcome of a new spirit, and in what respects its affiliations are with the old.

An important part of Thomson's poetical endowment was his

[1] Liberty, Part 3, ll. 514–526.
[2] Liberty, Part 4, ll. 348–362.
[3] The Castle of Indolence, Canto II, st. 3.

quick sensitiveness to the sights and sounds and odors of the
world about him.   He looked on nature with the

**Openness to
sense
impressions**

eye of an artist. but not of an artist in black and
white.   It was not form but color that attracted
him.   There are occasional descriptions, as of the
garden in *Spring*[1] and of the precious stones in *Summer*,[2] where
the lines glow like a painter's palette, and throughout *The Sea-
sons* there is a general impression of rich and varied coloring.
That this impression is stronger than a list of the color terms
used would seem to justify is due to two facts, both characteristic
of Thomson's work in general.   In the first place he did not care
for nicely discriminated shades or delicate tints.   He loved
broad masses of strong, clear color.   He dwells with ever new
delight on blue as seen in the sky or reflected in water, and on
green, "smiling Nature's universal robe."   In the second place
he is especially rich in such words as indicate color in general
without specification as to the kind.   "The flushing year," "every-
coloured glory," "the boundless blush of spring," "the innu-
merous-colored scene of things," "unnumbered dyes," "hues on
hues," are typical phrases.   Motion also caught his eye more
quickly than form.   The dancing light and shade in a forest
pathway, the waving of branches, the flow of water, the rapid
flight or slow march of clouds, the golden, shadowy sweep of
wind over ripened grain, count for much in the pleasurable
impression made upon his mind by different scenes.

It is evident that Thomson received more through his eye
than through his ear, but he was very far from being indifferent

Sound

to the sounds of nature.   The hum of bees, the
low of cattle, the bleating of sheep are frequently
noted.   The songs of birds, while often represented by some
general phase, as "the music of the woods," or "woodland
hymns," are now and then more minutely specified, as in the
fine description of the "symphony of spring."[3]   There is also

---

[1] Spring, 529–555.   [3] Spring, 574–613.

[2] Summer, 140–159.   Suggested probably by Mallet.   See Letter, August
2, 1726: "Your hint of the sapphire, emerald, ruby, strikes my imagination
with a pleasing taste, and shall not be neglected."

effective representation of the sounds heard in storms, as in the summer thunder-storm.[1] The most frequent sounds are, as is inevitable in an English poet whose facts come from actual observation, those made by water, as the plaint of purling rills, the thunder of impetuous torrents, or the growling of frost-imprisoned rivers.

While Thomson was not the first poet to speak of the odor of the bean-flower, his words show a keen appreciation of that perfume, and certainly the "smell of dairy," was a country odor first poetically noticed by him. His sensitiveness to odors is not especially marked, yet it is safe to say that he was in this respect more observant than his immediate predecessors or contemporaries.

In reading the poetry of nature after Dryden in historical sequence, there is, in coming to *The Seasons*, a sudden **Abundant first-hand knowledge** sense of freedom and elation, a sense of having at last come upon a poet who writes freely and spontaneously from a large personal experience, whose facts press in upon him even too abundantly. He knows many kinds of nature and under varying aspects. His garden picture, though somewhat too much in the floral catalogue style, shows how well he knew the cultivated flowers he described, and he speaks with no less loving minuteness of furze, the thorny brake, the purple heather, dewy cowslips, white hawthorn, and lilies of the vale. It is a pleasure to see how much he knew about birds. He describes their habits with remarkable accuracy and minuteness. He shows their tender arts in courtship,[2] their skill in nest-building,[3] and the " pious frauds" whereby they lure away the would-be trespasser.[4] In no poetry between Marvell and Thomson do we find birds so fully described, and Marvell has nothing so charming and sympathetic as Thomson's winter red-breast.[5] Thomson's scope is also wider in that he knew the birds of the seashore[6] as well as those of wood and meadow. Equally close attention is given to the various domestic

[1] Summer, 1116–1168.
[2] Spring, 614–630.
[3] Spring, 636–660.
[4] Spring, 690–701.
[5] Winter, 245–256.
[6] Spring, 21–25; Winter, 144–147.

fowl. The peacock had flaunted his painted tail through poetry for a hundred years, and is now for the first time outranked as an object of interested observation by the hen, the duck, and the turkey.[1] The frequent descriptions of domestic animals, especially the sheep,[2] the horse,[3] and the ox,[4] also show minute knowledge such as could not have been gained by books. It is, more-over, a significant fact that through these numerous and varied studies there runs a genuine love for animals. Thomson was, at least in poetic theory, a vegetarian, and he vigorously denounced the killing of animals for food as conduct worthy only of wild beasts.[5] His poetical invectives against hunting are as vigorous as Cowper's.[6] He objects to caging birds,[7] and his indignation waxes high over the bees "robb'd and murder'd" by man's tyranny.[8] The only unoffending animal that escapes Thomson's wide sympathy is the fish.[9] The skill with which the monarch of the brook is lured from his dark haunt and at last "gaily" dragged to land is described with a gusto in curious contrast to the pity lavished on the tortured worm that may have served for bait.[10]

Love for animals

As we have just seen, the animals that Thomson described were those that any country lad might know rather than those that had been canonically set apart for poetical service. The same independent judgment is evident in his study of other neglected realms in the world of nature. He gloried in storms and winter. Though he now and then falls into the conventional phraseology, and speaks of winter as drear and awful, he yet in the same breath exclaims that he finds its horrors congenial. The contrast of a first winter in London turns his mind with full emphasis to the days of his youth when he wandered with unceasing joy through virgin snows, and listened to the roar of the winds and the burst-

Enjoyment of winter

---

[1] Spring, 770–785.

[2] Summer, 371–422.

[3] Spring, 808–820; Summer, 506–515.

[4] Spring, 362–371; Summer, 489–493.

[5] Spring, 336–373.

[6] Autumn, 360–457; Winter, 788–793.

[7] Spring, 702–728.

[8] Autumn, 1172–1207.

[9] Spring, 394–442.

[10] Spring, 388–389.

ing torrent, and watched the deep tempest brewing in the grim sky. Such experiences he remembers with joy for they "exalt the soul to solemn thought."[1]   Through all the descriptive portions of the *Winter* there is a vigorous, manly enthusiasm as tonic and bracing as the bright, frosty days themselves. Thomson's pleasure in the sterner phenomena of nature is further shown by his evident delight in tracing the progress of any storm, whether the thunder storm of summer,[2] the devastating wind and rain of autumn,[3] or the black gloom of a winter tempest.[4] These fierce tempests certainly are of more comparative importance in *The Seasons* than they are in nature. Their frequent choice may be in part due to their dramatic qualities of rapidity and force. The crashing and hurtling of the elements was a subject not unsuited to Thomson's splendid but ponderous and swelling style. But in the main it is only fair to suppose that he wrote of storms well because he had many times watched them with an interest that had made him remember them.

With many other aspects of nature was Thomson familiar. He knew much of the sky both by day and by night. His few short descriptions of the starry heavens are worth **The sky** more than all Young's far-sought epithets.[5]   One phrase concerning the radiant orbs

> "That more than deck, that animate the sky,"[6]

seems a conscious turning away from the old artificial conception. One of the finest moon-light passages[7] is reminiscent of Milton in two lines,

> " Now through the passing cloud she seems to stoop,
> Now up the pure cerulean rides sublime,''

but the close,

> " The whole air whitens with a boundless tide
> Of silver radiance, trembling round the world,"

is Thomson's own, and is a good example of the full sweet har-

---

[1] Winter, 1–14.

[2] Summer, 1103–1168.

[3] Autumn, 311–348.

[4] Winter, 72–201.

[5] See as illustrative: Winter, 127, 738–741.

[6] Summer, 1704.

[7] Autumn, 1088–1102.

mony that marks his verse at its best.   There are many passages
and apparently casual phrases indicative of the closeness with which
he watched clouds.[1]   The doubling fogs that roll around the hills
and wrap the world in a " formless gray confusion " through which
the shepherd stalks gigantic is described with a Wordsworthian
felicity and precision.[2]

The descriptions referred to below of early morning,[3] of sun-
set,[4] of evening,[5] and of night[6] may be perhaps taken as among the
best examples of their sort in *The Seasons*. As a whole
they show conclusively from what long intimacy with
nature Thomson wrote. The very freshness of
morning breathes from the sunrise picture in *Sum-
mer* and the little picture in *Autumn* is more delicately sugges-
tive than many a more pretentious description of the dawning
day. The sunset after the rain in *Spring* is one of the best exam-
ples of Thomson's power to paint word pictures. It would be
difficult for any canvas to present a scene at once so mellow and
radiant, and so transfused with the joy of a renovated earth. As
exquisite in their way are the descriptions of the slow approach of
"Sober Evening" with her circling shadows and the softly swell-
ing breeze that stirs the stream and wood ; and the later description
of the strange uncertain mingling of light and darkness in a sum-
mer night in England. These passages and others that might be
quoted show to what fine issues Thomson's pen was sometimes
touched, but it cannot be denied that his really intimate and exact
knowledge of nature and her ways could not hold all his descrip-
tions subject to the charm of simplicity and truth.

As further illustrative of Thomson's knowledge of all that per-
tained to the country we have his admirably vivid
and detailed accounts of the homely labors of a
farmer's life, as plowing,[7] sowing,[8] reaping,[9] hay making,[10] and

[1] See as illustrative, Spring, 30–31. 139–141, 145–151, 398–444 ; Winter
54–57, 77–80, 195–196, 202–203, etc.

Autumn, 710–731. cf. Wordsworth: Prelude 8: 265.

[3] Autumn, 151·152. Summer, 47·66.   [7] Spring, 34·43.
[4] Spring, 189·202.   [8] Spring, 44·47.
[5] Summer, 1647·1659.   [9] Autumn, 153·169.
[6] Summer, 1682·1698.   [10] Summer, 352·370.

sheep shearing.[1] Of these the sheep shearing is the most simply
charming and natural. It is also the most noteworthy, because
sheep and shepherds had long been the very substance out of
which pastorals were woven so that in such descriptions the con-
trast between the new and the old way of looking at country life
is sharply defined. Thomson's pastoral queen and shepherd king
are at the opposite pole from the sentimental, affected, useless
nymphs and swains who had before posed as the guardians of
English sheep. His shepherds are sturdy fellows, doing hon-
est work and plenty of it, and as such they had no predeces-
sors in English classical poetry. The sheep, too, are real animals.
They have to be watched with a vigilance of which no flower-
crowned swain playing on an oaten pipe would be capable. And
they must be washed and sheared and branded. In winter they
must be housed and fed no matter what the dangers on the dark,
stormy hills. It is this strong, refreshing air of reality in Thom-
son's poetry, and his unfeigned respect and admiration for the
actual country life in England that completed the work begun by
the ugly satire of Swift and the mock pastorals of Gay, and made
the old, conventional, psuedo-classic pastoral from that time on an
impossibility in English poetry.

The phrase "dislike of boundaries" is perhaps not very apt, but
it may serve to describe what is certainly a pervasive quality of

Dislike of boundaries
Thomson's work, and a significant quality for if
there was one thing more pleasing than another to
an orthodox classicist it was a well defined limit.
Thomson preferred the blank verse to the couplet because the
unrhymed, flowing lines gave a certain freedom. There is an air
of abundance, of even undue exuberance about much of his work.
Even his diction presents this idea of lavishness. There is a sur-
prisingly large number of such words as effulgent, refulgent, effu-
sion, diffusion, suffusion, profusion from the roots *fundo* and
fulgeo with their idea of a liberal pouring out. Luxuriant, ample,
prodigal, boundless, unending, ceaseless, immense. interminable,
immeasurable, vast, infinite, are typical words.

[1] Summer, 371-442.

> " Profusely poured around,
> Materials infinite."

> " Infinite splendor wide investing all,"

> " To the far horizon wide-diffused,
> A boundless deep immensity of shade,"

> Night "a shade immense, magnificent and vast,"

are typical phrases. In one short description the birds are "innumerous;" they are "prodigal" of harmony; their joy overflows in music "unconfined"; the song of the linnets is "poured out profusely."[1] In another short passage the stores of the vale are "lavish," the lily is "luxuriant;" and grows in fair "profusion," the flowers are "unnumbered," beauty is "unbounded," and bees fly in "swarming millions."[2] When images come into his mind it is by the ten thousand. In spring the country is "one boundless blush," "far diffused around." He loves the "liberal air," "lavish fragrance," "full luxuriance," extensive harvests," "immeasurable," or "exhaustless" stores, "copious exhalations." All is superlative, exaggerated, scornful of limits. It was "the unbounded scheme of things" that most appealed to him.

The same point receives illustration in his sense for landscape. He rejoiced in a wide view.[3] He loved to seek out some proud eminence and there let his eye wander "far excursive," and dwell on "boundless prospects." Such scenes not only gave him a chance for picturesque enumerations without any especial demand for minute discrimination, but they satisfied his preference for grand, general effects.

Feeling for landscape

Closely connected with the sense for landscape is the use of geographical romance,[4] or the heightening of poetic effect by the accumulation of sounding geographical names.[5] The

[1] Spring, 589–608.

[2] Spring, 494–509.

[3] Spring, 107–113, 950–962; Summer, 1406–1441.

[4] W. D. McClintock; Unpublished notes.

[5] Summer, 819–829; Autumn, 781–804. cf. Shairp: Poetic Interpretation of Nature, p. 191, for the geographical use of nature in Milton.

finest example of this device is in the lines descriptive of the thunder re-echoed among the mountains.[1]   In this passage the impression of sublimity is due to the suggestions of mysterious elemental forces subtly associated with such names as Carnarvon, Penmanmaur, Snowden, Thule, and Cheviot.[2]   This mental following of the thunder from peak to distant peak, this endeavor to strengthen the impression by the use of the remote and the unknown, show a mind set toward romantic rather than classical ideals.

Geographical romance

A further indication of Thomson's defiance of limits is his curiosity.   His mind goes back of the present fact and restlessly strives after causes and origins.[3]   In imagination he seeks to penetrate to the vast eternal springs from which nature refreshes the earth.[4]   The most poetic example of this questioning spirit is in his address to the winds that blow with boisterous sweep to swell the terrors of the storm.

Intellectual curiosity

> " In what far-distant region of the sky,
>   Hush'd in deep silence, sleep you when 'tis calm ? "[5]

The classical spirit held itself to useful questions that could have some rational answer.   It is the romantic spirit that pushes its inquiries into the realms of the unknowable.

Throughout this study of Thomson's work there has been an implicit recognition of his strong love for nature.   This fact receives further definite confirmation from his letters.   It is interesting to note that his early life was almost as fortunate in its environment as Wordsworth's.   When he was a year old his father moved to Southdean, a small hamlet near Jedborough.   Here the lad remained till he entered the University at Edinburgh at fifteen,[6] and here he apparently passed most of his vacations

Personal enthusiasm for nature

[1] Summer, 1161–1168.

[2] Cf. Wordsworth: To Joanna, 54–65.

[3] Winter, 714–716; Spring, 849–852.

[4] Autumn, 773–776.

[5] Winter, 116–117.

[6] In 1720 there appeared in the *Edinburgh Miscellany*, a poem entitled,

till he went to London at twenty-five. One of his especial friends was Dr. Cranston of Ancrum, whose love of nature was equal to his own. Thomson's letters to Dr. Cranston, though somewhat stilted and high-flown, show clearly the eagerness with which they had together explored the picturesque country along the Tiviot and its tributary streams, the Ale and the Jed. In the first letter from London, under the date April 3, 1725, was written, "I wish you joy of the spring." In September of the same year Thomson wrote from Barnet:

"Now I imagine you seized with a fine romantic kind of melancholy on the fading of the year; now I figure you wandering, philosophical and pensive 'midst the brown, wither'd groves, while the leaves rustle under your feet, the sun gives a farewell parting gleam, and the birds

'Stir the faint note and but attempt to sing.'

"Then again when the heavens wear a more gloomy aspect, the winds whistle, and the waters spout, I see you in the well-known cleugh, beneath the solemn arch of tall, thick embowering trees, listening to the amusing lull of the many steep, moss-grown cascades, while deep, divine contemplation, the genius of the place, prompts each swelling awful thought. I am sure you would not resign your place in that scene at any easy rate. None ever enjoyed it to the height you do, and you are worthy of it. There I walk in spirit and disport in its beloved gloom. This country I am in is not very entertaining ; no variety but that of woods, and them we have in abundance ; but where is the living stream ? the airy mountain ? or the hanging rock ? with twenty other things that elegantly please the lover of nature. Nature delights me in every form."

Later in life Thomson was "more fat than bard beseems,"

"On a Country Life by a Student in the University." The poem is interesting as being Thomson's first poetical treatment of the theme which he was afterwards to adopt. The verse is in somewhat stiff and formal heroic couplets, and the poem is marked by classicisms. But there are lines and phrases suggestive of Thomson's later work and the plan and general tone are, as Sir Harris Nicholas has pointed out, strongly suggestive of *The Seasons*. The young poet's love of country life is quite clearly genuine.

and correspondingly indolent, and his biographers give the impression that no beauty of the world about him could compete with the charms of an easy chair. But his letters still bear witness to a love of nature as real if not as active as that of his youth. In July, 1743, he wrote to Mr. Lyttleton promising to spend some weeks with him at Hagley.

"As this will fall in Autumn, I shall like it the better, for I think that season of the year the most pleasing and the most poetical. The spirits are not then dissipated with the gaiety of spring, and the glaring light of summer, but composed into a serious and tempered joy. The year is perfect. . . . The muses, whom you obligingly say I shall bring with me, I shall find with you — the muses of the great, simple country, not the little, fine-lady muses of Richmond Hill."

Again four or five years later, he wrote to Paterson, " Retirement and nature are more and more my passion every day."[1]

This passion for nature finds frequent expression in the poems, but no citation of specific instances can be so convincing as the general impression of unforced personal enthusiasm made upon the reader of *The Seasons*. Moreover, Thomson's conception of the effect of nature on man, the next topic, may be fairly counted as but a transcript from his own experience, and therefore as further illustrative of his love for nature.

In *The Seasons* as in preceding poetry both man and nature have a place, but there is a great transfer of emphasis. Nature had been ignored or counted **His thought of the relation between man and nature** as the servant, the background, the accompaniment of man. Now the human incidents are few and unimportant and are used chiefly to lay additional stress by their tone on the spirit characteristic of each

[1] Cf. also remarks in Preface to second, third, and fourth editions of *Winter*: " I know no subject more elevating, more amusing ; more ready to awake the poetical enthusiasm, the philosophical reflection, and the moral sentiment, than the works of Nature. Where can we meet with such variety, such beauty, such magnificence ? All that enlarges and transports the soul ? What more inspiring than a calm, wide survey of them ?"

season. Nature is loved and studied and described purely for
her own sake. There is very little use of natural facts as similes
for human qualities, and there is, practically, no use of pathetic
fallacy. The effect of nature on the man sensitive to her high
ministration is represented as twofold. In the first place and
chiefly, she storms his senses with her ravishing delights. She
gives him pleasures of the most rich and varied sort. She
enchants him with color and harmony and perfume. These pleas-
ures are, however, of the eye and ear. They do not touch the
deeper joys of the heart. Of the appeal of nature to the soul
of man, in the true Wordsworthian sense, Thomson knew little.
Yet occasional passages indicate that he had received from nature
gifts higher than that of mere external, sensuous enjoyment.
He attributes to nature in at least a partially Wordsworthian
sense, the power of soothing, elevating, and instructing. He
sings the " infusive force " of spring on man.

> " When heaven and earth as if contending vie
> To raise his being, and serene his soul." [1]

It is his delight to " meditate the book of nature " for thence he
hopes to " learn the moral song." [2]   At the soft evening hour, he

> " lonely loves
> To seek the distant hills, and there converse
> With nature, there to harmonize his heart." [3]

Not only does he attend to Nature's voice from month to month,
and watch with admiration her every shape, but he

> " Feels all her sweet emotions at his heart." [4]

While these and a few other similar passages would hardly be
remarked in the poetry of nature after Wordsworth, they are of
great historical importance because they show the early begin-
ning of that spirit which received its final and perfect expression
seventy years later in *The Lyrical Ballads*.

Thomson's two dominant conceptions in his thought of God

[1] Spring, 868–874.
[2] Autumn, 670–672. Cf. Wordsworth : The Tables Turned, st. 6.
[3] Summer, 1380–1382.
[4] Autumn, 1309.

and Nature were the almighty Creator and the ever-active Ruler.

His thought of God in nature The whole tenor of his poems goes to show that he saw in nature not God himself but God's hand. Even his invocations to nature, animate and inanimate, to praise God in one general song of adoration, are but highly emotional and figurative statements of the conception that God is not all, but Lord of all. Now and then, however, in the midst of the old ideas there comes the breath of a new thought. In one line we find the cold, conventional idea, in the next, an intimation of divine immanence. God's beauty walks forth in the spring. His spirit breathes in the gales. The seasons "are but the varied God." God is the Universal Soul of Heaven and earth. He is the Essential Presence in all nature.[1] Such sentences as these, whether uttered consciously, or half unconsciously under the influence of poetic excitement, clearly prefigure the modern conception of the union and interpenetration of the physical and spiritual worlds.

Of the two general points to be kept in view in the study of Thomson as a poet of nature the second was a consideration of his affiliations with the classical spirit. It is surprising to observe in how few respects such affiliations can be justly predicated. There are occasional references to his Doric reed, and frequent invocations to his muse. As preliminary justification of his choice of themes are quotations from Virgil and Horace. The authority of the "Rural Maro" and the example of Cincinnatus lend added dignity to the English plow. Personifications of the conventional type often appear. There is one purely didactic description of the cure for a pest of insects, and another description of the method by which bees are robbed of their honey, that are evidently framed on Latin models. Nor do we miss the ever recurring advice to read the page of the Mantuan swain beneath a spreading tree on a warm noon.

His affiliations with the classical spirit

We also find that toward mountains and the sea Thomson held almost the traditional attitude. His nearness to the coast

[1] Compare Pope's rhetorical statement of the same speculative conception.

and his knowledge of shore birds show that he could not have
been entirely ignorant of the ocean, but it apparently made little
impression on him, for he seldom mentions it even casually, and
but once with any emphasis.   It is then one of the elements of a
wild, fierce storm that sweeps the coast.   A few of his epithets
for mountains, as "keen-air'd" and "forest-rustling," are new
though not especially felicitous, and he often mentions mountains
by name, or as bounding some distant prospect.   But in general
his conception and his phraseology are those of his contempo-
raries.   He speaks of the Alps as "dreadful," as "horrid, vast,
sublime," and again as "horrid mountains."   There is nowhere
any evidence of the modern feeling towards mountains, though
there are frequent expressions of appreciative love for green hills.

The point in which Thomson shows strongest traces of the
old influence is his diction.   He often has the new thought before
he has found the appropriate dress for it.   Birds are still the
"plumy" or "feathery people," and fish are the "finny race."
"Shaggy" and "nodding" are used of mountains and rocks
and forests, and "deformed" and "inverted" of winter, in
true classical fashion.   "Maze" is one of his most frequent
words.   "Horrid" still holds a useful place.   "Amusing" is
five times applied to the charms of some landscape.   Leaves are
the "honours" of trees, paths are "erroneous," caverns "sweat,"
and all sorts of things are "innumerous."   He also makes large
use of Latinized words such as turgent, bibulous, relucent, lucu-
lent, irriguous, gelid, ovarious, incult, concactive, hyperborean.
These words can hardly be said to belong to any received poetic
diction.   They are rather a mannerism of Thomson's style, and
an outgrowth of his delight in swelling, sounding phrases.

From this summary we at once perceive how few and compar-
atively unimportant were the characteristics held in common
by Thomson and the classicists in their treatment of external
nature.

This study of *The Seasons* shows that so far as intrinsic worth
is concerned the poems are marked by a strange
Summary   mingling of merits and defects, but that, con-
sidered in their historical place in the development of the poetry

of nature, their importance and striking originality can hardly be overstated. Though Thomson talked the language of his day, his thought was a new one. He taught clearly, though without emphasis, the power of nature to quiet the passions and elevate the mind of man, and he intimated a deeper thought of divine immanence in the phenomena of nature. But his great service to the men of his day was that he shut up their books, led them out of their parks, and taught them to look on nature with enthusiasm. This service is of the greater historical value because it was so well adapted to the times. To begin with, it was a necessary first step. People cannot love what they do not know. Lead them to nature, teach them to observe with amazement and delight, and the other steps follow in due course in accordance with the power of each soul to receive the deeper influences of nature. In the second place, men were just ready to take this first decisive step away from the artificial to the natural. The work of the poets who immediately preceded Thomson had been too slight and fragmentary to count for much in the way of influence, yet they were most clear indications of a tendency, a silent preparation of the general poetic mind, for such work as Thomson's. He was at once and easily understood because, while his poems in their spontaneous freshness and charm, their rich, easy fullness of description, their minute observation, their sweep of view, their unforced enthusiasm, must have come as a revelation, it was a revelation in no sense defiant or iconoclastic. In the main it was a revelation of new delights, not of disturbing theories, or vexing problems. A touch more of subtlety, of vision, of mystery, of the faculty divine, and Thomson might have waited for recognition as Wordsworth did.

John Dyer's more ambitious poems, *The Ruins of Rome* (1740) and *The Fleece* (1757), belong to a much later period than the

John Dyer
1700?-1758

present. Of these the first may be passed over as containing hardly a touch of nature. The second is a long didactic poem showing much technical knowledge of sheep-raising, weaving, dyeing, and home and foreign trade. It has frequent panegyrics of liberty and simplicity. It abounds with geographical details, and is notable as having so many full and often exact descriptive references to the rivers of Great Britain. The Avon, the Severn, the Thames, the Towy, the Vaga, the Ryddol, the Yftwith, the Clevedoc, the Lune, the Coker, the Ouze, and the Usk are chief among these. He is apparently always conscious of the rivers, rills, streams, or waterfalls in any landscape. But in general the poem is conventional in diction,[1] in the choice of similitudes, and in the occa sional descriptions. Its use of geographical details, though sometimes suggestive and stimulating, as in the lines,

> " Tempestuous regions, Darwent's naked peaks,
> Snowden and blue Plynlymmon and the wide
> Aërial sides of Cader-yddris huge,"[2]

is more often simply wearisome. It is true of Dyer, as it was of Thomson, that his really excellent poetry of nature was written when he was fresh from long and familiar knowledge of nature in her wilder forms, and that travel and contact with men served to dull the power of these early experiences. *Grongar Hill* and *The Country Walk* were published the same year as Thomson's *Winter*, and were doubtless written the year before. They could not have been in any sense due to the impetus given by Thomson to the study of nature. They are rather an original and independent contribution toward the same end. They were the expression of personal experience, and the direct outcome of native taste and singularly fortunate environment. Dyer's life before his school days at Westminster was spent in the wild and romantic country in Caermarthenshire, and during the years immediately preceding the publication of these two poems he was wandering through other parts of South Wales as an "itinerant painter." His previous study with Richardson had helped to develop that artistic sensitiveness to external impressions so apparent in his early work. He notes the colors and shapes of the trees grouped below him, the gloomy pine and sable yew, the blue poplar, the yellow beech, the fir with its slender, tapering trunk,

---

[1] Dyer uses almost as many words ending in "y" as Ambrose Philips. Stenchy, towery, framy, sleeky, thready, copsy, spiry, are illustrative.

[2] The Fleece. 1: 193.

the sturdy oak with its broad-spread boughs. The changing
horizon line as he climbs the hill, the long level lines of the
lawn, the various movements of rivers running swift or slow,
through sun and shade, the streaks of meadow, the close, small
lines of distant hedges, the curling spires of smoke, are observa-
tions that show the trained eye.[1] His colors seem to be rather
carefully discriminated. Yellow receives unusual emphasis. The
linnet's yellow plumage, the yellow foliage of the beech, the
mountain-tops shining yellow in the sun, and even the "yellow
barn" catch his eye. This preference for yellow characterizes
his later work. He speaks of "yellow corn," "yellow tillages,"
"yellowing plains," and the "yellow Tiber." He also liked the
words "golden" and "sunny." Purple is applied to evening
and to the groves at evening, and seems to be used with some
real sense of the modern specific meaning of the word. In later
work the color purple became almost a stock epithet with him ;

> " Purple Eve
> Stretches her shadows,"[2]

> " When many-colour'd Evening sinks behind
> The purple woods and hills,"[3]

> " The purple skirts of flying day,"[4]

> " When evening mild
> Purples the valleys,"[5]

> " Wide abroad
> Expands the purple deep,"[6]

are typical phrases. He also notices the "thousand flaming
flowers" in the fields, the silver and gold of the morning clouds,
the shining of lakes, the evening colors reflected in slow streams,
and the soft fair hues of distant mountain summits. He delights

---

[1] In Observations on the River Wye, by William Gilpin, pp. 103–108,
Dyer's *Grongar Hill* is, however, criticised for not accurately representing dis-
tance. The grove must be distant if it can be rightfully called purple, but the
castle beyond it "is touched with all the strength of a foreground; you see the
very ivy creeping upon the walls."

[2] Fleece, 1:577.
[3] Fleece, 2:55.
[4] Fleece, 2:510.
[5] Fleece, 2:518.
[6] Fleece, 2:241.

in the sounds of nature, especially in the songs of birds. Not for many years after Dyer is there so effective a bit of bird-song poetry as the closing lines of *Grongar Hill.* Nor is he indifferent to odors, for he notes the perfumed breeze from the valley, the fragrant brakes, and the sweet smelling honeysuckle. It is worthy of note that in these two short poems nearly a hundred natural facts are mentioned.

In this wide observation Dyer includes some features not hitherto counted as parts of a poetic landscape. The "windy summit wild and high," naked rocks, and barren ground, are mingled with the softer details, and

"Each gives each a double charm."

He nowhere dwells upon mountains in his descriptions, but the slight touches here and there and the general tone of the poems are sufficient to show his great delight in mountain scenery. He represents himself as climbing slowly and looking back often so as not to miss a single phase of the view unfolding before him. Once on the top he gazes out over the lovely prospect and exclaims,

"Now, even now, my joys run high
As on the mountain turf I lie."

In *The Fleece* are further indications of this love of mountains and wide views. The passage beginning

"Huge Breaden's stony summit once I climbed"[1]

is typical.

"Those slow-climbing wilds, that lead the step
Insensibly to Dover's windy cliff,
Tremendous height!"[2]

and

"By the blue steeps of distant Malvern walled,
Solemnly vast."[3]

have something of the modern touch.

The prevailing interest in these poems is in nature, but there are one or two charming pictures of homely life. The old man's hut and garden on the edge of the wood, and the barnyard scene are

[1] The Fleece. 1:555. [2] The Fleece. 1:41.
[3] The Fleece, 1:59.

as attractive as they are realistic. And surely the tattered old man digging up cabbage in the shade might have been expected to wait at least for Crabbe or Wordsworth to introduce him into the select company of the Muses. The same may be said of the tramp asleep by the roadside.[1]

In any tabulation Dyer's use of nature would seem to be much more abundant than it is for in *The Fleece* he of necessity used a large number of geographical details merely to mark out localities and with no more literary quality than there would be on a map. His chief use of nature is twofold, and is best seen in the short poems, *Grongar Hill* and *The Country Walk*. He describes a landscape with loving minuteness for its own sake, and he regards it as the occasion for a strain of half-melancholy reflection on human life. This gentle, quaintly precise moralizing is unlike the typical classical didacticism in that it seems to spring inevitably from the effect of natural objects on the poet's mind, instead of being itself the main thing and laboriously illustrated by such natural facts as came to hand.

The entire impression made by the two poems is that they were written by one who knew nature better then books. The negative as well as the positive qualities of the poem show this. There are almost no conventional phrases.[2] Of the personified abstract qualities, two at least, Pleasure and Quiet, are so imaginatively conceived as not to belong to the category of cold classical personifications. The only classical allusion is significant as being to the "fair Castalian springs" deserted now by all but 'slavish hinds.'[3] But the poems show something more than first-hand as opposed to bookish knowledge of nature. Their author evidently loved to linger over the charms of nature in solitude, to let them sink into his mind and heart. There is a power of quiet contemplation, of "wise passiveness," such as Thomson never knew. The closing lines of *Grongar Hill*,

[1] The Country Walk, 86-99; 33-40.

[2] He calls the sun "Phoebus" and "Apollo;" he occasionally uses such words as swain, bloomy, sylvan, verdant, flowery; and he speaks of "the wanton zephyr;" and he refers to a grove as the "haunt of Phyllis."

[3] The Country Walk, ll. 58-63.

> " Be full, ye courts ; be great who will ;
>   Search for Peace with all your skill :
>   Open wide the lofty door,
>   Seek her on the marble floor,
>   In vain you search, she is not there ;
>   In vain ye search the domes of care !
>   Grass and flowers Quiet treads,
> · On the meads, and mountain heads,
>   Along with Pleasure, close-ally'd,
>   Ever by each other's side :
>   And often, by the murmuring rill,
>   Hears the thrush, while all is still,
>   Within the groves of Grongar Hill,"

show a wonderfully true and delicate apprehension of the spiritual influences that speak through nature's forms. It is putting into plainer words what was the underlying conception in Parnell's *Hymn to Contentment*.

As has been observed, Dyer speedily left his first love and devoted himself to laborious, didactic blank verse. We cannot find that his two short poems attracted much attention at the time. Thomson's glory blazed forth so effulgently that lesser lights were but dimly seen. Now, however, as we go from poet to poet of the period, we cannot fail to be impressed by the unusual sincerity, simplicity, and truth with which Dyer wrote of nature. And we feel that while he lacked Thomson's power and fertility, he was quite equal to him in originality, and superior to him in delicacy.

David Mallet's chief poems in which there is use of external nature are *A Fragment*, *The Excursion*, and *Amyntor and Theodora*. The undated *A Fragment* reads like a poetical exercise in the style of Dyer's *The Country Walk* and *Grongar Hill*. The octosyllabic verse, the general plan of a walk at different times of day, the ascent of a hill for the view, the pleasure in the solitude of nature, the moralizing invocations to Health and Freedom, are all suggestive of Dyer. The description of the noontide woodland retreat, of the forest sounds, and of the poet's revery are like passages in *The*

David Mallet
(1705 (?)-1765)

Country Walk, while both the spirit and form of some passages in *Grongar Hill* are paralleled by such lines as,

> " On the brow of mountain high
> In silence feasting ear and eye,"[1]

or

> "And then at utmost stretch of eye
> A mountain fades into the sky ;
> While winding round, diffused and deep,
> A river rolls with sounding sweep."[2]

The Excursion and *Amyntor and Theodora* are interesting because of their relation to the work of Thomson. Thomson and Mallet were students together at Edinburgh, and there was evidently a close literary comradeship between them which lasted through the first years of their London life. During the summer of 1726 they were both engaged in literary work, the result of which was, on Thomson's part, *Summer*, and on Mallet's, about 300 lines of the first canto of *The Excursion*.[3] There was a vigorous interchange of letters concerning the two poems, each author giving advice and criticism on the passages sent him by the other.[4] A comparison of the poems shows numerous resemblances. As an illustration we may take the sunrise with which each poem opens. The order of occurrences is the same in each— night, faint gleams in the east, breaking clouds, rising mists, retreat of wild animals, song of birds, work of shepherds, full rising of sun, praise to God, reflections on the inspiration to be gained from nature. There are also many curious verbal similarities. In Thomson the meek-eyed *Morn*, mother of *dews*, comes *faint-gleaming* in the east to destroy night's *doubtful* empire, and before the *lustre* of her face the clouds break *white* away. In Mallet sacred *Morn pale-glimmering* comes with *dewy* radiance through the *doubtful* twilight and spreads a *whitening lustre* over the sky. In Thomson the powerful *King of Day looks* in boundless majesty *abroad*. In Mallet the *King of Glory looks abroad* on nature.

---

[1] Cf. Grongar Hill, l. 137.
[2] Cf. The Country Walk, l. 120.
[3] Thomson to Mallet, Sept. 1726.
[4] Thomson's Letters to Mallet in 1726.

These are but suggestions of the many unmistakable but baffling
and intricately interwoven similarities in the two poems. If we
had but these two poems it would be, perhaps, impossible to say
which poet exerted the stronger influence. Thomson's deference
to Mallet's judgment is evident. *Winter* was submitted to him for
correction,[1] and the splendid passage on precious stones in *Sum-
mer* was an addition proposed by him.[2] Thomson also greatly
admired Mallet's work.[3] Thomson's work, on the other hand, bears
the impress of a genuine enthusiasm and a many-sided personal
experience, while Mallet's work reads like that of a facile versi-
sifier speaking out of a meager experience and with a forced
enthusiasm. At any rate, when we come to *Amyntor and Theodora*,
published years after the full edition of *The Seasons*, Mallet is
clearly imitative in thought and phrase. The ocean, for instance,
is described as " through boundless space diffused, magnificently
dreadful." Again it is " diffused immense," and " magnificently
various." In its depths " immeasurably sunk," " ten thousand
thousand tribes endless range." Its stormy waves are " mountains
surging to the stars, commotion infinite" and they break in
" boundless undulation." Storms are presaged by " doubling
clouds on clouds." The earth glows with "the boundless blush of
spring." At sunset the sea shines with " an unbounded blush."
A comparison of these phrases with those quoted from Thomson
on pages 82 and 83 will serve to show in how exaggerated and
inartistic a form Thomson's mannerisms reappeared in the later
work of Mallet. Mallet's work, if it had been first in the field,
would have marked a distinct advance in the conception of nature.
As it is he is of real importance as indicating the influence of
Dyer, and especially of Thomson.

Richard Savage's *The Wanderer* appeared in 1729. Of this
poem Dr. Johnson says that it was " never denied
to abound with strong representations of nature,"
but a study of the five long, confused, formless can-
tos hardly confirms such an opinion. Most of the descriptions,

Richard Savage
(1698-1743)

[1] Letter to Mallet, July 10, 1725.
[2] Letter to Mallet, Aug. 2, 1726.
[3] Letters to Mallet, June 13 and July 10, 1726.

like those of Mallet's *Excursion,* are of scenes too remote for damaging comparisons with the reality, as of sunrise at the north pole, or of wide prospects from unknown mounts. The various details are brought together with little sense of unity. He called the poem a vision, and he had perhaps a right to dream-like combinations of facts, but the result is not a contribution to the study of external nature. His diction is vague and inexpressive. There is large use of stock poetic words, and there are many Thomsonian echoes. Most of the descriptions are tame, classical imitations. They show almost no first-hand knowledge of the country. There is, however, one characteristic of his poetry that cannot fail to arrest the attention, and that is his use of color. Not even Thomson is so lavish with bright tints, and they are sometimes nicely discriminated. Illustrative passages are referred to in the note.[1]   He observes the color of " crooked, sunny roads" that change "from brown, to sandy-red, and chalky hues." He perceives the "green grass yellowing into hay." His sunset sky has several colors that had not been noted in poetry. Some of the clouds had " the unripen'd cherry's die:" others were " mild vermilion," "streaked through white," and there was in the sky a tinge of " floating green," the result of the " blue veil'd yellow' of certain distant clouds. In a moonrise picture there are eight colors, besides twelve words indicative of brightness, and that in a description of thirteen lines. The best of these descriptions is that of the peas and beans in blossom. References such as those to the peas that with their " mixed flowers of red and azure " run in " colour'd lanes along the furrows," and to the beans that after a rain " fresh blossom in a speckled flower" bear the mark of first-hand observation. The same may be said of his brief touches descriptive of the roads and the fields and the sunset sky already referred to. There is also fairly abundant reference to birds, though but a single line.

> " The bullfinch whistles soft his flute-like note,"

[1] Cf. The Wanderer, 5:237, 238 (roads); 5:253–268 (fields and bushes); 5:230–235 (sunset); 5:363-374 (the rainbow); 4:59-63 (morning); 3:15–27 (moonrise); 5:8, 15-20 (foliage and flowers); 5:203–210 (bean fields); 1:195–198 winter landscape); 4:85-90 (sunrise).

exhibits any special felicity in expression.   On the whole, Savage
is important in the history of the poetry of nature merely for his
detailed insistence on color.

Among the minor poets of this period was Stephen Duck. He
spent most of his life on a farm where he early began to write
verses which attracted much local attention and
finally gained for their author substantial favor at
Stephen Duck
(1705-1756)
Court.   His *Thresher's Labour* is interesting simply
because it is a realistic treatment of a homely English theme.[1]
Duck's poems were popular in their own day, but his treatment
of nature is commonplace.

The poetry of these four years is interesting because it indicates
how early Thomson's influence made itself felt, as in the work of
Mallet and Savage; and also because it shows a use of nature
quite unlike Thomson's and is equally significant of coming tend-
encies, as in the work of Dyer.

THE POETS BETWEEN 1730 AND 1756.

The choice of 1756 as the date to mark the close of this
period is based on the appearance in that year of Joseph War-
ton's *Essay on Pope*.   In the twenty-six years between Thomson's
Seasons and this *Essay*, the most important literary works are
in prose, as the novels of Fielding, Richardson, and Smollett,
and the theological writings of Butler, Hume, and Warburton.
The period is marked by the establishment of numerous periodi-
cals, by the work of editors, and of compilers.   The most impor-
tant poetry of the period was the *Essay on Man*, *Moral Essays*,
and *The Dunciad* by Pope.   In writing of this sort there is, of
course, little use of external nature.   And it has already been
shown that the tragedies of Thomson and the later work of
Armstrong, Mallet, and Dyer which appeared during these years,
either ignore nature or treat it in a stiff or simply imitative man-
ner.   But there are in the twenty-six years poems that are not
only in accord with the changing attitude toward nature, but that
distinctly aid in the evolution of the new conception.   The chief

[1] In 1730 appeared a parody entitled *The Thresher's Miscellany* by "Arthur
Duck."

names are Somerville, Shenstone, Greene, Collins, Young, Akenside, Gray, and the Wartons. There are other authors whose works are not, as a whole, of importance in this study, but who have written single poems of some significance. Some of these minor poets are Boyse, Smart, Cawthorne, Jago, Whitehead, Dr. Dalton, Thompson, Mendez, Potter, Relph, Coventry, Mason, Cooper, and Dodsley.

Somerville, "a country gentleman and a skillful and useful Justice of the Peace," was a mighty hunter in his day, and found, in leisure hours, great pleasure in throwing into blank verse the accumulated wisdom of years in the field. *The Chace* he calls his "bold, instructive song," and it so well carries out the second epithet as to be of interest only to his "brethren of the couples" to whose kindness he commends it. There is the most minute description of the kinds of hounds, the breeding of dogs, the care of whelps, their habits, their diseases and the best remedies, and the most desirable kennels. In *Field Sports* we have almost as close a description of hawking. Both poems are, however, destitute of any real love of nature.' The diction, except for a free use of canine technicalities, is extremely limited and commonplace ; and we look in vain for the occasional happy touch, the felicitous epithet or line, that would indicate any original or appreciative knowledge of the external world. When this vigorous squire went out to hunt he had eyes but for the dogs and the game. His few descriptions are of the conventional type, as:

> " Hail, gentle Dawn! mild, blushing goddess, hail !
> Rejoic'd I see thy purple mantle spread
> O'er half the skies, gems pave thy radiant way,
> And orient pearls from every shrub depend." '

They are weak imitations, lifeless and vague. *Hobbinol* is a disagreeable poem. Its very ugly rural pictures might perhaps rank as realistic studies of English country life, but so far as any country atmosphere is concerned they are of no importance.

' The Chace, 2:79–82.

The smock-race, the wrestling match, the drunken affray, might as well have taken place in any city slums.

Somerville had a Catholic taste in poetry. He greatly admired Homer, Virgil, Pope, Allan Ramsay, and Thomson. The last poet he not only admired, but imitated. The passage beginning,

> " Justly supreme! let us thy power revere,"

is a pretty clear echo from Thomson's *Hymn*, and the closing twenty-five lines of *The Chace* must have been studied from the closing twenty-two lines of *Autumn*. Somerville is noteworthy in the present study only because he wrote on country themes, and imitated Thomson.

Shenstone is a much more important figure in the history of the poetry of nature. His sensitiveness to the new spirit and his reverence for the old form make him an interesting transitional influence. His *Prefatory Essay on Elegy* shows this Janus attitude and, what is more, his own consciousness of it. " If the author has hazarded throughout the use of English or modern allusions, he hopes it will not be imputed to an *entire* ignorance, or to the *least* disesteem, of the ancient learning. He has kept the ancient *plan* and *method* in his eye, though he builds his edifice with the materials of his own nation. In other words, through a fondness for his native country he has made use of the flowers it produced, though, in order to exhibit them to the greater advantage, he has endeavored to weave his garland by the best model he could find."[2] This statement is interesting as being directly opposed to the thought in Gay's experiment. Both poets mean to hold by the Latin form and use English materials, the one to show that the two are incompatible, the other to show that they may be united. Neither Gay nor Shenstone thought of discard-

William Shenstone (1714–1763)

---

[1] *To the Right Honorable Lady Anne Coventry.*

[2] An excellent example is *Nancy of the Vale* which takes as its model,

> " Nerine Galatea ! thymo mihi dulcior Hyblae !
> Candidior cygnis ! hedera formosior alba,"

but compares Nancy to the "wild-duck's tender young," to the water-lily on Avon's side, her eyes to the azure plume of the halcyon, etc.

ing the Latin form.   In the same *Essay* he claims that in his use
of nature he has drawn only on personal experience. "If he
describes a rural landskip, or unfolds the train of sentiments it
inspired, he fairly drew his picture from the spot : and felt very
sensibly the affection he communicates. If he speaks of his
humble shed, his flocks and his fleeces, he does not counterfeit
the scene : who having (whether through choice or necessity, is
not material) retired betimes to country solitudes, and sought his
happiness in rural employments, has a right to consider himself
as a real shepherd. The flocks, the meadows and the grottos are
his own, and the embellishment of his *farm* his sole amusement.
As the sentiments, therefore, were inspired by nature, and that in
the earlier part of his life, he hopes they will retain a natural
appearance." This plea for first-hand observation is important
because it is the most direct of the early critical remarks on the
poetical treatment of nature.

Shenstone's delight in nature was evidently genuine. He
grants that men may be dazzled by the city :

> " But soon the pageant fades away !
>   'Tis nature only bears perpetual sway,"[1]

and they learn again

> " the simple, the sincere delight —
> Th' habitual scene of hill and dale,
> The rural herds, the vernal gale,
> The tangled vetch's purple bloom,
> The fragrance of the bean's perfume."[2]

He speaks with scorn of those " bounded souls" who enjoy in
nature only the satisfaction of present needs, or the prospect of
future gain, and who can not on " the mere landscape" feast
their eyes, and apostrophizes them thus :

> " Athirst ye praise the limpid stream, 'tis true :
> But though, the pebbled shores among,
> It mimic no unpleasing song,
> The limpid fountain murmurs not for you.

[1] Rural Elegance, st. 20.
[2] Rural Elegance, st. 19.

> Unpleas'd ye see the thickets bloom,
> Unpleas'd the spring her flowery robe resume;
> Unmov'd the mountain's airy pile,
> The dappled mead without a smile."[1]

But to the true lover of nature,

> "Lo! not an hedge-row hawthorn blows,
> Or humble harebell paints the plain,
> Or valley winds, or fountain flows,
> Or purple heath is ting'd in vain:
> For such the rivers dash the foaming tides,
> The mountain swells, the dale subsides;
> Ev'n thriftless furze detains their wandering sight,
> And the rough, barren rock grows pregnant with delight."[1]

Shenstone also defends the doctrine that beauty is its own excuse
for being.

> "Let yon admir'd carnation own,
> Not all was meant for raiment, or for food,
> Not all for needful use alone."[2]

Though Shenstone's work is often undeniably tame and
diffuse, and though his interests were bounded by his farm, he is
of significance because of his thorough enjoyment of quiet
country places, his indignant rejection of the utilitarian view of
nature, and his courageous plea for truth to English scenes.

Green's chief poem, *The Spleen*, was published in 1737, after
his death. The subject is not one that would lead to much use
of nature, but there is at least one picture that
Matthew Green can not be passed over.[3] In his sketch of the
(1696-1737) ideal life he describes his ideal home. Its sur-
roundings are most charming and natural, and
the whole scene, in its unity and reality of effect, contrasts well
with such fanciful combinations as the garden in Tickell's *To a
Lady Before Marriage*. One line in this description,

> "Brown fields their fallow sabbaths keep,"[4]

is remarkable in that, in so few words, it not only presents a

---

[1] *Rural Elegance*, st. 4. 5. 6. 8.   [3] *The Spleen*. ll. 646-687.
[2] *Rural Elegance*, st. 16.   [4] *The Spleen*, l. 681.

complete picture, but also awakens the feeling that would be excited by the scene itself.

Hamilton's chief use of nature is in gentle little allegories of life. *The Rhone and the Arar*, though a description of two rivers, is obviously didactic in all its details. Spring, summer, and winter in *Ode III.* are but "moral shows," spread out for man's instruction. Though Hamilton's scenes are usually of the soft, delicious, vaguely pleasing sort, and his diction largely classical, yet now and then in his rather monotonous spring poetry we find a fresh line or phrase, as when he comments on spring's gift of beauty to "each nameless field." He finds joy in the prickly briar rose, the bright-colored weed, the lion's yellow tooth, in a thousand flowers never sowed by art.[1] He is filled with gratitude as he looks upon the smiling face of nature and the radiant glories of the sky, or listens to the music of the opening year.[2] In *Contemplation* he exclaims,

William
Hamilton
(1704-1754)

> "Mark how Nature's hand bestows
> Abundant grace on all that grows,
> Tinges, with pencil slow unseen,
> The grass that clothes the valley green;
> Or spreads the tulip's parted streaks."

More distinctive, however, than this love of the spring-time world, is Hamilton's sense of communion with nature. The lines,

> "As on this flowering turf I lie,
> My soul conversing with the sky,"

and this address to the passions that tyrannize over him,

> "This grove annihilates you all.
> Oh power unseen, yet felt, appear!
> Sure something more than nature's here."

are new evidences of the spirit that animated Lady Winchelsea, Dyer, and Parnell.

Hamilton's most important poem is *The Braes of Yarrow*.

[1] The Epistle of the Thistle.

[2] Contemplation.

In this ballad there is a remarkable blending of external nature with the tragedy of love and death. The use of the phrase, "the Braes of Yarrow," in the refrain adds a curiously subtle touch to the pathos of the poem. Tradition had so closely associated the sloping hills and the winding stream of Yarrow with stories of unhappy love in far off days that the name was in itself enough to strike the keynote of pathos in Hamilton's ballad. The tone or color that human experience had once given to the scenery was carried on by that scenery so that it became the appropriate background for a new tale of grief. The one descriptive stanza,

> "Sweet smells the birk, green grows, green grows the grass,
>   Yellow on Yarrow's banks the gowan,
> Fair hangs the apple frae the rock,
>   Sweet the wave of Yarrow flowan;"

and a single line in the maiden's lament,

> "I sang, my voice the woods returning,"

are an appropriate setting for the happy love of the bonny bride and her comely swain. But nature is also compelled, as it were, to share in the grief, and is implicated in the crime. On Yarrow's rueful flood floats the body of the slain knight; her doleful hills echo the cries of sorrow. And the desolate bride prays that rain and dew may forever forsake the fields where her lover was so basely slain.

The descriptive element in Hamilton's ballad is of further interest as having suggested some of the details in Wordsworth's *Yarrow Unvisited.*

The Deity, a poem by Samuel Boyse, and much praised in its own day,[1] is of importance here merely because of its Thomsonian imitations, and because of its conception **Samuel Boyse** of God in nature. This conception is, in the **(1708–1749)** main, the typical classical one, as in "Omnipotence," where the central idea is,

> "What hand, Almighty Architect, but thine
>   Could give the model of this vast design?"

[1] See Hervey: Meditations, II, 239. Fielding: Tom Jones, VII, ch. 1.

In "Providence," however, the modified classical conception is apparent, the ever-working power of God being dwelt upon. All nature is represented as being each moment derived from the Creator.

> "The sun from thy superior radiance bright
> Eternal sheds his delegated light ;
> Thou shedd'st the tepid morning's balmy dews,"

are characteristic lines.

That Boyse was an admirer of Thomson we know from the lines addressed to him,

> "When nature first inspired thy early strain
> To paint the beauties of the flowery plain ;
> The charming page I read with soft delight,
> And every lively landskip charmed my sight."[1]

In reading Boyse it is difficult to point out exact echoes from Thomson, but the impression remains that certain passages, especially in "Glory," are, in spite of their couplets, but weak paraphrases of some portions of Thomson's work, noticeably *The Hymn.*

Young's literary career lasted from 1712 to 1762. His *Ocean* and *Sea Pieces* and the only book of the *Night Thoughts,* in which there is much use of external nature, **Edward Young** have already been briefly characterized. They need **(1681-1765)** little further discussion here. The preface to *Ocean* is more worthy of note than the poem itself. In this preface Young deprecates slavish following of the models of antiquity, declaring that "originals only have true life." Due deference to the great standards of antiquity requires that "the motives and fundamental method of their working" should be imitated rather than the works themselves. He then defends his choice of the ocean as a subject, saying that it is, like the subjects chosen by the ancients, both national and great, and adds the significant phrase, "and (what is strange) hitherto unsung." "The crude ore of romanticism" which Mr. Gosse finds in Young, has to do with his despairing attitude towards

[1] To Thomson on Sophonisba.

life and death, not with his attitude towards external nature. His love of darkness, which seems at first thought akin to the sentimental melancholy of the romantic poetry, is really an unemotional choice of a fit background for his visions of gloom. His strongest lines on night represent not its beauty, nor its melancholy, but its divinity, or, rather, its theological import. The following are typical :

> " Let Indians　　　.　　.　　.
> 　　　.　　.　　.　　.　　the sun adore :
> *Darkness* has more divinity for me ;
> It strikes thought inward ; it drives back the soul
> To settle on herself."[1]

> " By night an atheist half-believes a God."[2]

At night the sense of sacred quiet is " the felt presence of the deity."[3] In occasional passages Young has more or less definite previsions of scattered ideas in later poetry,[4] but these are incidental, and of merely curious interest. Taken in the bulk, his work is so slightly and coldly concerned with the outer world as to offer no real contribution to the new feeling for nature.

[1] Night Thoughts, V:126–130.

[2] Night Thoughts, V:176.

Night Thoughts, V:171.

[4] See Night VI, where there is an interesting statement of the theory afterwards expounded in Coleridge's Ode to Dejection. Compare Young's,

> " Objects are but th' occasion ; ours th' exploit ;
> Ours is the cloth, the pencil, and the paint,
> Which nature's admirable picture draws,"
> 　　　　　　　　　Night VI : 431.

with Coleridge's.

> " O Lady! we receive but what we give,
> And in our life alone does nature live ;
> Ours is her wedding garment; ours her shroud."

In the same passage by Young is the line concerning the power of our senses that

> " Half create the wondrous world they see,"

from which Wordsworth took a line in Tintern Abbey. In Satire 1, l. 249 there are some lines that sound absurdly like certain stanzas in Peter Bell ;

> " On every thorn delightful wisdom grows ;
> In every rill a sweet instruction flows.

Collins possesses many of the qualities and the defects of the romantic spirit. He made plans almost as comprehensive and visionary as those of Coleridge. His indolence, **William Collins** his wavering, irresolute disposition, his morbid sen- **(1721–1759)** sitiveness, the intensity of his emotions, his love of liberty, his passion for "high romance and Gothic diableries," together with his new sense of the mystery of nature, set him quite apart from the men who were his friends, from Dr. Johnson, Armstrong, Aaron Hill, from Garrick, Quin, and Foote, even from Thomson. His interests were not those of his day, for his admiration turned to Æschylus, Sophocles, and Euripides, rather than to Virgil and Horace.[1] In English poetry he gave his allegiance to Spenser, Milton, and Shakespeare, rather than to Dryden and Pope.[2] He was devoted to music. He was also deeply interested in the remote history of his own country, and in the legendary lore and superstitions of any land. Dr. Johnson says of him : "He loved fairies, genii, giants, and monsters ; he delighted to rove through the meanders of enchantment, to gaze on the magnificence of golden palaces, to repose by the waterfalls of Elysian gardens."

Collins was a town-bred poet and could have known little of the country at first-hand. We might therefore expect all his imagery to be of the conventional sort in the *Eclogues* written in

> But some, untaught, o'erhear the whispering rill,
> In spite of sacred leisure, blockheads still."

The lines

> " In distant wilds, by human eyes unseen,
> She rears her flowers, and spreads her velvet green ;
> Pure gurgling rills the lonely desert trace
> And waste their music on the savage race,"

Satire V:229.

come between the similar passages by Gay and Gray.

Cf. also the simile of the eagle and the serpent (Vanquished Love, Bk. II : 226), with Shelley's Revolt of Islam, I : st. 8–10.

[1] Ode to Fear, Ode to Simplicity, An Epistle to Sir Thomas Hanmer, Ode to Pity.

[2] Ode to Fear, On the Poetical Character, Popular Superstitions, st. 11, An Epistle to Sir Thomas Hanmer.

his early school days. But such is not the case. In the later poems the use of nature, slight as it is, is marked by unusual originality and imaginative power. There is everywhere present a sense of delight in the wilder, freer, in the more remote and mysterious aspects of nature. He makes Fear sit

> " in some hollow'd seat
> 'Gainst which the big waves beat,"

and listen to

> " drowning seamen's cries in tempest brought."

His gifted wizard seers

> " view the lurid signs that cross the sky
> Where in the west the brooding tempests lie,
> And hear their first, faint, rustling pennons sweep."

Note also the description of the " wide, wild storm," in the *Ode to Liberty*, and especially the skillful mingling of landscape details and superstitious terrors in the *Ode on Popular Superstitions*. The " bewitch'd, low, marshy, willow brake," " the spot where hums the sedgy reed," the " dim hill that seems up-rising near," " Uist's dark forest," " the watery strath or quaggy moss," " the damp, dark fen," are slight touches, but they serve perfectly to suggest the fit home of the kelpie, the will-o'-the-wisp, the mischievous fairy folk, and the phantom train of gliding ghosts. But Collins's most appreciative use of nature is in the *Ode to Evening*. That poem was doubtless the result of personal experience, for it notes facts, such as the rising of the beetle in the path at twilight, that were not yet stock poetical property. The lines

> " Thy dewy fingers draw
> The gradual dusky veil,"

could hardly have been written by one unfamiliar with the slow disappearance of a landscape as night comes on. More remarkable are the simplicity and directness of touch by which the few details are made to stand for complete pictures. The cloudy sunset, the silence of evening, the calm lake amid the upland fallows, the fading view, the windy day in autumn, are all excellent examples of the stimulative as opposed to the delineative description. But the final impression made on the mind is powerful mainly because in some way that escapes analysis the very mood and spirit of evening, its calm, its tender melancholy, breathe through the unpretending lines. We seldom find in the eighteenth century, personifications so high and spiritual, description so essentially poetical, or workmanship so perfect in its simplicity.

Dr. Akenside's *The Pleasures of the Imagination*, though not published till 1744, was begun in 1738 when the author was but seventeen, and completed when he was twenty-one. In 1757 it was remodeled and many additions were made. In its first form the poem was essentially a product of the author's precocious, brilliant youth. Yet it has little of the fire and passion of youth. It is a smooth, correct, rather frigid exposition of certain philosophical principles. The whole poem seems like an illustration of Akenside's belief that poetry is true eloquence in metre.[1] It is not marked by any especially rich or faithful portrayal of nature, nor is there much description. In point of fact, such descriptions as occur are often marred by eighteenth century periphrases such as calling honey "ambrosial spoils;" the sun, "the radiant ruler of the year;" flowers, "the purple honors of the spring;" water, "a delicious draught of cool refreshment;" and frogs, "the grave, unwieldly inmates of the neighboring pond." There is also frequent use of stock words and of worn-out similitudes. But in spite of its coldness, this poem is an important contribution to the development of the poetry of nature because of its new conception of the relation between man and nature.

Dr. Akenside (1721-1770)

When the poet endeavors to explore the "secret paths of early genius," he imagines inspiration as coming to the lonely youth from some " wild river's brink at eve," or from " solemn groves at noon,"[2] and there is one passage that lays a Wordsworthian emphasis on the effect of nature on the soul of a child.

> " O ye Northumbrian shades, which overlook
> The rocky pavement and the mossy falls
> Of solitary Wensbeck's limpid stream;

[1] Mason: Memoirs of Gray, p. 261.
[2] Pleasures of Imagination, Bk. IV: 26 (1770).

> How gladly I recall your well-known seats
> Beloved of old, and that delightful time
> When, all alone, for many a summer's day,
> I wandered through your calm recesses, led
> In silence by some powerful hand unseen.
>   Nor will I e'er forget you; nor shall e'er
> The graver tasks of manhood, or the advice
> Of vulgar wisdom, move me to disclaim
> Those studies which possessed me in the dawn
> Of life, and fix'd the color of my mind
> For every future year." [1]

But the great scene of nature does not appear the same to all. It is only to the finer spirits that the true meaning of the outer world is revealed.[2] These nobler souls are all "naked and alive"[3] to the influences of nature to which they respond as Memnon's image to the touch of the morning.[4] Form, color, sound, motion, detain the enlivened sense, and soon the soul perceives the deep concord between these attributes of matter and the mind of man.[5] The passions are lulled to a divine repose. The intellect itself suspends its graver cares. Love and joy alone possess the soul

> "Whom nature's aspect, nature's simple garb,
>   Can thus command." [6]

For the happy man whom neither sordid wealth nor the gaudy spoils of honor can seduce to leave the sweets of nature,

> " Each passing hour sheds tribute from her wings:
>   And still new beauties meet his lonely walk,
>   And loves unfelt attract him. . . . .
>   . . . . Nor thence partakes
>   Fresh pleasure only; for the attentive mind,
>   By this harmonious action on her powers,

[1] Pleasures of Imag., Bk. IV: 38–51 (1770); cf. Hymn to the Naiads, 243–249; cf. Wordsworth: Prelude, Bk. I:402, and many other passages concerning the silent power of nature over him in his youth.

[2] Pleasures of Imag., Bk. I: 136–140 (1757).

[3] Pleasures of Imag., Bk. I: 120 (1744).

[4] Pleasures of Imag., Bk. I: 150 (1757).

[5] Pleasures of Imag., Bk. I: 153–160 (1757).

[6] Pleasures of Imag., Bk. I: 168–175 (1757); cf. Wordsworth: Tintern Abbey ll. 41–49.

> Becomes herself harmonious; wont so oft
> In outward things to meditate the charm
> Of sacred order, soon she seeks at home
> To find a kindred order, to exert
> Within herself this elegance of love." [1]

If men feel themselves cramped by custom, by sordid policies let them appeal

> " to Nature, to the winds
> And rolling waves, the sun's unwearied course,
> The elements and seasons."

All these call us to beneficent activity.

> " Thus the men
> Whom Nature's works can charm, with God himself
> Hold converse; grow familiar, day by day,
> With his conceptions, act upon his plan,
> And form to his the relish of their souls." [2]

But even the susceptible soul must come to nature in an open, receptive mood. The sacred rights of the Naiads are sought in vain by the "eyes of care." No vision is granted to the preoccupied guest.[3] There is also an independent life in nature, or at least a spirit that is no reflection of man's moods, but with qualities of its own whereby man is influenced.

> "Throned in the sun's descending car,
> What power unseen diffuseth far
> This tenderness of mind ?
> What Genius smiles on yonder flood ?
> What God, in whispers from the wood,
> Bids every thought be kind? "[4]

> " Who can tell,
> Even on the surface of this rolling earth,

[1] Pleasures of Imag., Bk. III: 591–605 (1744). This "sacred order" of the universe is one of the points on which Wordsworth dwells, and he refers frequently to the tranquilizing, steadying effect which the contemplation of this order and harmony will have on the mind of man. See Excursion, Bk. IV: 1198–1219; 1254–1265.

[2] Pleasures of Imag., Bk. III: 615–633 (1744).

[3] Odes, Book I, Ode 14, stanzas 4–6; cf. Wordsworth's statement that nature reveals herself to the heart that " watches and receives."

Odes: Bk. I, Ode 5, st. 8.

> How many make abode?   The fields, the groves,
> The winding rivers and the azure main,
> Are rendered solemn by their frequent feet,
> Their rites sublime."[1]

The power of nature over man is constant and varied. She is endowed with such enchantment, made up of forms so exquisitely fair, breathed through with such ethereal sweetness, that she can at will "raise or depress the impassioned soul."[2] Her dark woods rouse him to solemn awe. Her gay landscapes with blue skies and silver clouds give an impression of winning mirth. There is in the rising sun something kindred to man's spirit. At evening the "breath divine of nameless joy," that steals through the heart, is but another message from the spirit of love that rules the world. All the forms of the external world are but visible expressions of such thoughts of God as the mind of man is fitted to receive. The soundness of this interpretation of nature is not here in question. We are merely concerned with the fact that in the middle of the century we find a statement of poetical creed which, so far as the thought is concerned, might come from *The Excursion* or *The Prelude*. Akenside is one of the first of the poets of the age to insist on the beauty of all nature,[3] and to show an abiding sense of the spiritual elements that give significance to the external forms of nature. He was also the first one to emphasize the Platonic doctrine of the identity of truth and beauty,

> For Truth and Good are one ;
> And Beauty dwells in them, and they in her."[4]

A minor poet, John Gilbert Cooper, must be mentioned because of one poem, *The Power of Harmony* (1745). In execu-

---

[1] Pleasures of Imag., Bk. I: 670–675 (1757).

Pleasures of Imag., Bk. III: 484 (1757).

[3] Pleasures of Imag., Bk., I: 576–589 (1757).

[4] Pleasures of Imag., Bk., I: 432–437 (1757).

Akenside's presentation of this doctrine has led Gosse to call him a "sort of frozen Keats," but Akenside's pleasure in nature was philosophical rather than sensuous. His scientific delight in the analyzed rainbow (Pleasures of Imag., 2: 103–120 [1744]) would have filled Keats with horror.

tion it is heavy and involved. It is a clumsy attempt to work out a theory of beauty. The preface is more interesting than the poem. In this preface he says: "It is the design of the poem to show that constant atten-tion to what is perfect and beautiful in nature will, by degrees, harmonize the soul to a responsive regularity and sympathetic order." In the poem he ascribes to "each nat-ural scene a moral power," and traces even the song of birds and the frisking of cattle to the effect

John Gilbert Cooper (1723–?)

> " Of beauty beaming its benignant warmth
> Through all the brute creation."

He believes also that all parts of nature are beautiful. Shagged rocks, barren heaths, precipices, sable woods, headlong rivers, all are examples of the principle of harmony and so of beauty.

Somewhat earlier in the period is another minor poet who would be today practically unknown had not Southey preserved his work. This is Joseph Relph, the son of a Cum-berland statesman. He was born in Shergham, where he spent most of his unhappy life. His *Cumbrian Pastorals* were, Southey says, transcripts from real life. They are among the very earliest attempts to represent the Cum-berland dialect, and they are a close record of Cumberland super-stitions and games and customs. The poems show an original study of the scenery about Shergham, as in the following lines:

Joseph Relph (1712–1743)

> " A finer hay-day was never seen,
> The greenish sops already luik less green
>
> .   .   .   .
>
> And see how finely striped the fields appear,
> Striped like the gown 'at I on Sundays wear.
> White show the rye, the big of blaker hue ;
> The bluimen pezz greenment wi' reed and blue."

Blair's one important poem is *The Grave* (1741). Its aim is a moral one, and it makes but slight use of the outer world. There is, however, one interesting realistic descrip-tion of a row of ragged elms

Robert Blair (1699–1746)

> " Long lash'd by the rude winds. Some rift half down

> Their branchless trunks ; others so thin atop,
> That scarce two crows could lodge in the same tree."

These elms, the cheerless unsocial yew, the wan moon, the howling wind, the screech owl, the moss-grown stones skirted with nettles, are descriptive details that serve very well to add the desired "supernumerary horror" to the scene. *The Grave* is one of the earliest poems to give to melancholy reflections on man's mortality the nature setting that was later recognized as the conventionally appropriate one.

William Thompson is best known by his *Epithalamium* (1736), *Sickness* (1746), and especially his *Hymn to May*, written " not long after." His poems were published in a volume in 1757. His *Milkmaid* is a stilted, artificial pastoral filled, in with homely details. Colin begs politely and on his knees that Lucy will smile upon him ;

William Thompson (1712?–1760?)

> " So may thy cows forever crown
> With floods of milk thy brimming pail ;
> So may thy cheeze all cheeze surpass,
> So may thy butter never fail."

Lucy, of course, sighed and blushed a sweet consent. This pastoral, together with his admiration of Pope's Alexis, who was so

> " Gently rural ! without coarseness plain ;
> How simple in his elegance of grief !
> A shepherd but no clown,"

would hardly lead one to suspect much satisfactory study of nature in Thompson's poetry. But there is apparent in the *Hymn* and even in *Sickness*, through all the florid. exuberant diction and obscure forms of expression, a genuine delight in the beauty and freshness of the outer world. He was a great admirer of Thomson, who as

> " Nature's bard the seasons on his page
> Stole from the year's rich hand,"[1]

and his poems show Thomson's influence in expression and general conception. Such phrases as the "boundless majesty of

[1] *Sickness*, 5:5.

day," the "sun's refulgent throne," the "vernant showery bow profusive," clouds of "ten thousand inconsistent shapes," are suggestive.   Here is a typical Thomsonian passage:

> "What boundless tides of splendor o'er the skies,
> O'er flowing brightness! stream their golden rays!
> Heaven's azure kindles with the varying dyes." [1]

Or take this one:

> "And what a prospect round
> Swells greenly grateful on the cherish'd eye;
> A universal blush, a waste of sweets!" [2]

There are many other suggestions of Thomson in these " tender and florid" descriptions of "the beauties, the pleasures, and the loves" of spring. William Thompson is of importance in this study merely because he is one more poet who loved nature, who wrote of her with enthusiasm, and who imitated Thomson. His chief use of nature is in similitudes and in frequent enthusiastic summaries of the charms of nature.

Moses Mendez published in 1751 four poems named in imitation of Thomson, *Spring*, *Summer*, *Autumn*, and *Winter*. There

Moses Mendez
d. 1758

is some first-hand observation in such lines as,

> "The pool-spring gnat on sounding wings doth pass
> And on the ramping steed doth suck his fill,"

or:

> "The patient cow doth, to eschew the heat.
> Her body steep within the neighboring rill;"

but more often the observations are of the conventional imitative sort, as in this couplet:

> "On every hill the purple-blushing vine
> Beneath her leaves her racy fruit doth hide,"

which is hardly true of an English scene. On the whole the passages in which Mendez treats of nature, while rather fanciful and decorative, are not indicative of any real knowledge of nature.

[1] Hymn to May, st. 20.

[2] Sickness, 5:17.

Jago's most important poems are *Edge Hill* (1767), *The Swallow* (1748), *The Blackbirds* (1752) and *The Goldfinches.*

Richard Jago
(1715-1781)

The last two are love stories of the birds named, each love story being disastrously ended by the cruelty of man in taking innocent life. *The Swallow* is an allegory of life and death. *Edge Hill* is notable for its pleasure in wide views which are minutely traced, and, alas, made " generally interesting by reflections, historical, philosophical, and moral." The new note is struck by the exceptional frequency and evident appreciation with which the poet notes the mountains in the different views. Of "Dafset's ridgy mountain," he says:

> " Like the tempest-driven wave,
> Irregularly great, his bare tops brave
> The winds."

To the west

> "Braids lifts his scarry sides,
> And Ilmington, and Campden's hoary hills,
> Impress new grandeur on the spreading scene,
>
> .   .   .   .   .   .
>
> While distant, but distinct, his Alpine ridge
> Malvern erects o'er Esham's vale sublime."

In 1750 appeared Francis Coventry's *Pens-hurst,* a poem in rhymed octosyllabics, notable chiefly for its many imitations of

Francis Coventry
(d. 1759?)

Milton. Another poem written by Coventry to the Honorable Wilmot Vaughan indicates that the two friends had found some pleasure in mountain climbing:

> " Dost thou explore Sabrina's fountful source,
>   Where huge Plinlimmon's hoary height ascends:
> Then downwards mark her vagrant course
>   "Till mixed with clouds the landscape ends?
> Dost thou revere the hallowed soil
>   Where Druids old sepulchred lie?
> Or up cold Snowden's craggy summits toil
>   And muse on ancient savage liberty?
> Ill suit such walks with bleak autumnal air."

In the *World,* April 12, 1753, Coventry also had an article entitled " Strictures on the absurd Novelties introduced in Gardening," which was a plea for simplicity and naturalness.

William Mason, who is a poet known chiefly because he had insight enough to appreciate Gray, may, in this study, be lightly passed over. His dramas *Elfrida* (1752), and *Caractacus* (1751) were written on the model of the ancient Greek tragedy. They have little to do with external nature, although in order to introduce " touches of pastoral description" such as had especially delighted him in *Comus* and *As You Like It* he had laid the scene of *Elfrida* in " an old romantic forest." *Caractacus* is a Druid play the action of which takes place on or near "majestic Snowden," but there is only a single passage in which the wild scenery is made effective in the poem, and that is the ode beginning,

William Mason (1725 1797)

> " Mona on Snowden calls:
> Hear, thou King of Mountains, hear."

Later on the ode allies itself with romantic work by its use of the supernatural but it makes slight use of nature. Mason's chief significance in this study is in what he had to say about gardens. In *To a Water Nymph* (1747), there is a protest against the elaborate Gothic fountains then fashionable, and also against shell work and mineral grottos. His long work *The English Garden* will be spoken of later.

The greatest name in this period is that of Thomas Gray. His prose will be taken up under *Travels*. His poetry falls into three periods.' The first or classical period, in spite of an occasional good line, such as

Thomas Gray (1716-1771).

> " The untaught harmony of Spring,"

is entirely conventional in its use of nature, the prevailing tone being exemplified in such phrases as "the attic warbler," "the purple year," and " Venus' train." But in the two poems of 1742, we find close and appreciative study of the country about Windsor and Stoke Pogis. In the ode on *Eton College* the wistful pleasure with which the poet recalls his childhood is intensified by his memory of the beloved hills and fields, the silver-winding

---

' Phelps : The Beginnings of the English Romantic Movement.

stream, and the pleasant paths inseparably associated with the care-free days of his youth.   In the *Elegy* the use of nature is highly artistic.   The purpose of the poem is a human one—the sympathetic representation of the honorable labor, the innocent joys, the tender and wholesome affections of the poor, the general tone being that of a pensive melancholy induced by the thought of death.   Nature is used in due subordination to the theme, and with exquisite fitness.   Every detail of the opening twilight picture contributes its own touch to prepare the mind for the succeeding reflections on death.   The sounds, the tinkling of the distant folds, the droning of the beetle, the complaining of the owl, are such as emphasize silence, which is itself an accompaniment and ·an emblem of death.   The ivy-mantled tower, the rugged elms, the black yews, have been immemorially associated with death.   There is also a subtle analogy in the withdrawal of light, the life of nature.   So, too, each detail in the first picture of morning, has its human purpose.   The stirring sounds are interesting and of pathetic import because they once waked an answering throb of life in the hearts of men who now hear them no more.   The enumeration of homely country tasks has its chief value in the suggested delight of the workman in his occupation and the resultant emphasis by contrast on the pathos of death.

In the last six stanzas of the poem we find the true romantic conception of the relation between man and nature.   The poet is represented as a shy, solitary being in communion with nature, and drawing his inspiration from her.   In the morning he hurries to some hillside that he may watch the sunrise ; at noon he stretches himself at full length under some beech-tree by the side of a brook, and pores over the waters as they babble by ; or he wanders through the woods, murmuring to himself his wayward fancies.   This poet is certainly far enough removed from the typical town-bred poet of the classical régime.   He is rather of the same race as Warton's Enthusiast, and he at least suggests Wordsworth's Poet who murmurs by the running brooks a music sweeter than their own.[1]   In these stanzas nature is not only the

[1] Wordsworth : A Poet's Epitaph. st. 10.

appropriate dramatic background.   It is taken up into the mental action and becomes at least in part the occasion of the poet's moods, and it is entirely through the relation of the poet to nature that these moods are revealed to the reader.

Nature is thus throughout the poem made strictly subservient to the human theme, but the intrinsic beauty of the brief descriptions, quite apart from the context, cannot pass unnoticed.   Separate lines have the power of suggesting whole pictures.   For example in

"How bowed the woods beneath their sturdy stroke,"

the ringing blow of the ax, the crash of the falling tree, smite upon the ear.   "Oft did the harvest to their sickle yield"

is full of color and life.   There is a wide, peaceful landscape effect in   "The lowing herds wind slowly o'er the lea."

And the line

"The swallow twittering from its straw-built shed"

brings up all the details of a humble farmyard.   These and other descriptions in the *Elegy* are distinctively English inspirit and detail.   They are the result of first-hand knowledge, they are drawn with a firm hand, and they are used with an instinctive recognition of artistic fitness.

A new range of sympathies, however, appears in the poems of Gray's third or purely romantic period.   Here he writes of northern mythologies and superstitions or gives transcripts of Norse tales, and the pictures interwoven with the human elements are of a wild and savage character.   In *The Bard* mountain, precipice, and torrent form a setting without which the fiery denunciation of the poet would lose half its force.   The storm and the whirlwind sweep through these poems.   Rough and frowning steeps, foaming floods, warring winds, the heights of Snowdon and huge Plinlimmon, darkness, cold, make up the terrible but dramatically appropriate environment for the fierce, imprecatory elegy which the bard utters over his lost companions, for the fatal and dreadful song of the gigantic sisters weaving "the loom of Hell."

In one or two other poems there is effective use of nature. The joy of a convalescent able at last to go out of doors was not an uncommon subject through this period, but there is no better expression of it than in *A Fragment* by Gray. The feeling, and in passages, the phraseology, are almost Wordsworthian.

> " The meanest flowret of the vale,
> The simplest note that swells the gale,
> The common sun, the air, the skies,
> To him are opening Paradise,"

is an illustrative stanza. There are also some exquisite lines on birds, as,

> " But chief, the Sky-lark warbles high
> His trembling thrilling ecstacy;
> And, lessening from the dazzled sight,
> Melts into air and liquid light,"[1]

and.

> " There pipes the wood-lark, and the song-thrush there
> Scatters his loose notes in the waste of air."[2]

Though undated these lines in their spirit and workmanship ally themselves at once with the period of the *Elegy* rather than with the later work. They also more accurately represent Gray's dominant attitude towards nature, his knowledge of sweet, homely things, and the delicate perfection of his literary touch.

The Rev. R. Potter's chief poem is *A Farewell Hymn to the Country, Attempted in the Manner of Spenser's Epithalamion* (1749).

R. Potter
(1721–1804)
The poem shows much sympathetic knowledge of some parts of nature, especially of birds and trees· He speaks of the quail that "runnes piping o'er the land," of the "mavis-haunted grove," and of the nightingale that delights "the stillness of the night." He declares that his entire orchard, plums, pears, grapes, permains, and all, is at the service of these, his "fellow-poets." At evening

> " The slum'bring trees seem their tall tops to bow
> Rocking the careless birds that on them nest
> To gentle, gentle rest."

[1] On the Pleasure arising from Vicissitude.
[2] Couplet about Birds.

He does not often refer to specific trees, but he gives little sug-
gestive pictures as of "the uncertain shaded grove," or

> "the doubtfull shade
> By quivering branches made,"

or of delightful resting places roofed with "inwoven branches."
The stream for which he cared most was "the gentle Tave" in
Norfolk.   He mentions many flowers, but in no new or finely
descriptive manner.   His sensitiveness to perfumes we may see
in such lines as,

> "Sweet is the breath of heaven with day-spring born,"

> "Where the fresh hay-cock breathes along the mead,"

or in such phrases as "this flowre-perfumed aire."   The poem is
rich in color, as in the descriptions of sunrise, and of various
kinds of fruit.

Though it would be difficult to quote specific lines to prove
the statement, it is nevertheless true that the whole poem con-
veys in a quite unusual degree a sense of warm, abiding affection
for the simple scenes of the country.   "Smit with the peacefull
joys of lowly life," he gives thanks for "the unmoved quiet of
his silver daies," and thinks with dread of "the cares and pains
in mad citties."   His use of nature is almost entirely in a running
assemblage of sweet sights and sounds to justify his preference
for country life.

Another of the minor poets of this period is Dr. John Dalton.
In 1755 he wrote a *Descriptive Poem*, inscribed to Two Ladies,
the daughters of Lord Lonsdale.   It is long,
Dr. John Dalton rambling, tedious, but it is of historical impor-
(1709–1763) tance as being probably the first poetical tribute
to the beauty of Westmoreland and Cumberland.

> "Then change the scene : to Nature's pride,
> Sweet Keswick's vale, the Muse will guide.
> The Muse, who trod th' enchanted ground,
> Who sail'd the wonderous lake around,
> With you will haste once more to hail
> The beauteous brook of Borrodale."

He speaks of the streams that

> " rejoice to roar
> Down the rough rocks of dread Lodore,"

and says that

> " Horrors like these at first alarm,
> But soon with savage grandeur charm,
> And raise to noblest thoughts your mind.
> Thus by thy fall, Lodore, reclin'd,
> The cragged cliff, inpendent wood,
> Whose shadows mix o'er half the flood,
> The gloomy clouds, which solemn sail,
> Scarce lifted by the languid gale
> O'er the cap'd hill and darken'd vale
>
> .   .   .   .
>
> I view with wonder and delight,
> A pleasing tho' an awful sight."

Of Keswick and Skiddaw he writes,

> "Thy roofs, O Keswick, brighter rise!
> The lake and lofty hills between,
> Where giant Skiddow shuts the scene.

> " Supreme of mountains, Skiddow, hail!
> To whom all Britain sinks a vale!
> Lo, his imperial brow, I see
> From foul usurping vapors free!
> 'Twere glorious now his side to climb,
> Boldly to scale his top sublime."

There are several passages in the poem indicative of Dr. Dalton's unusually close study of streams, especially those near Lowther Castle, and in the picturesque valley of Borrowdale. With evident delight he traces the stream from its mountain source, over tuneful falls, under broad spreading boughs, along silent meadows, to the wide lake. There is also a fine passage descriptive of a patriarchal oak near Lowther. It is the first sustained description of a specific tree with anything like the modern feeling. It is represented as standing in a "sunny plain alone." Its reverend age, its majesty, are especially dwelt upon. The poem shows some excellent first-hand observation. Dr. Dalton is ahead of Wordsworth in noticing the " azure roofs " of the lowly cottages.   And he should have the credit of discovering the beauty of the vale of Derwentwater, and the majesty of giant Skiddaw, fourteen years before Gray made his famous tour, and nearly half a century before the lake poets set up their monopoly.

The most important work of this period was doubtless that of the Warton brothers.   Their father was also a poet, and he struck the romantic note in his hatred of city **Joseph Warton** life and his longing for solitude in the country. **(1722-1800)**   Joseph Warton had a long literary career during which he edited books, wrote poems, and contributed articles to periodicals.   Those of his poems that were of especial note in the history of Romanticism were written early in life, between 1740 and 1756.   *The Enthusiast* (1740), *Odes on Various Subjects* (1746), and *Ode on Mr. West's Translation of Pindar* (1749) are the chief ones to be studied.   In these poems there are many summaries of such objects in nature as give pleasure, but there is little actual description.   In details and phraseology there are frequent echoes from Milton and Thomson.[1]

In general, though unoriginal in expression, the poems are marked by an unmistakably genuine love of nature, and of nature untouched by man.   The poet dislikes Versailles whose fountains cast

> " The tortur'd waters to the distant heav'ns." [2]

Even Kent—

---

[1] "All-beauteous Nature! by thy boundless charms," "the vast, various Landscape," "sight-refreshing green," "the thousand-colored tulip," are typical Thomsonian phrases.

" Liquid lapse of murm'ring waters "—Enthusiast, l. 93, Paradise Lost, 8:263;

" Mountain shagg'd with horrid shades "—Enthusiast, l. 75, Comus, l. 429;

> " When young-eyed spring profusely throws
> From her green lap the pink and rose."
>
> —Ode to Fancy, l. 106.   Song on May Morning ;
>
> " Then lay me by some haunted stream,
> Rapt in some wild poetic dream."
>
> —Ode to Fancy, l. 41.   L'Allegro, l. 129 ;

are some of the characteristic instances of the echoes from Milton.

[2] The Enthusiast.

> " Though he, by rules unfettered, boldly scorns
> Formality and method, round and square
> Disdaining, plans irregularly great," [1]

cannot design like nature. No gardens however artfully adorned can charm like "unfrequented meads and pathless wilds." The poet finds peculiar pleasure in all the wild, solitary, mournful aspects of nature. He loves "hollow winds" and "ever-beating waves," and hoary mountains where

> " Nature seems to sit alone." [2]

He wishes for

> "·some pine-top'd precipice
> Abrupt and shaggy, whence a foamy stream
> Like Anio, tumbling roars ; or some black heath
> Where straggling stands the mournful juniper,
> Or yew-tree scath'd." [3]

He escapes from the hated city's "tradeful hum" and seeks for solitude at "the deep dead of night" under the pale light of the moon. He is alive to all the mysterious, romantic suggestions of nature. He is charmed by the little dancing Fayes that sip night-dews and "laugh and love" in the dales. In storms he hears demons and goblins shrieking through the dark air. He is also deeply conscious of the effect of nature on man. He finds himself even oppressed by the boundless charms of "brooks hill, meadow, dale," and it is his belief that all nature conspires

> " To raise, to soothe, to harmonize the mind."

Nature can give happiness beyond that of luxury or gratified ambition. These poems mark a new phase in the feeling towards nature, because, with little description, with no theory to propound, no moral to teach, no human interest to exemplify, the poet with a rapt fervor and intensity cries out for solitary communion with nature as a necessity of his own being. Warton is also, I think, the first of the romantic poets to advocate a return to nature in the sense in which Rousseau used the phrase.

> " Happy the first of men, ere yet confin'd
> To smoaky cities ; who in sheltering groves,
> Warm caves, and deep-sunk vallies liv'd and lov'd.

[1] The Enthusiast.   [2] Ode to Fancy.   [3] The Enthusiast.

> Yet why should man mistaken deem it nobler
> To dwell in palaces and high-roof'd halls,
> Than in God's forests, architect supreme!"[1]

Joseph Warton's exceptionally strong love of nature is emphasized by the testimony of Bowles who traces his own love of nature to companionship with Dr. Warton, and by the testimony of his brother Thomas in a poem, *An Ode Sent to a Friend.* In this poem Thomas Warton tells of his brother's delight in walks at morning and evening through unfrequented grassy lanes, or in the deep forest, or up steep hills " to view the length of landscape ever new."

A part of the service which Warton rendered to the poetry of nature rests in the fact that he led the attention from Pope to poets who had treated of nature with imaginative power. He had only scorn for

> "The fearful, frigid lays of cold and creeping Art,"

'the courtly silken lay," "the polished lyrics," of his own day. But it is in his prose that we find the best evidence of his break with the classicists. In the dedication prefixed to the *Essay on Pope* (1756) he divided English poets into four classes, putting in the first class only Spenser, Shakespeare, and Milton. Of Pope he said, " I revere the memory of Pope; I respect and honor his abilities, but I do not think him at the head of his profession." He then proceeded to show the difference " betwixt a man of wit, a man of sense, and a true poet." In the first and second sections of the *Essay* he minutely discusses Pope's descriptive poetry showing that his idea of pastoral poetry as representing some golden age was but "an empty notion," and commenting severely on his mixture of British and Grecian ideas. He condemns *Windsor Forest* because its images are " equally applicable to any place whatsoever." In contrast with Pope he puts Thomson, of whose *Seasons* he gives a most discriminating eulogy. It is too long to quote entire, but a part of it must be given if only to show its remarkably modern tone.

" Thomson was blessed with a strong and copious fancy ; he

[1] The Enthusiast.

hath enriched poetry with a variety of new and original images, which he painted from nature itself, and from his own actual observations ; his descriptions have, therefore, a distinctness and truth, which are utterly wanting to those of poets who have only copied from each other, and have never looked abroad on the objects themselves. Thomson was accustomed to wander away into the country for days, and for weeks, attentive to ' each rural sight, each rural sound,' while many a poet, who has dwelt for years in the Strand, has attempted to describe fields and rivers, and generally succeeded accordingly. Hence that nauseous repetition of the same circumstances ; hence that disgusting impropriety of introducing what may be called a set of hereditary images, without proper regard to the age, or climate, or occasion in which they were formerly used. . . . . And if our poets would accustom themselves to contemplate fully every object, before they attempted to describe it, they would not fail of giving their readers more new and complete images than they generally do."[1]

Wordsworth himself was hardly more emphatic in his scorn of vague descriptions and hereditary images, and in his plea for simple truth to nature. The passages already quoted are sufficient to show how self-conscious and theoretical was Warton's romanticism. He was not, however, so far as the study of nature alone is concerned, the first self-conscious worker in the new field. Ramsay and Shenstone had already, apologetically to be sure, but none the less distinctly, entered their protest against the conventional imitations of their day. But Warton uttered no apology. His theory was fully established in his own mind. He came down on the classicists with hammer and tongs, and enunciated in 1756 at least two of the cardinal doctrines of the poets of nature who wrote forty years later.

Thomas Warton's poems seem at first reading to be but a patchwork of phrases from Milton.[2] *The Pleasures of Melancholy* (1745)

[1] An Essay on the Genius and Writings of Pope.

[2] Note such lines as

    " Haste thee nymph, and hand in hand,
    With thee lead a buxom band ;

was written when he was but seventeen.   The theme of this poem is a defense of solitude against various social pleasures, and it has the customary note of delight in darkness, tombs, pale shrines, "fav'rite midnight haunts," "pale December's foggy glooms," and "the pitying moon." *The First of April, Ode on the Approach of Summer, and Morning, an Ode,* are of more importance so far as the love of nature is concerned. The lines on the opening spring show close observation.

Thomas Warton (1728-1790)

> " Reluctant comes the timid spring."
>
> " Fringing the forest's devious edge
>   Half rob'd appears the hawthorn hedge."
>
> " Scant along the ridgy land
>   The beans their new-born ranks expand."

The rooks swarm with clamorous call and

> " Wreathe their capacious nests anew."

The fisher " bursting through the crackling sedge "

> " Startles from the bordering wood
>   The bashful wild-duck's early brood."
>
> " And so loud the blackbird sings
>   That far and near the valley rings."

He notes also the kite that sails above the crowded roof of the dove-cote, the plumy crest of thistles, the russet tints and gleams of light in the tops of trees at sunset, the faint, varying shades of green when the new foliage appears on the trees, and the blue tint of the unchanging pine standing in their midst. Warton's pleasure in wide views is indicated in several passages where he speaks of climbing a hill for the sake of the broad prospect of field and stream. He had also an appreciation of wild nature, as we see from the descriptions in *The Grave of King Arthur.* Warton's work is of interest because of the many attractive details scattered through his poems, but there is

> Bring fantastic-footed joy," etc.,
> " But ever against restless heat," etc.,
> " Let not my due feet fail to climb," etc.
>
> Approach of Summer.

little unity of effect. The general impression is that he saw nature first through Milton's eyes, and that when he afterwards made many charming discoveries for himself he tried to express them in the *Il Penseroso* manner.

His chief influence was in his *Observations on the Faerie Queen* and in his *History of Poetry*, but except as attention was thus directed to older writers, these works had no effect on the poetry of nature.

In Joseph Warton's *Enthusiast* (1740) the love of solitary communion with nature was supreme. About fourteen years later appeared William Whitehead's *Enthusiast*, which is of interest here because it shows so well the typical eighteenth century view in contrast to the pure romanticism of Warton. In Whitehead's *Enthusiast* the poet yields instinctively to the new spirit, but is suddenly recalled to himself, is rendered sane by the wise admonitions of Reason. It is a bright day in May. The poet, entranced by the beauty about him, walks forth,

William Whitehead (1715–1785)

> " With loit'ring steps regardless where,
> So soft, so genial was the air,
> So wond'rous bright the day.
>
> And now my eyes with transport rove
> O'er all the blue expanse above,
> Unbroken by a cloud !
> And now beneath delighted pass, ·
> Where, winding through the deep-green grass,
> A full-brim'd river flow'd."

> " These, these are joys alone, I cry ;
> 'Tis here, divine Philosophy,
> Thou deign'st to fix thy throne !
> Here Contemplation points the road
> Through Nature's charms to Nature's God !
> These, these are joys alone !"

Then Reason whispers " monitory strains," and teaches the Enthusiast that " light, and shade, and warmth, and air," that the " philosophic calmness," the visionary sense of " universal love," which come to man from nature, must sink into insignificance before the exalted joys of Virtue, and reminds the poet that

" man was made for man." The intrinsic value of this poem is slight, but it is noteworthy because we see the two tendencies contending for mastery. Whitehead was no poet. He simply reflected in a turbid fashion what more original men were saying. His tolerably full statement of the romantic attitude towards nature, with his subsequent assertion of the triumphant good sense of Classicism is, therefore, valuable testimony to the two-fold spirit of the age.

In general we may say that we find during this period, rural didactic poetry treating of English subjects in the manner of John Philips in *Cyder*, as in Somerville and Smart. There is good local color in some descriptive poems as in Shenstone, Gray, Dr. Dalton, and Relph. There is throughout the period first-hand observation, but it is not so abundant, nor is the openness of the poet's mind to sensuous impression so apparent as in some preceding work. There is, however, delicate and poetic handling of material as in the poems of Gray and Collins and Greene. There is a self-conscious endeavor to break away from ancient models, as in Ramsay's *Preface* and Shenstone's *Preface*, and from existing poetic domination as in Warton's protest against Pope. Truth to nature, independence of observation, as necessary poetic qualities, are for the first time openly and theoretically insisted on in Warton's *Essay*. There is scorn of the utilitarian view of nature, as in Shenstone. The debt of man to nature is dwelt upon with new emphasis by Young, Shenstone, and especially Akenside. The sense of a divine spirit in nature is clearly expressed by Akenside, and less clearly by Young. The purely romantic love of nature in connection with sentimental melancholy is fully exemplified in Joseph Warton. There is strong personal enthusiasm for nature in Shenstone, Akenside, and Joseph Warton. There is love of animals in Shenstone and Jago. There is notable representation of country people in Relph and Gray and Somerville.

THE PERIOD FROM 1756 TO 1798.

From the *Essay on Pope* to the *Lyrical Ballads* is a long period but any subdivision would be purely arbitrary. It is chiefly characterized by the development and emphasis of influences already manifestly operant. The most valuable work is that of Macpherson, Beattie, Burns, Cowper, and Blake. Goldsmith is of less importance. Brown, Langhorne, Logan, and Bowles, though minor poets, are significant in their poetry of nature. Of less note are Mickle, Grainger, Bruce, Cunningham, Graeme, and Scott.

John Brown, otherwise unimportant, is interesting because of his early appreciation of the scenery of the English

John Brown (1715-1766) Lakes. He wrote a description of Keswick[1] in a letter to Lyttleton, and his undated *Fragment of a Rhapsody Written at the Lakes of Westmoreland* is probably the outcome of the same visit. The *Fragment* is short and may be quoted entire as well because of its beauty, as because of its subject and early date :

> " Now sunk the sun, now twilight sunk, and night
> Rode in her zenith; nor a passing breeze
> Sigh'd to the groves, which in the midnight air
> Stood motionless; and in the peaceful floods
> Inverted hung; for now the billow slept
> Along the shore, nor heav'd the deep, but spread
> A shining mirror to the moon's pale orb,
> Which, dim and waning, o'er the shadowy cliffs,
> The solemn woods and spiry mountain tops
> Her glimmering faintness threw. Now every eye
> Oppress'd with toil, was drown'd in deep repose,
> Save that the unseen shepherd in his watch,
> Propt on his crook, stood listening by the fold,
> And gaz'd the starry vault and pendant moon.
> Nor voice nor sound broke on the deep serene
> But the soft murmur of swift gushing rills,
> Forth issuing from the mountain's distant steep
> (Unheard till now, and now scarce heard) proclaimed
> All things at rest, and imag'd the still voice
> Of quiet whispering to the ear of night."

For a curious coincidence compare Wordsworth's lines written thirty years later:

[1] See page 195, under Travels.

> "The song of mountain streams, unheard by day,
> Now hardly heard, beguiles my homeward way."

John Langhorne was born at Kirby-Stephen in Westmoreland. His best poems were published in 1759-60, though his *Fables of Flora* did not appear till 1771. Langhorne had an enthusiastic personal love for nature. He dwelt with rapture on stream and flower and field and sky.[1]   His wish was,

John Langhorne
(1735-1779)

> "Oh let me still with simple nature live,
> My lowly field flowers on her altar lay;
> Enjoy the blessings that she meant to give
> And calmly waste my inoffensive day."[2]

Or again,

> "Slow let me climb the mountain's airy brow;
> The green height gained, in museful rapture lie,
> Sleep to the murmur of the woods below
> Or look to nature with a lover's eye."[3]

His preference for nature untouched by art is seen in the charming little *Fable*[4] showing the superiority of the wild rose to the more splendid cultivated rose. And in another *Fable* he says;

> "Come let us leave the painted plain,
> This waste of flowers that palls the eye;
> The walks of nature's wilder reign
> Shall please in plainer majesty."[5]

That he had a tender feeling towards animals is shown by his poems on birds and by his protest against the cruelty of confining birds in cages. The most striking characteristic of Langhorne's poems is his direct expression of the excellence of the gift that nature's hand bestows. A part of this excellent gift is the inspiration to poetry. The young shepherd was inspired with "poetic charms" as he wandered through the wild scenes

> "By Yarrow's banks or groves of Endermay."

In his own experience

[1] Hope.
[2] Vision of Fancy, Elegy 3.
    Vision of Fancy, Elegy 3.
[4] Fable IV.
[5] Fable, The Bee Flower.

> " The nameless charms of high poetic thought,"

were born of "spring's green hours," and the murmuring shore
spoke to him "divine words,"[1] while in earlier days "each lay
that falter'd from his tongue" had been "from Eden's murmurs
caught."[2]   In an ode to the "Genius of Westmoreland," he
says that she kindled the "sacred fire" in his heart, that she gave
him "thoughts too high to be exprest."   Again he speaks of
an hour in his youth when

> " The woodland genius came
> And touched me with his holy flame."[3]

Statements still more remarkable as foreshadowing later doctrines
are found in such lines as,

> " Whatever charms the ear or eye,
> All beauty and all harmony,
> If sweet sensations they produce,
> I know they have their moral use.
>
> I know that nature's charms can move
> The springs that strike to virtue's love."[4]

Or these lines,

> " Has fair philosophy thy love ?
> Away ! she lives in yonder grove.
> If the sweet muse thy pleasure gives,
> With her, in yonder grove, she lives.
> And if religion claims thy care,
> Religion fled from books is there.
> For first from nature's works we drew
> Our knowledge and our virtue too."[5]

Langhorne's perception of the power of nature over man, and
his passionate sense of personal indebtedness to nature are
the keynotes of his work.   In a narrow way and with feeble
speech he shows a mental and spiritual experience of the same
type as that which Wordsworth records of his own youth.   His
motive in writing, "an unaffected wish to promote the love

[1] To the Rev. Lamb.   [3] Autumnal Elegy.
[2] Fable IV.   [4] Fable X.
[5] Inscription on the Door of a Study.

of nature and the interests of humanity," is likewise Words-worthian.

In Christopher Smart's one great poem, the *Song to David* (1763), the use of nature is of so strange a character that it refuses classification under the customary categories. The **Christopher Smart (1722-1770)** chief thought of the poem in the parts where nature is used has to do with the creative energy of God, the song of praise that is eternally his from all existence, and the exceeding sweetness, strength, beauty, and glory of the Spirit of God in man. These themes are not new with Smart in this poem. In his prize poems ten years before he had taken the attributes of God as his subject, and the general line of thought, and the method of proof by the rapid accumulation of illustrative images drawn from nature are practically the same as in the *Song to David*. Here and there are instances of the same noble conceptions and striking phrases, as in this picture of a tree:

> "The oak
> His lordly head uprears, and branching arms
> Extends—behold in regal solitude
> And pastoral magnificence he stands
> So simple! and so great! The underwood
> Of meaner rank an awful distance keep." [1]

Or this description of the Leviathan that,

> "The terror and the glory of the main,
> His pastime takes with transport proud to see,
> The ocean's vast dominions all his own." [2]

It is, however, only in the *Song* that the early themes are treated with sustained energy of thought and splendor of imagery. In this poem each thought is abundantly illustrated from nature. The details are brought together from every clime and season. They are poured forth with impetuous ardor. The excited imagination of the poet does not hesitate and choose. The universe is laid under contribution. There is a prodigal

[1] The Immensity of the Supreme Being.

[2] The Immensity of the Supreme Being, l. 56. Cf. also the similar lines in Hymn to the Supreme Being, st. 16. It was apparently a favorite image. See Browning's reference to it in his poem on Smart.

heaping up of the treasures of nature, an almost barbaric splendor
of images.   Does the poet wish to say that all nature praises
God?   The earth passes before him as in a vision.   The great
song of adoration swells upon his ear from every form of harmo-
nious activity.   Seasons change, almonds glow, tendrils climb,
fruit trees blossom, birds build their nests, bell-flowers nod, the
spotted ounce and her cubs play, harvests ripen, wild carnations
blow, the pheasant shows his glossy neck, the squirrel hoards nuts,
the map of nature is crowded with scenes of beauty, the crocus
"burnishes alive" upon the snow-clad earth, the bullfinch sings
his flute note, the redbreast balances on the hazel spray, silver
fish glide through rivers, cataracts fall, fruits are luscious, gums give
out incense, all to "heap up the measure, load the scales" with
praise to the Lord who is great and glad.   In this rapid summary
there is a pomp, an energy, an activity that is indescribable.   A
later stanza on strength is almost terrifying in its powerful ima-
gery.

> "Strong is the lion—like the coal
> His eyeball--like a bastion's mole
> His chest against the foes:
> Strong the gier-eagle on his sail,
> Strong against tide the enormous whale
> Emerges as he goes."

I know nothing like it except Blake's *Tiger* which is marked by
the same tenseness and abrupt energy.

Many of the details in Smart's poems were drawn from his
reading, especially from the Hebrew Scriptures.   They could not
have come from observation for they have little to do with the
"old, oft catalogued repository of things in sky and wave and
land."   The images are fresh, original, daring.   They startle the
mind out of passivity.

Another point to be noted is the peculiar combination of
facts.   Bears, sleek tigers, ponies, and kids, are the beasts assem-
bled to illustrate God's creative activity, and so in other combi-
nations.   Objects the least likely to suggest each other are brought
together.   In the same way facts from nature and from human
nature are strangely mingled.   Among beauteous things are reck-

oned a fleet before a gale, a host in glittering armor, a wild garden, a moonlight night, and a virgin before her spouse.

Amidst the prettinesses, decencies, timidities, of the eighteenth century poetry of nature, this poem by Smart sounds out like a trumpet. The marshaled facts move forward like a cohort of soldiers with a splendid tread that shakes the earth. The whole effect is Hebraic, apocalyptic.

Mickle's chief poems are *Syr Martyn* (1767) *Pollio* (1762) and some shorter pieces. In *Pollio* Mickle makes frequent references to his own love of nature. The country he knew best was that about Roslin Castle where he was brought up, but he was not unfamiliar with other parts of southeast Scotland as is shown by his references to the Forth, the Annan, the Wauchope, the Ewes, to the dales of Tiviot, and to various country seats. His interest in nature was varied in character. In *Almada Hill* and *May Day* there are frequent appreciative lines on mountains, as;

> " Where Snowden's front ascends the skies,"
>
> " The tower-like summits of the mountain shore."

There are briefer references in such phrases as, " the hills of Cheviot," " the thyme-clad mountain," " the mountains gray," " Old Snowden," " Snowden's hoary side," " the curving mountain's craggy brow," which serve at least to show that Mickle was not unconscious of the scenery about him. One or two lines indicate the effect of the sea on his mind. As he stood on Almada Hill and looked out over old Ocean,

> " By human eye untempted, unexplored,
>   An awful solitude,"

it was

> the last dim wave, in boundless space
> Involved and lost " [1]

that held his impatient imagination. Even so brief a passage serves to illustrate the awakened curiosity, the new sense of pleasure in the infinite and the unknown, that characterized the romantic impulse. Another modern note in Mickle is his inter-

[1] **Almada Hill**, l. 330.

est in moonlight and stars. There are several picturesque descrip-
tive lines, as,

> " When sudden, o'er the fir-crown'd hill
> The full orb'd moon arose."[1]

> " How bright, emerging o'er yon broom-clad height
> The silver empress of the night appears."[2]

> " While on the distant east
> Led by her starre, the horned moone looks o'er
> The bending forest, and with rays increast
> Ascends."[3]

> " The star of evening glimmers o'er the dale
> And leads the silent host of heaven along."[4]

In spite of the classical note in such a phrase as "silver empress"
these lines show not only genuine pleasure in the loveliness of
night, but also first-hand knowledge of its phenomena. Close-
ness of observation is further indicated in the lines on birds, as in
the description of the "sootie black-bird," that chaunts his shrill
vespers from the topmost spray of some tall tree, or of the eagle
that sails through the sky with "wide-spread wings unmov'd " till
suddenly he "sheer descends " on the brow of Snowden.

In his representation of flowers Mickle notes the " daisie-
whitened plain," and " the white and yellow flowers that love the
dank," but he was especially attracted by flowers growing among
rocks or upon cliffs. One close observation is of the twinkling
lines of gossamer that on summer mornings hang from spray to
spray.

Mickle's poems show a genuine love of nature. He abounds
in reminiscences of his happy youth

> " By the banks of the crystal-streamed Esk,
> Where the Wauchope her yellow wave joins."[5]

His chief use of nature is in the passages where he gives these
early associations, and in the many similitudes in his *Elegies*.
He always sees nature in a pathetic or joyous union with past
experiences in his own life or in that of others.

[1] The Sorceress, st. 4.   [4] Pollio, st. 3.
[2] Elegy, st. 4.   [5] Eskdale Braes, st. 1.
[3] Syr Martyn, 2:31.

Grainger's chief poem, *The Sugar Cane*, appeared in 1764. The theme and outline are presented in the first four lines:

> "What soil the cane affects; what care demands;
> Beneath what signs to plant; what ills await:
> How the hot nectar best to crystallize;
> And Afric's sable progeny to treat"

James Grainger
(1724–1767)
Grainger recognizes as his poetical masters, Maro, the "pastoral Dyer" (*The Fleece*), "Pomona's bard" (*Cyder*), Smart (*The Hop Garden*), and Somerville (*The Chace*). *The Sugar Cane* is a purely didactic poem and is no real contribution to the new feeling towards nature. The first part of the *Ode to Solitude*, a long ode beginning,

> "O Solitude, Romantic maid,"

is another example of the sentimental view of nature, with frequent and obvious imitations of Milton; but the last half of the poem declares that only the old and feeble should seek the solitude of the country, that shades are no medicine for a troubled mind, and, in general, that the proper business of mankind is man.

James Macpherson (1738–1796)
Chronologically Macpherson's *Poems of Ossian* belong in the five years before the publication of Percy's *Reliques* (1765), and they are a part of the same general stream of influence, the revival of folk-lore. These poems are epic in character, their aim being the celebration of the exploits of Celtic heroes. They are of importance in this study because the adventures of Fingal, Ossian, Oscar, and Gaul are throughout closely associated with natural scenery of a wild and romantic sort.[1] Mist-covered mountains, storm-swept skies, rough streams, desolate shores, dim moonlight nights, are the most frequent scenic details, and they are so wrought into the story that the human tragedy and the scene where it was enacted cannot be thought of apart. The three ways in which nature is used in these poems, as dramatic background, in similitudes, and in apostrophes, will serve to

[1] See Life and Letters of James Macpherson, by Bailey Saunders, p. 14.

illustrate both the prominence given to nature and the close union between human emotions and the varying phenomena of the external world. A fine example of a bright description to usher in a sudden contrasting portent of disaster is in the opening lines of *Temora*:

"The blue waves of Erin roll in light. The mountains are covered with day. Trees shake their dusky heads in the breeze. Gray torrents pour their noisy streams. Two green hills, with aged oaks, surround a narrow plain. The blue course of a stream is there." The song that was "lovely, but sad, and left silence in Carric-Thura," has an autumn picture as its fit setting.

"Autumn is dark on the mountains; gray mist rests on the hills. The whirlwind is heard on the heath. Dark rolls the river through the narrow plain. A tree stands alone on the hill and marks the slumbering Connal. The leaves whirl round with the wind and strew the graves of the dead." [1]

The description of the desolation of Balclutha is the prelude to the song of mourning for the unhappy Moina. [2]

The use of nature in apostrophes is characteristic of the Ossian poems. Of these the most famous is the address to the sun. [2] There are frequent apostrophes to winds, streams, and tempests, to stars, and especially to the moon. Two good examples are the poet's address to the evening star in *The Songs of Selma*, and to the moon in *Dar Thula*. Of these the second may be quoted as fairly typical:

"Daughter of heaven, fair art thou! the silence of thy face is pleasant! Thou comest forth in loveliness. The stars attend thy blue course in the east. The clouds rejoice in thy presence, O Moon! they brighten their dark-brown sides. Who is like thee in heaven, light of the silent night? The stars are ashamed in thy presence. . . . But thou thyself shalt fail one night, and leave thy blue path in heaven. The stars will then lift their heads. . . . Thou art now clothed with thy brightness. Look from thy gates in the sky. Burst the cloud, O wind! that the daughter of night may look forth; that the shaggy mountains may brighten, and the ocean roll its white waves in light."

[1] Carric-Thura.   [2] Carthon.

It will be observed that in almost every apostrophe there is beautiful external description together with an underlying analogy to the thought of the poem. In the passages quoted above the triumphant brightness of the moon in her blue path, and the suggestion of the coming night when she shall fail in heaven, are but types of the beauty of Dar Thula and of the day when, though the winds of spring shall be abroad, though the flowers shall shake their heads on the green hills, and the woods shall wave their growing leaves, the white-bosomed maiden shall not again move in the steps of her loveliness.

Dr. Blair in his full study of the similitudes of Ossian admits that they are too "thick-sown," and that they are drawn from a narrow range of objects. But he claims, on the other hand, that the similes have the exceptional vividness that comes from first-hand observation,[1] and that they show an imaginative perception of subtle analogies.[2] Dr. Blair's recognition of beauty and congruity was so quickened by his partisanship of Ossian that his conclusions usually need to be scrutinized in the cold light of facts. The subtlety of the analogies certainly often escapes the ordinary reader, but no one can fail to observe the pathetic beauty of the little pictures into which the similitudes are often elaborated. Music, for instance, is compared to "the rising breeze, that whirls at first the thistle's beard, then flies dark-shadowy over the grass." Again a song is "like the voice of a summer breeze, when it lifts the head of flowers and curls the lakes and streams." The heroes contended "like gales of spring, as they fly along the hill, and bend by turns the feebly-whistling grass." The warriors are "bright as the sunshine before a storm; when the west wind collects the clouds, and

[1] Dr. Blair has a significant comment on the truth in the poems of Ossian. "The introduction of foreign images betrays a poet copying not from nature, but from other writers. Hence so many lions and tigers, and eagles and serpents which we meet with in the similes of modern poets; as if these animals had acquired some right to a place in poetical comparisons for ever, because employed by ancient authors. They employed them with propriety, as objects generally known in their country; but they are absurdly used for illustration by us, who know them only at second-hand, or by description."

[2] Blair's Critical Dissertation, in Tauchnitz ed. of the Ossian Poems.

Morven echoes over all her oaks." In these and many similar comparisons we see how the beauty of the suggested natural picture led the poet into a use of details not necessary for his illustrations. The importance of the poetry of Ossian in the evolution of the poetry of nature rests on its early date, its close interweaving of human emotions and natural scenes, and its abundant and appreciative use of wild, free nature.

Percy's *Reliques* appeared in 1765. The publication of these ballads was of great importance to the cause of the romantic revival in general. The ballads were, however, of **Bishop Percy** somewhat less significance in their influence on the **(1729–1811)** new feeling toward nature. A ballad would never interrupt the story for a description, and there would, of course, never be any hint of a philosophy of nature. But throughout the ballads there are casual touches of description showing a genuine love for some forms of nature, especially the forest, green hills, and moors. "Upon the wide moors," "on moors so broad," "over the fields so brown," "over the lea," "over the downs," are characteristic phrases. The castles are usually on a hill and command a wide view.[1] The love of the hills is indicated by such little pictures as

> "Robin sat on a gude grene hill.
> Keipand a flock of fie."[2]

or,

> "Lord Thomas and fair Annet
> Sate a' day on a hill,
> When night was cum and sun was sett
> They had not talkt their fill."[3]

But it is the forest that most often appears.

> "Until they came to the merry green wood,
> Where they had gladdest bee,"[4]

gives the fresh, open-air setting of most of these tales of love and heroism;

[1] See Child of Elle, Edom o' Gordon, Hardyknute, and others.
[2] Robin and Makyne.
[3] Lord Thomas and Fair Annet.
[4] Robin Hood and Guy of Gisborne.

> Mery it was in the grene forest
> Amonge the leves grene;"[1]

> " All in the merrye month of May,
> When greene buds they were swellin;"[2]

> " And wee'll away to the greene forest;"[3]

> " Gil Morice sate in gude grene wode,
> He whistled and he sang;"[4]

> " In summer time when leaves grow greene,
> And blossoms bedecke the tree;"[5]

> " To the greene forest so pleasant and faire;"[6]

> " He myght have dwelt in grene foreste,
> Under the shadowes greene;"[7]

> " The woodweele sang, and wold not cease,
> Sitting upon the spraye,
> Soe lowde, he wakened Robin Hood
> In the greenwood where he lay ;"[8]

are typical forest pictures.[9] But the gude green wood is not always fresh and blooming, as we see from occasional lines such as

> " Now loud and shrill blew the westlin' wind,
> " Sair beat the heavy shower;"[10]

> " About Yule quhen the wind blew cule;"[11]

> " Oft have I ridden thro Stirling town
> In the wind both and the weit;"[11]

> " No shimmering sun here ever shone;
> No halesome breeze here ever blew;"[12]

Trees are not often mentioned individually except the oak and the willow, the latter always representing sorrow.

[1] Adam Bell.   [2] Barbara Allan's Cruelty.

[3] The Marriage of Sir Gawaine.   [4] Gil Morice.

[5] King Edward IV and Tanner of Tamworth.

[6] The King and the Miller of Mansfield.

[7] Adam Bell.   [8] Robin Hood and Guy of Gisborne.

[9] For the Forest in Mediæval poetry see Vernon Lee, Euphorion, p. 122.

[10] Hardyknute.   [11] Young Waters.   [12] The Heir of Linne.

There is occasional use of nature in simple comparisons, as, " White as evir the snaw lay on the dike," "drye as a clot of claye," "light of foot as stag that runs in forest wild," his "een like gray gosehawk's stair'd wyld."

There are also some homely pictures of everyday country life, as in *Take Thy Old Cloak About Thee*, *Plain Truth and Blind Ignorance* (Somersetshire dialect). *The Ewe-Bughts Marion*, and *The Auld Good Man*.

The use of nature in the *Ballads*, slight and limited as it is gives an impression of vivid reality. It is what Schiller would call the simple as opposed to the sentimental love of nature, the first being characteristic of early races who *are* nature, and the last of the moderns who *seek* nature.[1] On eighteenth century readers who, as a class, knew little about the external world out-side their parks and gardens, the effect of the descriptive touches in the *Ballads* would be to lead them into lovely regions where nature was as spontaneous and free as the knights and fair ladies themselves.

Michael Bruce imitated Milton's *Lycidas* in an Elegy called *Daphnis*, and imitated Gray in some *Runic Odes*, which were lauded as "truly Runic and truly Grayan." In **Michael Bruce** these poems the use of nature is slight and conven-**(1746-1767)** tional. His *Lochleven* (1766) is more significant. In this poem he celebrates

" The pastoral mountains, the poetic streams "

of his native land. He finds all nature full of joy.

" The vales, the vocal hills,
The woods, the waters, and the heart of man
Send out a general song ; 'tis beauty all
To poet's eye and music to his ear."

Clouds arrested in their swift course by lofty mountains, lakes that hold a mirror to the sky, songsters twittering o'er their young, waters glowing beneath western clouds, hoary-headed Grampius clad in snow, are counted among his pleasures. He prefers life in the country, for there

[1] Schiller : " Ueber die Naive und Sentimentale Dichtung."

> " All in the sacred, sweet, sequestered vale
> Of solitude, the secret primrose-path
> Of rural life, he dwells."

He loved especially the Gairney, a stream that flows into Loch Leven, because, as a lad, he lay on its banks and composed poetry. He speaks with evident knowledge of other streams, the gulfy Po, "slow and silent among its waving reeds," and the rapid Queech rushing impetuous over broken steeps. It is natural that Bruce should know, as he did, especially water birds. The " wild-shrieking gull," " patient heron," " dull bittern," the " clamorous mew," and the " slow-wing'd crane " moving heavily along the shore, were doubtless birds that he had often seen. Bruce's pleasure in wide views is shown by this poem, *Lochleven*, for it is a description of the prospect spread out before him as he stands on " Mount Lomond." Bruce's *Elegy* was written when he felt himself dying of consumption. It represents his delight in all forms of nature's life and his deep melancholy at bidding farewell to the springtime world.

By a process of selection we find in Bruce's poems his real love for the outer world. This is not, however, the impression made by his poems as a whole. His knowledge of nature was limited, and his expression was often rigid and formal. He died young, before he had really attained the mastery of his own thought, and his importance lies not so much in actual accomplishment as in scattered suggestions of his tendencies and possibilities.

Bruce's most intimate friend was John Logan, who, in 1770, published an edition of Bruce's poems and included some " wrote by other authors." In 1781, when he published **John Logan** his own works, he laid claim to a number of the **(1748-1788)** poems that had appeared in the edition of Bruce's poems in 1770. Among these the most important was *The Cuckoo*,[1] a poem well worth the sharp controversy waged over it by the respective friends of the two authors. There is nothing else in this period that rings so fresh and clear as this little ode. One stanza may be quoted to illustrate its beauty, its simplicity, and naturalness. This stanza is also of peculiar

---

[1] The poem is quoted entire by Gosse in his Eighteenth Century Literature.

interest because it so definitely foreshadows Wordsworth's *To the Cuckoo.*

> " The schoolboy, wandering through the wood,
> To pull the primrose gay,
> Starts, the new voice of spring to hear,
> And imitates thy lay."

Logan's other poems, though he has nothing equal to the cuckoo song in spontaneity and exquisite simplicity, are yet of real value. His *Braes of Yarrow* is an effective presentation of the ancient, sorrow-laden Yarrow *motif.* As is fitting in a ballad the touches of description are of the briefest sort, but the forest, the bonny braes, and the sounding stream are felt through all the plaintive story. *Ossian's Hymn to the Sun* is a poetical paraphrase of the famous apostrophe in *Balclutha.* It has some fine lines, but is inferior in strength to the original. The *Ode Written in Spring* is a laudation of a certain fair Maria in the true classical fashion, but the new note is struck in the first five stanzas descriptive of spring.

> " The loosen'd streamlet loves to stray
> And echo down the dale,"

> " The hills uplift their summits green,"

> " The cuckoo in the wood unseen,"

> " At eve the primrose path along,
> The milkmaid shortens with a song,
> Her solitary way,"

> " The sudden fields put on the flowers,"

are lines showing fresh observation and easy, natural expression. Another passage characterizes autumn as " the Sabbath of the year." Limited in compass as is Logan's good work it is of value, because marked by exceptional purity and sweetness.

Most of James Graeme's poems were written before he was twenty. His tastes are thus referred to by his friend, Dr. Robert Anderson : "A passion for romantic fiction

James Graeme
(1747-1772)
and fabulous history, appeared in him very early in life. . . . . Of the Gothic, Celtic and Oriental mythology he was a warm admirer ; and frequently attempted

imitations of the wild and flowery fictions of the northern and eastern nations.   .   .   .   Like other votaries of the Muses, he was passionately fond of rural scenery, and delighted in walking alone in the fields."

His chief poems of nature are some descriptive elegies. Occasionally there is a fairly good line, as

> " The torrents, whiten'd with descending rain,"

or

> " The blue-gray mist that hovers o'er the hill,"

showing at least a hint of first-hand observation. But on the whole the poems are a composite of phrases belonging to the typical poetry of sentimental melancholy. His characteristic attitude towards nature is shown by his constant preference for chilly midnight when howlets scream and ravens croak, and when he, with pensive care, tunes the voice of woe and sheds "teary torrents " over grass-green graves. One poem, on *Curling*, is, however, quite different in tone, for it is a crudely realistic and technical description of the game and the peasants who engage in it.

The tastes of Graeme and his attempts are of more significance than his actual work, which is of little value.

The bent of Goldsmith's mind was towards the study of man in social relations. His use of nature is accessory and limited. In *The Traveller* the real interest is in manners and customs.[1] When the pilgrim is in the Alps with a wide prospect before him, it is the thought of man's grand heritage that impresses him. In the account of Switzerland there is only a vague general description of the country, but a full, sympathetic description of the peasant. So, too, in Italy, France, Holland, and even in England. In the few descriptions that do occur there are occasional lines indicative of first-hand observation, as in this picturesque couplet on the scenery in Holland :

Oliver Goldsmith
(1728-1774)

---

[1] In this poem about 16 per cent. of the lines have something to do with nature. In Wordsworth's Descriptive Sketches over 50 per cent. of the lines treat of nature.

> " The slow canal, the yellow-blossomed vale,
> The willow-tufted bank, the gliding sail."

We also find effective combinations of geographical names that give a certain charm of remoteness and melody; and there is a sense of space and movement conveyed by the rapidly presented and wide landscapes.

In *The Deserted Village* the central thought is still man, and the purpose didactic, but there is effective though not abundant use of nature. Even here, however, it is only nature inseparably associated with man. Nine tenths of the poem has to do directly with human nature. The other tenth merely gives charming pictures of the country close about a village. Scattered lines are of perfect workmanship, as that one descriptive of the straggling fence,

> " With blossomed furze unprofitably gay,"

and

> " The breezy covert of the warbling grove."

In the picture of desolation the details are selected with delicacy and precision. Each touch helps the general impression. The value of such work becomes more apparent when put into contrast with the description of torrid climes. In Goldsmith and in Thomson what was seen at first-hand had the grace and power of truth, but scenes in remote lands, known only through the distorting spectacles of books, were credited with an odd mixture of incongruous details. Except for one use of mountains in a simile there is no indication that Goldsmith knew any but tame scenery.

In general we may say that Goldsmith showed a direct, simple-hearted pleasure in the open-air world, that he was a sympathetic observer of the more obvious facts of nature, and that he had a bright, easy way of recording those facts. The simplicity of his work is combined with a quick perception of artistic form. But he has hardly a touch of what Matthew Arnold calls " natural magic," and he is in no sense a revealer. He was on the surface of things. Of the higher ministry of nature to man's spiritual needs he knew nothing. In his prose works Goldsmith has several vigorous attacks on falseness and affectation in poetry.

In 1759 he characterized Italian poetry at it lowest ebb, as " no longer an imitation of what we see, but of what a visionary might wish. The zephyrs breath a most exquisite perfume; the trees wear eternal verdure; fauns, dryads, and hamadryads stand ready to fan the sultry shepherdess . . . . who is so simple and inno- cent as often to have no meaning." This attack on the falseness and affectation of Italian poetry might be quoted verbatim by a modern critic of the popular eighteenth century pastorals. Gold- smith also praised Gay's poems saying that " he has hit upon the true spirit of pastoral poetry." Goldsmith has other keen criti- cal remarks that point in the direction of the new spirit but they do not bear directly on the study of nature. He is important chiefly because of his interest in man as man, his close and sympa- thetic delineation of the poor and ignorant.

In 1766 James Beattie had written 150 lines of *The Minstrel.* The poem was then laid aside for the *Essay on Truth* and not taken up again till 1770. The first book was pub- **James Beattie** lished anonymously in 1771. The second book (1742-1803) appeared with the author's name in 1774. The poem consists of 122 Spenserian stanzas. Its design is " to trace the progress of a poetical genius . . . . till that period when he may be supposed capable of appearing in the world as a minstrel,"[1] and its theme is really the effect of mountain scenery on a poet- ically sensitive mind. The child, Edwin, is brought up in a remote village among the Scotch hills, and his genius is devel- oped through the varied influence of wild natural scenery until he becomes "itinerant poet and musician." As a lad his chief pleas- ure was to follow

> " Where the maze of some bewilder'd stream
>   To deep untrodden groves his footsteps led."

He loved to climb craggy cliffs

> " When all in mist the world below was lost.
>   What dreadful pleasure! There to stand sublime
>   Like shipwreck'd mariner on desert coast
>   And view the enormous waste of vapour, toss'd

[1] The Minstrel, Preface.

> In billows, lengthening to the horizon round,
> Now scoop'd in gulfs, with mountains now emboss'd."

> And oft he traced the uplands, to survey,
> When o'er the sky advanced the kindling dawn,
> The crimson cloud, blue main and mountain gray."

He was

> " Fond of each gentle, and each dreadful scene.
> In darkness and in storm he found delight."

He listened

> " with pleasing dread, to the deep roar
> Of the wide-weltering waves."

When storms came up in black array

> " He hastened from the haunt of man,
> Along the trembling wilderness to stray."

He visited haunted streams by moonlight and let his imagination dwell on graves and ghosts. His soul was possessed by the " mystic transports " born of " melancholy and solitude." He scanned all nature with a "curious and romantic eye," and his imagination was stirred by ' old heroic ditties,' by

> " What'er of lore tradition could supply
> From gothic tale, or song, or fable old."

The second stage of Edwin's education comes through his companionship with a wise hermit, who, like Wordsworth's Solitary, had " sought for glory in the paths of guile," but finally, dissatisfied with success and stung with remorse, had hidden himself in a deep retired abode in the mountains, there to commune with nature. From a lofty eminence Edwin chanced to look down one day upon this savage dell, shut in by mountains and rocks piled on rocks ,and he saw the "one cultivated spot " with its garden of roses and herbs, and he heard the voice of the hermit soliloquizing on the vanity of human life. In subsequent interviews the hermit discoursed learnedly on history, art, and sciences.

The intrinsic value of this poem is not great. It is important because of the conception which it embodies. Edwin finds in nature adequate instruction and inspiration; the hermit, adequate consolation. His words are,

> " Hail, awful scenes, that calm the troubled breast,
> And woo the weary to profound repose !
> Can passion's wildest uproar lay to rest,
> And whisper comfort to the man of woes !"

Now the power of wild scenery over the plastic mind is exactly Wordsworth's idea in his account of the Wanderer's youth,[1] and the power of nature to minister to a mind diseased is one of the leading thoughts in his account of the Solitary,[2] while the thought of tracing a child's experiences with nature until under her tutelage he becomes a poet is the fundamental idea of the *Prelude*.[3] It is certainly of more than merely curious interest thus to find in the rather vague, ineffective stanzas of the earlier poet general conceptions which afterwards appear as the ruling ideas of the poet confessedly greatest in his treatment of nature.

The character of Edwin was autobiographic and shows Beattie's personal love of nature. In a letter to the Dowager Lady Forbes, October, 1772, he wrote :

" I find you are willing to suppose that, in Edwin, I have given only a picture of myself as I was in my younger days. I confess the supposition is not groundless. I have made him take pleasure in the scenes in which I took pleasure, and entertain sentiments similar to those of which, even in my early youth, I had repeated experience. The scenery of a mountainous country, the ocean, the sky, thoughtfulness and retirement, and sometimes melancholy objects and ideas, had charms in my eyes, even when I was a schoolboy : and at a time when I was so far from being able to express, that I did not understand my own feelings, or perceive the tendency of my own pursuits and amusements."

Beattie never lost this keen delight in nature. When he was schoolmaster at Fordoun, at the foot of the Grampian Hills, his greatest pleasure was found in the neighboring mountains and wooded glens. His biographer also says that he would frequently " pass the whole night among the fields, gazing on the

---

[1] Wordsworth : The Excursion, 1 : ll. 108–300.
[2] Wordsworth : The Excursion, 4 : ll. 466–600.
[3] Wordsworth : The Prelude. " Advertisement."

sky, and observing the various aspects it assumed till the return
of day." Beattie's poems bear conclusive evidence of his love
of nature in all her forms. Mountains, and the sea, wild scenes
of various sorts, storms, torrents, night, clouds, the sky, streams,
meadows, groves, summer and winter, wide views, are regarded
with genuine delight. But there are certain curious limitations.
There are almost no specific flowers, birds, or trees mentioned in
all this abundant study of the external world. This use of the gen-
eral instead of the specific is one element of an effect too often
perceived, an indefiniteness of outline, a vague blurring of
edges, the result of which is not mysterious suggestiveness but
simply dimness and confusion. There is also an unexpected
feebleness of vocabulary and lack of direct observation. The
old word "murmur," for instance, is applied with wearisome
insistence to springs, rills, water, the ocean, pines, woods, groves,
and gales. So the interest in wild nature, when analyzed, shows
a rather monotonous and undiscriminating succession of cliffs
and precipices. But it would be unfair to press these limitations
too far. There are many true observations happily presented, as
in the following lines which are selected as illustrative :

"While waters, woods, and winds in concert join."

"The wild brook babbling down the mountain side."

" Torrents
Heard from afar amid the lonely night."

" And now the storm of summer rain is over
And cool and fresh and fragrant is the sky."

" When by the winds of autumn driven
The scatter'd clouds fly 'cross the Heaven.
Oft have we from some mountain's head
Beheld the alternate light and shade
Sweep along the vale."

" The scared owl on pinions gray
Breaks from the rustling boughs
And down the lone vale sails away
To more profound repose."

He finds pleasure in old oak trees that

"from the stormy promontory tower

> And toss their giant arms amid the skies."

In winter he watches

> " The cloud stupendous, from the Atlantic wave
> High towering, sail along the horizon blue."

Lines such as these show knowledge both fresh and close, and the expression is marked by picturesque effectiveness.

But Beattie's real contribution to the study of nature lies, as has been indicated, in his own personal enthusiasm, and his steadfast belief in the effect of nature on man. In one stanza he even set forth the doctrine, held to be sufficiently startling forty years later in Wordsworth's day, that country rustics from their familiarity with nature, gain a nicer sense of moral purity than is known among the poor of a city.[1] Upon all men he urged the study of nature as a moral duty.

> "These charms shall work thy soul's eternal health,
> And love, and gentleness, and joy impart."[2]

The message of nature is one not to be ignored.

> " O how canst thou renounce the boundless store
> Of charms which Nature to her votary yields !
> The warbling woodland, the resounding shore,
> The pomp of groves, and garniture of fields ;
> All that the genial ray of morning gilds,
> And all that echoes to the song of even,
> All that the mountain's sheltering bosom shields,
> And all the dread magnificence of Heaven,
> O how canst thou renounce and hope to be forgiven !"[3]

[1] The Minstrel, 1 : 52.   [2] The Minstrel, 1 : 10.

[3] The Minstrel, 1 : 9.

Of this stanza Gray said in a letter to Beattie, March, 1771,

"But this, of all others, is my favorite stanza. It is true poetry; it is inspiration; only (to show it is mortal) there is one blemish; the word garniture suggesting an idea of dress, and, what is worse, of French dress." Beattie said he had often wished "to alter this same word, but had not been able to hit upon a better."   Dyce's Memoir of Beattie, p. xxxvii.

Gray's praise of Beattie was faint compared to Beattie's admiration of Gray. In 1765 he declared that he had "long and passionately admired " Gray's writings. He thought Gray's poems finer than those of his contemporaries in any nation. He thought his taste most exact, his judgment most sound, and his learning most extensive. See Dyce's Memoir of Beattie, p. xvi. and p. xviii.

Though less popular than the *Essay on Truth*, Beattie's *Minstrel* met with almost immediate favor. Lyttleton said to Mrs. Montagu who sent him the first book in 1771 :

"I read your 'Minstrel' last night, with as much rapture as poetry, in her noblest, sweetest charms, ever raised in my soul. It seemed to me that my once most beloved minstrel, Thomson, was come down from heaven, refined by the converse of purer spirits than those he lived with here, to let me hear him sing again the beauties of virtue."[1]

And Cowper wrote in 1784 :

"Though I cannot afford to deal largely in so expensive a commodity as books, I must afford to purchase at least the poetical works of Beattie."[2]

Mr. Dyce says that the success of *The Minstrel* (Book First) "was complete. The voice of every critic was loud in its praise; and before the second book appeared, four editions of the first had been dispersed throughout the kingdom."[3]

The Minstrel is of importance in the historical development of the poetry of nature because of the ideas it emphasizes, and its immediate popularity is an indication of the change in taste since the beginning of the century.

Most of John Scott's poems were on rural subjects,[4] and he is of especial interest because of his abundant and close observation of natural facts. Mr. Hoole says of him, "He was certainly no servile copyist of the thoughts of others; for, living in the country, and being a close and accurate observer, he painted what he saw;" and again, "He

John Scott
(1730-1783)

---

[1] Dyce : Memoir of Beattie, p. xxxvi.

[2] Cowper : Letter to Rev. William Unwin, April, 1784.

[3] Dyce : Memoir of Beattie, p. xxxv.

[4] His chief poems are : Four Moral Eclogues (1773); four Elegies (pub. 1760 but written earlier); Amwell, A Descriptive Poem (pub. 1776 but written 1768); and Odes and Amœbæan Eclogues (1782). His Epistle on the Garden and Essay on Painting will be spoken of later.

It is interesting to note the spirit of apology with which Scott's friends and admirers comment on his choice of subjects. In such poetry there is little opportunity for genius, for, says Mr. Hoole, "A hill, a vale, a forest, a rivulet, a cataract, can be described only by general terms; the hill must swell, the vale sink,

cultivated the knowledge of natural history and botany, which enabled him to preserve the truth of nature with many discriminating touches, perhaps not excelled by any descriptive poet since the days of Thomson." It was Scott's avowed purpose to enrich poetry by the use of many natural facts not before observed. In the introduction to the *Amœbœan Eclogues* he said, "Much of the rural imagery which our country affords, has already been introduced in poetry, but many obvious and pleasing appearances seem to have totally escaped notice. To describe these is the business of the following Eclogues." After this explicit announcement, two gentle youths, in responsive verse, call attention to over two hundred rapidly stated natural facts. A fact to a line is about the average, as in these lines :

> " These pollard oaks their tawny leaves retain,
> These hardy hornbeams yet unstripped remain ;
> The wint'ry groves all else admit the view
> Through naked stems of many a varied hue."

> "Old oaken stubs tough saplings there adorn."[1]

> "Straight shoots of ash with bark of glossy gray,
> Red cornel twigs, and maple's russet spray."

> " There scabious blue, and purple knapweed rise,
> And weld and yarrow show their various dyes."

> " In shady lanes red foxglove bells appear
> And golden spikes the downy mullens rear."

The second of these *Eclogues* has to do with the care of farms and is as minute as Cowper's treatise on the cucumber. There is nowhere in these poems any poetical fusion of facts. They read rather like the notebooks of a professional observer. Yet it is certainly significant to find at this date so persistent and sys-

the rivulet murmur, and the cataract foam." Mr. Hoole recognizes the "slight estimation " in which descriptive poetry is commonly held, but thinks there are devices to render it attractive and calls attention to the skill with which Mr. Scott has made his poems "interesting by the introduction of historical incidents, apt allusions, and moral reflections."

[1] At this line Mr. Hoole's admiration broke down. He could only regret that Mr. Scott's desire for novelty had led him to admit such circumstances as no versification can make poetical.

tematic a search for natural facts, and that not in the service of science but of poetry. In *Amwell* Scott calls on the Muse of Thomson, Dyer, and Shenstone for his inspiration. The poem is a description of the prospect from a certain "airy height" near Amwell. A single illustration will show the minute observation and catalogue style in this commemoration of "lonely sylvan scenes."

> "How picturesque
> The slender group of airy elm, the clump
> Of pollard oak, or ash, with ivy brown
> Entwin'd ; the walnut's gloomy breadth of boughs,
> The orchard's ancient fence of rugged pales,
> The haystack's dusty cone, the moss-grown shed,
> The clay-built barn ; the elder-shaded cot,
> Whose whitewashed gable prominent through green
> Of waving branches shows ;   .   .   .   .
> .   .   .   .   the wall with mantling vines
> O'erspread, the porch with climbing woodbine wreath'd,
> And under sheltering eves the sunny bench
> Where brown hives range, whose busy tenants fill
> With drowsy hum the little garden gay,   .
> Whence blooming beans, and spicy herbs, and flowers,
> Exhale around a rich perfume !   Here rests
> The empty wain ; there idle lies the plough."

There is a pleasant homely grace in these lines about the cottage, worth more than all the historical episodes "introduced to secure interest." In the *Elegies* and *Odes* there is no use of nature different from that observed in the other poems, unless, indeed, mention should be made of Scott's belief that nature gives her fairest smiles to those "who know a Saviour's love." One further characteristic is to be found in a large number of the poems, and that is enjoyment of a wide view. He describes views as seen from "Musla's corn-clad heights," from "Grove Hill," the cliff at Bath, from "Chadwell's cliffs," from "Widbury's prospect-yielding hill," from "Upton's elm-divided plains," from "Clifton's rock," from Amwell, and other spots. The poems read as if he had spent many days climbing hills and prospecting for views.

William Blake's *Poetical Sketches*, published in 1783, were written between 1769 and 1777.[1] The *Songs of Innocence* appeared in 1788-9 ; *Book of Thel*, 1789 ; *The Marriage of Heaven and Hell*, 1790 ; and *Songs of Experience* in 1794. In the first volume nature was the leading subject ; in the next human interests were in the ascendant, and nature was used only in fresh, ballad-like touches. In the later work nature is slightly used and for the most part in the form of mystical symbolism.

**William Blake
(1757-1827)**

It was Blake's theory that man is "imprisoned in his five senses," and he counted it his mission to reveal to closed eyes the spiritual as the only real fact of existence. In his early work this theory, as yet unexaggerated in application, led to a treatment of nature, not untrue to facts, but characterized especially by qualities of simplicity and vision such as are not found again before Wordsworth. In these years of his youth Blake was essentially the poet of childhood and spring in all their sweet potent, indefinable charm.

> " And I made a rural pen,
>   And I stained the water clear,
> And I wrote my happy songs,
>   Every child may joy to hear,"[2]

gives the keynote to these songs of delight. The joy of nature is everywhere insisted on. The sun makes the sky happy ; the vales rejoice ; spring cannot hide its joy when buds and blossoms come ; the happy blossoms look on merry birds ; groves are happy and green woods rejoice ; dimpling streams, the air, green hills, meadows, and birds laugh with delight. Here is one exquisite example :

> " The moon like a flower
>   In heaven's high bower,
> With silent delight,
>   Sits and smiles on the night."[3]

He contrasts the clamour and destruction of city streets with

[1] See " Advertisement " to Poetical Sketches.
[2] "Introduction " to Songs of Innocence.
[3] Night.

the true joy in nature. In the silent woods, "Delights blossom around. Numberless beauties blow. The green grass spring, in joy, and the nimble air kisses the leaves. The brook stretches its arms along the silent meadow; its silver inhabitants sport and play. The youthful sun joys like a hunter roused to the chase."[1]

Blake cared much for sleep as the time when man was most free from the tyranny of the senses. Many of his characters are represented as asleep, and the conception is transferred to many lovely scenes in nature. He pictures summer as sleeping beneath oaks; flowers shut their eyes in sleep; the west wind sleeps on the lake; and dawn sleeps in heaven. With this is associated an evident pleasure in the silence of nature, apparently the pathetic complement of its joys. There is a silent sleep over the deep of heaven; the evening star speaks silence to the lake. At night the moon is silent, and the earth, and the sea.

Occasional passages show the character of Blake's own love of nature, as,

> "I love to rise on a summer morn,"
> "I love the laughing vale,"
> "I love the echoing hill."

His feeling towards flowers was as intimate, as tenderly protecting, as was that of Burns towards small animals. Sun and stars, winds, clouds, dew, and angels are represented as caring for the happy blossoms.

All of Blake's poetry of nature is as freshly beautiful as the dewy mornings, the springtime green, the shining skies, as clear and transparent as the limpid, dimpling streams he loved. There are also frequent passages that beside their metrical flow and exquisite charm of external suggestion seem to reveal the essential spirit of the object described. One of the loveliest examples is the word of the Lily of the Valley.

> "I am a watry weed,
> And I am very small and love to dwell in lowly vales:
> So weak the gilded butterfly scarce perches on my head.
> Yet I am visited from heaven; and He that smiles on all
> Walks in the valley, and each morn over me spreads his hand.

[1] Contemplation.

> Saying, Rejoice, thou humble grass, thou new-born lilly flower,
> Thou gentle maid of silent valleys and of modest brooks;
> For thou shalt be clothed in light and fed with morning manna."[1]

For fine contrasts, each poem perfect of its kind, see *The Lamb* and *The Tiger*. The modest simplicity of the one is as adequately portrayed as the dread magnificence of the other. There is no description. There is interpretation of the most penetrating sort.

He has also frequent similes worked out with picturesque detail, as in this one from *The Couch of Death:*

"He was like a cloud tossed by the winds, till the sun shine, and the drops of rain glisten, the yellow harvest breathes, and the thankful eyes of villagers are turned up in smiles; the traveller that hath taken shelter under an oak, eyes the distant country with joy."

One secret of the effectiveness of Blake's best work is his recognition of the unity of all existence. The prefatory stanza to *Auguries of Innocence,*

> " To see a world in a grain of sand,
> And a heaven in a wild flower;
> Hold infinity in the palm of your hand,
> And eternity in an hour,"

is a brief poetic statement of the creed afterwards elaborated in Wordsworth's *Primrose on the Rock* and Tennyson's *Flower in the Crannied Wall.* The thought back of the lines is the one in Wordsworth's mind when he looked on "the meanest flower that blows."— It is this underlying consciousness of essential spiritual unity in all existence that gives to the work of both Blake and Wordsworth its subtle power.

There could hardly be two more dissimilar ways of approaching nature than those of John Scott and William Blake. They stand at opposite poles, the one with no sense of unity, no power of poetic fusion or interpretation, but with a wide, accurate, and often picturesque assemblage of natural facts; the other with a prevailing tone of unreality and mysticism, a fine scorn of the actual, but with a swift recognition of the spirit of nature, and

[1] Book of Thel.

an abiding sense of cosmic unity. Yet each represents a characteristic phase of the new feeling for nature as seen in Wordsworth. On the one hand, the practised eye and the inevitable ear; on the other, the vision and the faculty divine.

In its significance as a prophecy of Wordsworth and Shelley the early poetry of William Blake is of especial importance.

Crabbe's poetry falls into two periods, the first one closing with *The Newspaper* in 1785, and the second beginning with *The Parish Register* after an interval of twenty-two years. In the first of these periods we find but slight use of external nature. The occasional similitudes are of a formal conventional type. The two longest descriptive passages are of a dismal winter scene,[1] and of some sterile summer fields that mock man's need with profitless blooms.[2] There is no expression of pleasure in nature. It is her pitiless, anti-human aspects that Crabbe sees. The charm of nature independent of utility seems to have no meaning for him. He consciously repudiates

George Crabbe 1754–1832)

> " Clear skies, clear streams, soft banks, and sober bowers,
> Deer, whimpering brooks, and wind-perfuming flowers,"

as unworthy poetic material.[3] Rough or barren nature as the background or occasion of man's misery is the thought of these early poems.

Crabbe's second period does not properly belong in a study of development which has *The Lyrical Ballads* as its *terminus ad quem*, but it may be briefly spoken of here because of the interesting contrast it offers to the first period. A suggestive study might be made of the descriptive element in *The Village* (1783) as compared with that of *The Borough* (1810). The scene of each is a seaside village on the Suffolk coast, but we note many changes in the presentation. In the first place, in *The Borough* nature plays a much more important part than in *The Village*. There is a leisurely elaborateness of description as if the poet enjoyed the work for its own sake. There is, to be sure, insistence on the ugly realistic details of the scenes about a

---

[1] Inebriety. [2] The Village. [3] The Choice.

country town, but there is in addition a recognition that even along this rocky coast and in these barren fields where nature defies man's industry there may be found her gift of beauty. The "greedy ocean" of *The Village* is now "a glorious page of nature's book" on which the poorest may gaze with delight. The firm, fair sands on quiet summer evenings, the lovely "limpid blue and evanescent green" as shadows run over the waves on a fresh day, serene winter-views where strange effects of fog add mystery to the scene, the majesty of a storm at sea — all these are now reckoned a part of the pleasures of the poor in a seaside village. The sterile fields, too, have rare blossoms and curious grasses. There are pleasant walks with every scene rich in beauty. The evening twilight is sweet with jasmine odors.[1] *The Borough* is as realistic as *The Village*, but it has a broader outlook and depicts the attractive as well as the forbidding aspects of the Suffolk coast near Aldborough. In later poems the scope becomes still wider. Besides the frequent strong and truthful ocean pictures there are some beautiful descriptions of autumn days, moonlight nights, and soft, rich inland scenes. It is especially noteworthy that though there are seldom any gay or bright aspects of nature presented, yet nature is no longer represented as a force inimical to man. On the contrary, there is something in even her most useless forms that gives to man a strangely profound pleasure. The simple music of a cascade has in it a soothing power that words will not express. In the clear, silent night there is a quiet joy that lessens the sting of mortal pain. These positive expressions of pleasure in nature are not numerous, but they are important as marking a distinct change of tone. They are the more significant because they occur chiefly in the poems after 1819.

Yet it must not pass unnoticed that what Crabbe wrote in these late poems, he had perceived and felt in his youth. In his description of Richard he gives an account of his own boyhood. Of the ocean he says,

> "I loved to walk where none had walked before,
> About the rock that ran along the shore.

[1] The Borough: especially Letters 1 and 9.

> Here had I favorite stations, where I stood
> And heard the murmurs of the ocean flood,
> With not a sound beside, except when flew
> Aloft the lapwing, or the gray curlew.
>
> Pleasant it was to view the sea-gulls strive
> Against the storm, or in the ocean dive
> With eager scream, or when they dropping gave
> Their closing wings to sail upon the wave.
>
> Nor pleased it less around me to behold
> Far up the beach the yesty sea-foam rolled;
> Or from the shore upborne, to see on high
> Its frothy flakes in wild confusion fly:
> While the salt spray that clashing billows form
> Gave to the taste a feeling of the storm."[1]

He recalls how he explored every creek and bay, how he took long walks over the hilly heath and mossy moors. Most of the scenery in *The Borough* as well as that in *The Village* is a memory picture of the country he knew so well in boyhood. It seems strange that this genuine love and accurate knowledge of nature should not have found fuller expression in his early poetry. The explanation is perhaps twofold. His interest was primarily in man. He said that the finest scenes in nature were less attractive to him than faces on a crowded street. He meant to be the portrait painter of poor people as he had seen them in a seaside village. His bitter pictures of country vice and ignorance and folly had in them no touch of patronage or contempt. He simply gave a hard, truthful representation of sordid life, and nature had no meaning for him except as it is brought into connection with that life. When in after years his own lot was a happier one, and when a wider experience had brought him into contact with thrifty country folk, the bitterness of his early thought of man was greatly modified. With new views of man came an openness of mind to the gentler aspects of nature. The real love of his boyhood, no longer crushed down by an overmastering sense of human misery, was allowed free play. Furthermore his later

[1] Tales of the Hall, Bk. 4.

work was doubtless influenced by the new spirit of poetry about him.   His son says that while at first but a cool admirer of the Lake poets, he came soon to love them and took no books oftener in his hands.   All of Crabbe's work in which there is much use of nature comes more than ten years after the *Lyrical Ballads*, hence his growingly full use of nature might easily be due in part to the influence of the new school of poetry.   His free life, the different class of peasants he saw, the new poetry he was reading, would all have their effect in turning his attention to nature.   But the nature he chose to write about was that which he had known and loved as a boy.

William Cowper as a poet of nature, is marked first by the narrowness of the limits within which he writes.   Mountains[1] are merely mentioned.   Night is nowhere described.   Moonlight plays no part in his poetry.[2]   The stars are occasionally spoken of, but only in a conventional manner as " shining hosts," " fair ministers of light," or "beamy fires."   Of wild scenery there is none.   The nearest approach to it is in two brief descriptions of rocky bluffs on the seashore.[3]   His references to the ocean are brief and not of much importance; nor are there any storms except in a few lines about " a driving, dashing rain " with thunder and lightning used as an "apt similitude."[4]   The one winter storm is merely a gentle fall of snow that comes after the evening curtains are tight drawn.[5]   The similitudes, though often carefully elaborated, show little if any new use of nature, and they are drawn from a small number of natural facts.[6]

William Cowper (1731-1800)

[1] In a letter to Newton, Nov. 16, 1791, he wrote:

" I would that I could see some of the mountains which you have seen ; especially because Dr. Johnson has pronounced that no man is qualified to be a poet who has never seen a mountain.   But mountains I shall never see, unless, perhaps, in a dream, or unless there are such in heaven."

[2] See Task, 1:764; 4:254-258.   The best lines on the moon are in Task, 4:3,

" the wintry flood, in which the moon
Sees her unwrinkled face reflected bright."

[3] Task, 1:520; 6:495.   [4] Truth, 238.   [5] Task, 4:322.

[6] Illustrative similitudes are those drawn from the thunder-storm (Truth,

The explanation of this narrowness of limit is twofold. Cowper described only what he had seen,[1] and he had seen no country but his own, and only a very small and comparatively uninteresting portion of that. The Downs about Bath, where he seems to have been for a short time when he was about eighteen, was the nearest approach to wild scenery that he had ever known. During the seventeen years before the writing of *The Task* he had seldom left Olney, and never for a fortnight together.[2] His knowledge was further limited by his continued ill health. He was ignorant of certain phases of the out-door world simply because his physical infirmities kept him in the house.

This explanation of the narrow range of the nature in Cowper's poetry is not entirely satisfactory, for when we come to his letters we find suggestions of a wider experience and sympathy than the poems would indicate. In a letter to Joseph Hill he wrote :

"I was always an admirer of thunderstorms, even before I knew whose voice I heard in them ; but especially an admirer of thunder rolling over the great waters. There is something singularly majestic in the sound of it at sea, where the eye and the ear have uninterrupted opportunity of observation, and the concavity above, being made spacious, reflects it with more advantage. . . . . We have indeed been regaled with some of those bursts of etherial music. . . . But when the thunder preaches, an horizon bounded by the ocean is the only sounding board."

To the Rev. William Unwin, Sept. 26, 1781, he wrote :

"I think, with you, that the most magnificent object under heaven is the great deep ; and can not but feel an unpolite species of astonishment when I consider the multitudes that view it without emotion, and even without reflection. In all its various forms it is an object of all others the most suited to affect

---

238), deer (Task, 3: 108), peacocks and pheasants (Truth, 58), elm and vine Retirement, 129), moles (Task, 1:276), etc.

[1] In a letter to Rev. William Unwin, Oct. 1784, Cowper wrote "My descriptions are all from nature ; not one of them second-handed."

[2] To Lady Herbert, Oct. 12, 1785.

us with lasting impressions of the awful power that created and controls it. I am the less inclined to think this negligence excusable, because, at a time of life when I gave as little attention to religious subjects as any man, I yet remember that the waves would preach to me, and that in the midst of dissipation I had an ear to hear them. One of Shakespeare's characters says, 'I am never merry when I hear sweet music.' The same effect that harmony seems to have had upon him I have experienced from the sight and sound of the ocean, which have often composed my thoughts into a melancholy not unpleasing nor without its use."

He had also, during these years at Olney, made many an imaginary evening journey to remote lands by means of books of travel, of which he was especially fond. But when he came to write poems, only what he had known at first hand and with long familiarity occurred to him. Experiences merely casual, or remote in time, and facts gained from books slipped away. He remembered only what he habitually saw. The scenes about Olney he knew, literally, by heart, and of these he wrote.

A characteristic excellence of Cowper's treatment of nature is that, within his narrow circuit, his knowledge is of unusual fulness and accuracy. The charm of truthful description is everywhere apparent. In pictures of homely country occupations, such as feeding the hens,[1] foddering the cattle,[2] cutting wood,[3] plowing,[4] threshing,[5] there are no false touches, no hasty work. All is the result of first-hand, leisurely, sympathetic observation. His description of the garden is from memory, but it almost seems as if he were walking from flower to flower and taking notes, so minute is the characterization, so exact each epithet in the representation of the various colors, forms, odors, and ways of growth of the flowers in this garden that the poet sees under the snows of winter.[6]

The same love of precise detail is illustrated in his descriptions of trees. In noting their color he does not, like Thomson,

[1] Task, 5:58.
[2] Task, 5:27.
[3] Task, 5:41.
[4] Task, 1:161.
[5] Task, 1:358.
[6] Task, 6:147.

enjoy general, broadly inclusive words, but he gives the exact shade and tells to what tree it belongs. When he takes a walk he sees that the trunks of the ash, the lime, and the beech shine distinctly under their shadowy foliage. The willow is a "wannish gray." The poplar is likewise gray, but there is a touch of silver in the lining of the leaves. The elm is deeper green than the ash, and the oak of a deeper green still. The maple, the beech, and the lime have glossy leaves that shine in the sun. The sycamore changes from green to tawny, and then to scarlet, according to the season.[1]

This highly differentiated knowledge is evident also in various passages on the sounds of nature. In a letter to Newton he wrote : " The notes of all our birds and fowls please me, without one exception ; . .   and as to insects' . . . in whatever key they sing, from the gnat's fine treble to the bass of the humble bee, I admire them all."

Equally specific is his record of the sounds from winds and waters, as in these lines :

> " Rills that slip
> Through the cleft rock, and chiming as they fall
> Upon loose pebbles, lose themselves at length
> In matted grass that with a livelier green
> Betrays the secret of their silent course." [2]

Or these about forest sounds :

> " Mighty winds
> That sweep the skirt of some far-spreading wood
> Of ancient growth, make music not unlike
> The dash of ocean on his winding shore." [3]

In wider descriptions, as of extended views, there is absolutely no blurring of edges. The picture is as clear. distinct, and exact as a photograph. There is no inartistic mixing of foreground and background. A good example is the view described in the first book of *The Task*.[4] The eye travels over the landscape with its river shining like molten glass ; on its

[1] Task, 1 : 304.   [3] Task, 1 : 185.
[2] Task, 1 : 195.   [4] Task, 1 : 159.

banks droop the elms. on either side are level plains sprinkled with cattle, beyond is the sloping land covered with hedgerows, groves, heaths, with here and there a square tower or tall spire, and in the distance smoking towns ; and at last the scene is lost in the clouds on the horizon.

Many little pictures, complete in a few lines, serve even better to illustrate the exquisite truth of Cowper's work.   Note this description of the shifting lights in a forest pathway :

> " While beneath
> The chequered earth seems restless as a flood
> Brushed by the wind. So sportive is the light
> Shot through the boughs, it dances as they dance,
> Shadow and sunshine intermingling quick,
> And darkening and enlightening, as the leaves
> Play wanton, every moment, every spot." [1]

Or this of the squirrel just come from winter quarters in some lonely elm :

> " Flippant. pert, and full of play :
> He sees me. and at once, swift as a bird,
> Ascends the neighboring beech ; there whisks his brush,
> And perks his ears, and stamps, and cries aloud,
> With all the prettiness of feign'd alarm
> And anger insignificantly fierce." [2]

Equally felicitous are the descriptions of tall grass fledged with icy feathers on a frosty morning,[3] or of the red-breast in a sheltered woodland path in winter.[4] These pictures and other similar ones immediately take a permanent place in one's mental picture gallery. It would be difficult indeed for a painting to make the light dance as it does in that forest path. The squirrel absolutely tingles with life. The right word comes easily and the lines show exquisite deftness of literary touch. It is rare in any poetry to find more excellent examples of pure description than these and other passages in *The Task*. Cowper had a mind that watches and receives. He looked about, wrote down in simple, sincere words the loveliness he found. He took notes, but they were of the right sort, mental and uncon-

[1] Task, 1 : 346.
[2] Task, 6 : 310.
[3] Task, 5 : 22.
[4] Task, 6 : 77.

scious, the inevitable imprint on a sensitive mind of scenes that had ministered to his deepest need.

The ministry of nature to human needs is a cardinal principle in Cowper's poetry. Nor was this conception merely theoretic. It was rather a transcript from his own experience. From childhood he had loved nature,[1] and poems about nature,[2] and he had always planned to live in the country.[3] After years of disappointment and terrifying fears comparative peace came to him amid quiet country scenes. The instincts of his early days revived. Nature offered him a paradise of rich delights. She enchanted him. She gave him heart-consoling joys. She sweetened his bitter life, alluring him with smiles from gloom to happiness. The glory of each new morning was a lesson in hope. He found in nature the nurse of wisdom, a power that could compose his passions and exalt his mind. He felt that in the country God spoke directly to his heart.[4]

The obverse of this genuine love of the country is an equally genuine detestation of the town and town standards. The crowds that swarm to city streets are the subjects of repeated invectives, and there is even more emphatic scorn of sham lovers of nature, as cockneys in suburban villas; girls who but for the show and dress-parade of the country would hurry back to the city; men who love hunting and fishing, and call it a love of nature; sentimentalists, who exclaim over Thomson's poetry, but prefer to read it in the city.[5] His own relationship with nature was too intimate and too sacred to admit of indifference or profanation on the part of others.

Cowper's literary use of nature was largely determined by his

[1] Task, 1; 109, 142.   [2] Task, 4:700.   [3] 4: 695.

[4] See Hope, ll, 39-60; Task, 3:721; 4:780; 3:301; and other passages.

[footnote] In the passage from Hope compare the line:

for grou   "She spreads the morning over Eastern hills,"
descri .   orth's

       "A boy I loved the sun
. . . . for this cause that I had seen him lay
His beauty on the morning hills."   —Prelude, 2:183.

[5] See Retirement, 481, 563; Task, 3:314; 3:306.

purpose in writing.   His p. .ical thesis received its dogmatic summing up in the famous dictum,

"God made the country and man made the town."[1]

and to the establishment of this thesis nearly all his use of nature is made more or less directly subservient.

This is clearly seen in his use of summaries.   He has a habit of analyzing nature into separate facts and then classifying these facts under topics. For instance, to make a list of his sounds one hardly needs to search through the poems. They will be found already grouped together. So, too, the garden flowers, the greenhouse flowers, the colors of trees, country occupations, and country pleasures, are arranged under heads instead of being scattered through various descriptions. Then there are many summaries of miscellaneous facts. Now the literary purpose of nearly every assemblage of details is the establishment or illustration of some point connected with the general conception of the superior attractions of the country. The catalogues of facts have a definite argumentative value, and the artistic selection of these facts out of the mass known is determined by the especial point under consideration. In *Retirement* there is a rapid enumeration of many phases of nature in various seasons, the purpose being to show that all forms of nature are pleasing to a poet's mind The following passage is a good example of a summary the purpose of which is to present a concrete, picturesque, amplified statement of the creed that nature gives a wisdom higher than can come from books:

> "But trees, and rivulets, whose rapid course
> Defies the check of winter, haunts of deer,
> And sheep-walks populous with bleating lambs,
> And lanes, in which the primrose ere her time
> Peeps through the moss that clothes the hawthorn root,
> Deceive no student. Wisdom there, and truth,
> Not shy, as in the world, and to be won
> By slow solicitation, seize at once
> The roving thought, and fix it on themselves."[2]

[1] Task, 1:749.
[2] Task, 6:109; cf. lines 84-117 Wordsworth in The Tables Turned;

Frequent summaries are used to show that in the country God gives especial revelations of his power. The long flower catalogue is to show that the beauty of the flushing spring but speaks to man of the indwelling of God.[1] The ceaseless activity of nature is attested by another summary.[2] Still further summaries illustrate the power of nature over the man wearied with cares of state.[3] The beautiful summary of rural sounds is to show the exhilarating effect of nature on the languid mind and heart.[4] It is this underlying purpose that gives unity to passages which would otherwise be hardly more than catalogues.

Another characteristic way in which Cowper presents nature is in descriptive passages used as a background for his own meditative figure. The beautiful description of the sheltered path where he walked in winter[5] would lose much of its meaning if we were not throughout conscious of the poet's presence and his delighted response to all the influences about him. Nearly all the passages that might otherwise be called pure description are given warmth and tone by the fact that we go with the poet, and, as it were, hear him talk about the scene as one he has long known and loved, until it takes from him the interest of personality, or we seem to see him in semi-identification with the scenes. It is the apparent equality, the comradeship, between

> " Books! 'tis a dull and endless strife,
>
> . . . . . .
>
> Come forth into the light of things,
> Let Nature be your teacher.
> She has a world of ready wealth
> Our minds and hearts to bless.
>
> . . . . . .
>
> Sweet is the lore which Nature brings ;
> Our meddling intellect
> Mis-shapes the beauteous forms of things."

See also, To My Sister:

> "One moment now may give us more
> Than years of toiling reason."

[1] Task, 6: 121–197. [3] Retirement, 419. [5] Task, 6:59.
[2] Task, 1: 369. [4] Task, 6: 181.

the hare, the squirrel, and the poet in the solitary winter retreat that adds to the beauty of the spot the needed human touch. Nature is thus suffused with human experience and takes on a new interest. But it usually happens that these descriptions become, further, either the appropriate setting for a certain train of reflections on the part of the poet, or they directly suggest these suggestions. In the winter retreat just spoken of the fearless, innocent animal life becomes the occasion of a long disquisition on the lesson of benevolence taught by nature to man. In the sheltered walk the poet finds his mind soothed and prepared for a Wordsworthian contemplation on nature as the teacher of the wise, so that ultimately many of Cowper's descriptions, as well as his summaries, become contributary to his main purpose.

Cowper's knowledge of natural facts was not more remarkable than John Scott's. His range was much narrower than Thomson's. Other men had loved nature with passionate intensity. To other minds nature had suggested deep thoughts of God and man. Cowper came when many elements of the new attitude towards nature had been voiced. What marks him out as holding a unique position is not only that he gave body and emphasis to the new thought, but especially that be became its propagandist. He analyzed the effect of nature on man, he translated his personal experiences into a theory which he set himself to interpret and promulgate. He wrote with the zeal of a convert. Joy such as had come to him late in life was man's natural heritage. Men must be called back from the perverted and ruinous life of towns to the simplicity of nature. His theme is stated abstractly, repeated in concrete form, illustrated and amplified with the patience and ardor of absolute conviction. He was the preacher of the new religion of nature.

Robert Burns was deeply sensitive to the charms of nature. In a letter to Mrs. Dunlop he said :

Robert Burns
(1759–1796)

"I have some favorite flowers in Spring, among which are the mountain-daisy, the harebell, the foxglove, the wild brier-rose, the budding birk and the hoary hawthorn, that I view and hang over, with particular delight. I never hear the loud, solitary whistle of the curlew in a Summer noon, or the wild mixing cadence of a troop of grey-plover, in an Autumnal morning, without feeling an elevation of soul like the Enthusiasm of Devotion or Poetry.[1] Again he says:

"I have various sources of pleasure which are in a manner peculiar to myself. . . . . . . Such is the peculiar pleasure I take in the season of Winter more than in the rest of the year. . . . . . . There is scarcely any earthly object gives me more—I don't know if I should call it pleasure, but something which exalts me, something which enraptures me, than to walk in the sheltered side of a wood or high plantation in a cloudy winter day, and hear a stormy wind howling among the trees and raving o'er the plain. It is my best season for devotion; my mind is rapt up in a kind of enthusiasm to *Him* who . . . . . walks on the wings of the wind."[2]

Note also what Mr. Walker, his companion on the Border Tour, says of him:

"I had often, like others, experienced the pleasures which arise from the sublime or elegant landscape, but I never saw those feelings so intense as in Burns. When we reached a rustic hut on the river Tilt, where it is overhung by a woody precipice, from which there is a noble waterfall, he threw himself on the heathy seat, and gave himself up to a tender, abstracted, and

[1] Burns: Works, Vol. 5, p. 185.

[2] Burns, Works, Vol. 1, p, 28.

Cf. lines in the Epistle to William Simson.

> " Ev'n winter bleak has charms to me,
> When winds rave thro' the naked tree;
> Or frosts on hills of Ochiltree
> > Are hoary gray;
> Or blinding drifts wild-furious flee
> > Dark'ning the day!
> O Nature! a' thy shews and forms
> To feeling, pensive hearts hae charms,
> Whether the summer kindly warms
> > Wi' life an' light;
> Or winter howls, in gusty storms,
> > The lang, dark night."

voluptuous enthusiasm of imagination. . . . . . . It was
with much difficulty that I prevailed upon him to leave the spot."[1]

This susceptibility to nature was one of the signs by which
" Coila " knew that Burns would be the poet of Scotland.   He
represents her as saying to him :

> " I saw thee seek the sounding shore,
>   Delighted with the dashing roar ;
> Or when the North his fleecy store
>   Drove thro' the sky
> I saw grim Nature's visage hoar
>   Struck thy young eye.
>
> " Or when the deep green-mantled earth
> Warm cherished ev'ry floweret's birth,
> And joy and music pouring forth
>   In ev'ry grove ;
> I saw thee eye the general mirth
>   With boundless love."[2]

In his Commonplace Book, Burns records his eager desire to
write verse that shall make " the fertile banks of Irvine, the roman-
tic woodlands & sequestered scenes on Aire, and the healthy,
mountainous source, & winding sweep of Doon emulate Tay,
Forth, Ettrick, Tweed, &c."[3]   And his love of nature was limited
in scope to just these scenes of which he speaks.   He had no
interest in mountains or the sea.   Mr. Douglas calls attention to
the fact that, "living in full face of the Arran hills he never names
them."[4]   He was as narrow in his limits and as vividly local in
the nature he chose to represent as was Cowper, but what he
loved he loved with intensity.   In the beautiful and picturesque
scenery about Ayr he found poetic inspiration.   To William
Simson he said,

> [1] Burns : Works, Vol. 4, p. 272.   [3] The Vision.
> [2] Burns: Works, Vol. 4, p. 91.
> [4] Burns: Works, Vol. 1, p.18
>   In one poem Burns declares that he prefers "wild mossy moors " to
> ,' Forth's sunny shores," but a characteristic reason,
>   " For there by a lanely sequestered stream
>   Resides a sweet lassie, my thought and my dream,"
> forbids the use of the passage as a proof of real enjoyment of the wild in nature.

> " The muse, nae poet ever fand her,
> Till by himself he learn'd to wander,
> Adown some trottin burn's meander,
> An' no think lang ; "

and in *The Brigs of Ayr* he says the simple bard may learn his tuneful trade from every bough.

Burns's knowledge of the nature about him was abundant and exact, and he was keenly critical of any note of falsity in the poems of others. He objected to the "Banks of the Dee" because of the line,

> " And sweetly the *nightingale* sang from the *tree*."

"In the first place," he said, "the nightingale sings in a low bush, but never from a tree ; and in the second place, there never was a nightingale seen or heard on the banks of the Dee, nor the banks of any other river in Scotland. Exotic, rural imagery is always comparatively flat."[1]

Again he said of another song, "It is a fine song, but for consistency's sake, alter the name 'Adonis.'" Was there ever such banns published, as a purpose of marriage between *Adonis* and *Mary*? These Greek and Roman pastoral appellations have a flat, insipid effect in a Scot song."[2] He gives especial praise to Rev. Dr. Cririe, because "like Thomson," the poet had "looked into nature for himself," and had nowhere been content with a "copied description."[3]

When Burns wrote a descriptive poem of set purpose he was comparatively commonplace and uninteresting as in *The Fall of Foyers* or *Admiring Nature*. His best descriptions come in, by chance as it were, in the midst of some vivid human interests. One of the most beautiful is a stanza in *Halloween*.

> " Whyles owre a linn the burnie plays,
> As thro' the glen it wimpl't ;
> Whyles round a rocky scaur it strays,
> Whyles in a wiel it dimpl't ;
> Whyles glitter'd ta the nightly rays,
> Wi' bickerin, dancin dazzle :

[1] Burns: Works, Vol. 6, p. 242.   [3] Burns: Works, 5, p. 165.
[2] Burns: Works, 6, p. 241.

> Whyles cookit underneath the braes,
>   Below the spreading hazle
>   Unseen that night."

Work so perfect as this is rare in any age. The beauty of the poem is simply the beauty of the stream itself.

Burns's chief use of nature, however, is in connection with man. External nature is illustration, background, frame, for human emotions. *The Lass of Cressnock Banks* was written at twenty-two and is the first one of his poems in which there is any distinct use of nature. It is merely an assemblage of twelve formally drawn out similes to represent the beauty of the lassie. Some of these similes are conventional and unmeaning, as when her hair is likened to curling mist on a mountain side,[1] her forehead to a rainbow, her lips to ripe cherries, and her teeth to a flock of sheep. In later poems the similitudes are simpler and sweeter, but they are drawn from a small number of facts and those of the more obvious sort, as the "simmer morn," "the flower in May," "the opening rose." A much more effective use of nature is as dramatic background either by congruity or contrast. As fine examples of the use of nature to give the keynote of the human emotion it accompanies we have the opening lines of the *Elegy*, *Farewell Song to the Banks of Ayr*, *Raving winds around her blowing*, and *Farewell to Ballochmyle*. The more usual form is to represent a natural picture in contrast to the human emotion, as in *The Chevalier's Lament*, *The Lament of Mary, Queen of Scots*, or, best of all, *The Banks of Doon*.

> "Ye banks and braes o' bonny Doon,
>   How can ye bloom sae fresh and fair ?
>   How can ye chant ye little birds,
>   And I sae weary, fu' of care!"

It is characteristic of Burns that his knowledge was wider and his sympathy keener in the realm of animate than of inanimate nature. He apparently thought of animals almost as if they had been human. The address to a mouse is as tenderly and genuinely sympathetic as if it had been to a hurt child. On

---

[1] Burns warmly admired Ossian, and this phrase sounds like an echo from one of the Ossian poems.

winter nights he listens to the wind and cannot sleep for think-
ing of the "ourie cattle" and "silly sheep" and helpless birds
that "cow'r" with "chittering wing."[1] He scorned hunting and
said there was no warm poetic heart that did not inly bleed at
man's savage cruelty.[2] He found it impossible to reconcile
so-called "sport" with his ideas of virtue.[3] He knew animals,
especially birds, in an intimate, friendly fashion. In the descrip-
tion of their manners and habits there is the most minute real-
ism. The following phrases are illustrative : "Ye grouse that
crap the heather bud," "Ye curlews calling thro' a clud;" "Ye
whirring paitrick brood;" "Ye fisher herons watching eels;"
"sooty coots;" "speckled teals;" "whistling plover;"

> "Clam'ring craiks at close o' day
> 'Mang fields o' flow'ring clover gay;"

and

> "Ye duck and drake, wi' airy wheels
> Circling the lake."[4]

In accurate first-hand observation, in abundant knowledge, in
the use of felicitous descriptive epithets, in great personal joy
in nature, in delight in winter, in love for animals, and in a criti-
cal estimate of the value of truthful portrayal Burns represents
the new spirit.

William William Lisle Bowles is another of the reputed "fathers"
of modern poetry. His slender title to the distinction
thus conferred upon him by Charles Cowden
William
Lisle Bowles Clarke,[5] rests on the admiration of Coleridge,[6]
(1762-1785) Southey, and Lovel[7] for his early poems.[8] From
1798 to the end of his life Bowles wrote con-

[1] Burns : Works, Vol. 2, p. 33.   [4] Burns : Elegy on Captain Henderson.

[2] Burns : The Brigs of Ayr.   [5] Bowles : Poetical Works, Vol. 2.

[3] Burns : Works, Vol. 5, p. 231.   [6] See Sonnet by Coleridge.

[7] "My friend Mr. Crutwell, the printer, wrote a letter saying that two young
gentlemen, strangers; one a particularly handsome and pleasing youth, lately
from Westminster School, and both literary and intelligent, spoke in high
commendation of my volume." See preface to ed. of 1837, Bowles' Poems.

[8] Fourteen Sonnets, 1789. The same with additions, 1790. The same
reproduced with illustrations. 1798.

stantly, so the list of his works is a long one ; but in the present study we are concerned only with the poems before 1798, the ones that stirred Coleridge to abandon metaphysics for poetry.

From fourteen to nineteen years of age Bowles was in Winchester school under the tutelage of Dr. Joseph Warton, who won the boy's confidence and inspired him with his own tastes. In the *Monody on the Death of Dr. Warton*, written eighteen years after these school days, Bowles says of Warton,

> "Thy cheering voice,
> O Warton ! bade my silent heart rejoice,
> And wake to love of nature ; every breeze
> On Itchin's brink was melody ; the trees
> Waved in fresh beauty ;   .   .   .
> .   .   .   .   . And witness thou
> Catherine, upon whose foss-encircled brow
> We met the morning, how I loved to trace
> The prospect spread around.   .   .   .
> So passed my days with new delight."

Warton also taught him to love literature. He learned to read Greek poets with "young-eyed sympathy," and he went with "holier joy" to

> "The lonely heights where Shakespeare sat sublime."

Charmed, the lad bent his soul

> "Great Milton's solemn harmonies to hear."

"Unheeded midnight hours" were beguiled by the wild song of Ossian. and his fancy found a " magic spell " in the Odes of his master. Dr. Warton.

The influences of these early school days had awakened Bowles to love of nature and of poetry, and when sorrow came it was to nature and to poetry that be turned for relief. His *Sonnets* are the direct and genuine expression of a personal grief. They were composed, he says. during a tour in which he "sought forgetfulness of the first disappointment in early affections,"[1] and they are pervaded by a melancholy unmistakably real. But along with this deep sadness is a frequent recognition of the power of nature

---

[1] Bowles: Poems, Introduction to edition of 1837.

to give at least temporary respite from grief. Not only does she
"steep each sense in still delight,"[1] but she bestows "a soothing
charm."[2] The lovely sights and sounds of morning

> "Touch soft the wakeful nerve's according string." [3]

The river Itchen brings "solace to his heart."[4] After visiting
the Cherwell he says:

> " Whate'er betide, yet something have I won
> Of solace, that may bear me on serene." [5]

In the midst of sorrow he is

> " Thankful that still the landscape beaming bright
> Can wake the wonted sense of pure delight."[6]

What Bowles saw in nature was largely determined by his state
of mind. His own sadness led him to a quick perception of the
pensive or melancholy suggestions in any scene. He loved
sequestered streams, romantic vales, the hush of evening. The
sounds he heard were soft and plaintive. The river Wainsbeck
makes "a plaintive song among its "mossy-scattered rocks."[7]
He listens to the wind and seems to hear a plaint of sorrow.[8] Sea
sounds are

> " Like melodies that mourn upon the lyre."[9]

> " There is strange music in the stirring wind
> When lowers the autumal eve." [10]

Of the bells at Ostend he says :

> "And hark! with lessening cadence now they fall ;
> And now, along the white and level tide,
> They fling their melancholy music wide ;
> Bidding me many a tender thought recall

[1] Hope.
[2] The Tweed Visited,
[3] Elegy Written at the Hotwells. Bristol.
[4] To the River Itchen.
[5] The River Cherwell.
[6] Elegy Written at the Hotwells. Bristol.
[7] The River Wainsbeck. cf. Akenside.
[8] The River Wainsbeck.
[9] At Tynemouth Priory.
[10] Absence.

> Of summer days, and those delightful years
> When from an ancient tower, in life's fair prime,
> The mournful magic of their mingling chime
> First waked my wondering childhood into tears."[1]

Again, his own striving after self-control leads him to look with pleasure on such natural objects as have withstood the shock of tempests. Rugged Malvern Hill, on which the "parting sun sits smiling," teaches him a lesson of victory over grief, and he exclaims,

> "Ev'n as thou
> Dost lift in the pale beam thy forehead high,
> Proud mountain! whilst the scattered vapours fly
> Unheeded round thy breast — so, with calm brow
> The shades of sorrow I may meet, and wear
> The smile unchanged of peace, though pressed by care!"[2]

Some of the brief descriptions in these sonnets are beautiful in themselves, as

> "How shall I meet thee, Summer, wont to fill
> My heart with gladness, when thy pleasant tide
> First came, and on the Coomb's romantic side
> Was heard the distant cuckoo's hollow bill."[3]

Or this from Dover Cliffs,

> "On these white cliffs, that calm above the flood
> Uprear their shadowing heads, and at their feet
> Hear not the surge that has for ages beat,
> How many a lonely wanderer has stood!
> And, whilst the lifted murmur met his ear,
> And o'er the distant billows the still eve
> Sailed slow, has thought of all his heart must leave
> Tomorrow,"[4]

But here, as elsewhere in the poems, the chief thought is human grief; and the most important characteristic of the poems, taken as a whole, is the intimate union between the spirit of a man and the spirit of nature. It was always Bowles's theory, says

---

[1] The Bells, Ostend.
[2] At Malvern.
[3] The Approach of Summer.
[4] Dover Cliffs.

Clark,[1] that nature is the true subject of poetry ; but he does not, in his later work, strike so true and simple a note as in these early sonnets.

Such general statements as are to be drawn from this study of specific poets can be more conveniently made after the studies in Gardening, Fiction, Travels, and Painting, for these four studies, brief as they are, yet offer facts that modify or confirm the impression gained from the poetry.

[1] Bowles's Memoir.

CHAPTER III.

Up to the beginning of the eighteenth century the garden that had satisfied public taste was some form of the Ancient, Geo-**Gardening** metrical, Roman, Architectural, or Regular Garden, as it has been variously styled. In English literature this garden plays but a small part. In Evelyn's *Diary* we find many descriptions of French and Italian gardens which are eminently suggestive as showing the taste of the age. His approbation is always given to proofs of ingenuity in the way of mechanical devices. We find the same general tone in a letter by Mallet. He had been traveling in Wales for six weeks, and had found the journey simply "tedious" till he came to Sir Arthur Owen's garden, which consisted of an acre and a half, laid out like a mariner's compass with a tree in the centre for the needle and a grove cut into thirty-two sections by paths answering to the points in the compass. This was the only remarkable thing Mallet saw in Wales.[1] The classical and the only important article on the Formal Garden before 1700 is by Sir-William Temple.[2] According to his taste Moor Park was the sweetest garden known. It was divided into quarters by gravel walks, and adorned with two fountains and eight statues in each quarter. Its terrace walk had a summerhouse at each end. On each side of the parterre was a cloister, over each cloister an airy walk, and so on. "Among us," he explains, "the beauty of building and planting is placed chiefly in some certain proportions, symmetries, or uniformities, our walks and our trees ranged so as to answer one another and at exact distances." This sentence is especially interesting as show-

[1] Mallet in Letter to Pope (1734).

[2] Temple ; On the Gardens of Epicurus ; or of Gardening in the year 1685.

ing how completely the ideal garden represented the thought of the age. "Certain proportions, symmetries, and uniformities" is a phrase characteristic of Classicism in all its manifestations. Equally characteristic and interesting is Temple's reason for approving of this style of gardening. In exact figures, with regular and definite intervals, it is, he says, "hard to make any great or remarkable faults." In this sentence there is surely a suggestion of one reason for the love of order, of limits clearly set, that marked the classical spirit. Symmetries and proportions and uniformities were a specific against great and remarkable faults such as had resulted from the undue license of a romantic age. The beaten path had legitimate attractions for an age that had lost its way among the pleasures of the pathless woods.

In the poetry between Marvell and Pope the garden hardly appears at all. Perhaps the gardens in Dryden's plays are as significant of the spirit of the age as any that could be found. Take especially *The Tempest*, in the modernization of which all the exquisite nature setting is lost. The beautiful part of the island where Prospero lived is to be represented thus : " 'Tis composed of three walks of cypress trees : each side walk leads to a cave." In his plays the scene is often laid in a garden, but it is always stiff and formal. An interesting comparison might be made between these garden scenes and those in *Faust*.

The distinctive characteristics of the formal garden were high walls shutting out the surrounding country, flights of stairs going up and down terraces, trees planted in long straight lines, flower beds in geometric patterns, water in straight canals or geometric basins, and elaborate topiary work.[1]

The break from this formal garden to the Natural Garden (known also as the Modern, English, Irregular, or Landscape

[1] Quarterly Review Jan. 1817. Article on H. Repton's Theory and Practice of Landscape Gardening.

Reginald Blomfield and F. Inigo Thomas : The Formal Garden in England.

Lecky : England in the Eighteenth Century, Vol. 1, ch. 4.

Walpole : On Modern Gardening (an excellent summary). Works, Vol. 2.

Famous Parks and Gardens of the World Described and Illustrated. (T. Nelson & Sons, London, 1880.)

Garden) began early in the eighteenth century. The three gardeners who by theory and practice established the new ideas were Bridgeman who was first in the field, Kent who is the most famous, and Brown who, though less known, is said to have had the most genius. The specific credit that belongs to each is not beyond dispute but apparently Bridgeman was the first to protest against "artificially trained and sculptured greenery." He also showed distaste for the "mathematical exactitude and rectilinear designs of the preceding age." Walpole ascribes to him the destruction of the walled enclosures—"the decisive step that led to all that followed." Bridgeman's work was, however, rather tentative and theoretic. It was left for Kent to make bold experiments along the same lines. Walpole calls Kent "the father of modern gardening." What Bridgeman had thought of, Kent thought of and did. His fundamental idea was to make "natural pictures." He cut down the fences and showed that the garden should be ruralized and the surrounding country somewhat cultivated so that all might unite in a harmonious whole. He wished "to bring nature to the parlor windows." His underlying principle was to study nature and to follow out her laws.[1] It must be confessed that the iron-clad and undiscriminating application of this theory led to results often as artificial and unnatural as the formal garden had been. For instance, nature apparently abhors a straight line, so all paths and avenues and streams were sent serpentining about in the most tedious and unmeaning fashion. Francis Coventry said that no follower of Kent would be willing to go to heaven on a straight line. The desire to get rid of all "remnants of old formalities" led to the destruction of many fine old straight avenues. The desire to follow nature led even to such extravagances as the planting of dead trees.[2]   "Capability" Brown

----

[1] There is a discriminating eulogy of Kent in Coventry's paper in The World, April 12, 1753.

[2] Sir Walter Scott: Review of Stewart's The Planter's Guide, The Quarterly Review, 37:303.

Francis Coventry: Strictures on the Absurd Novelties Introduced into Gardening, and a Humorous Description of Squire Mushroom's Villa, The World, No. 15, 1753.

was Kent's successor. He carried out the principles of Kent with greater skill and breadth of design. Kent's chief gardens were Richmond, Esher, Claremont, Stowe, and Rustham. Blenheim was formed by Brown who was kitchen-gardener at Stowe when Bridgeman and Kent made it over.[1]

In this brief outline of the beginnings of the new school of gardening the points to be emphasized are that before the eighteenth century the fundamental principle on which gardens were made was the display of art, of triumphant human mastery over nature; that the fundamental principle on which the new gardens were made was the close study and imitation of nature and the concealment of art; that this change was made early in the century, while the classical spirit was apparently at its height; and that the new ideas in gardening are similar to the first turnings from the classical conventions regarding nature on the part of the poets, and are contemporary with them. Gardening was unlike poetry in that, from the very nature of the art in gardening, some enunciation of theories preceded any possible practical illustration. All change in the art of gardening was conscious and attended by more or less discussion, while in poetry a similar change is largely unconscious, or at least seldom accompanied by formal statements of theory. But both changes grow out of and illustrate the same mental restlessness under the limitations imposed by the formal or classical conception of nature.

In this revolt from the formal garden the gardeners mentioned play hardly so important a part as do Pope and Addison. The great influence of their work, coming as it did at a crisis time, has been recognized by most students of the garden. Blomfield says:[2] "It now became the fashion to rave about nature, and to condemn the straightforward work of the formal school as so much brutal sacrilege. Pope and Addison led the way with about as much love of nature as the elegant Abbé Delille some three generations later." In *Famous Parks and Gardens* Pope is spoken of as "the prophet of the new school."

[1] Thomas Whateley or Wheatley: Observations on Modern Gardening, 1770.
[2] Blomfield & Thomas: The Formal Garden in England, p. 80.

Mason in his *English Garden* calls Kent "Pope's bold associate." Walpole dwells on the assistance Kent had from Pope and he thinks that the ideas of Kent's best works were really borrowed from Pope's garden at Twickenham. Hazlitt emphasizes "the healthy and important influence for good in this direction"[1] exercised by Pope. In the Review of Repton's work in *The Quarterly* for 1816 we find the following : "Pope attacked the prevailing style with his keenest shafts of ridicule.   .   .
.   .   He so completely developed the true principles of gardening that the theories of succeeding writers have been little more than amplifications of his short general precepts." Courthope says that the principles laid down in Pope's writings and exemplified in his garden[2] were really the basis on which the new school worked. And finally,[3] Biese quotes Pope's famous maxim and attributes to him and to Addison much influence in bringing about the return to nature in the art of gardening.

A few brief quotations will serve to illustrate the tone adopted by Pope and Addison.

"There is something more bold and masterly in the rough careless strokes of nature than in the nice touches and embellishments of art. The beauties of the most stately garden or palace lie in a narrow compass, the imagination immediately runs them over, and requires something else to gratify her : but, in the wild fields of nature, the sight wanders up and down without confinement, and is fed with an infinite variety of images."[4]

"I do not know whether I am singular in my opinion, but, for my own part, I would rather look upon a tree in all its luxuriancy and diffusion of boughs and branches, than when it is thus cut and trimmed into a mathematical figure : and can not but fancy that an orchard in flower looks infinitely more delightful than all the little labyrinths of the most finished parterre."[5]
"My compositions in gardening are altogether after the Pindaric

---

[1] Hazlitt : Gleanings in Old Garden Literature. p. 66 (ed. 1887).

[2] Famous Parks and Gardens, p. 134 (description of Twickenham).

[3] Biese : Die Entwickelung des Naturgefühls, pp. 290–293.

[4] Addison : The Spectator, No. 414 (1712).

[5] Addison : Spectator, 414 (1712).

manner, and run into the beautiful wildness of nature without affecting the nicer elegancies of art."[1]   Of more importance is Pope's scornful *Essay on Verdant Sculpture.*[2]   "There is certainly something," he says, "in the amiable simplicity of unadorned Nature that spreads over the mind a more noble sort of tranquillity, and a loftier sensation of pleasure, than can be raised from the nicer scenes of Art.   .   .   .   I believe it is no wrong observation that persons of genius, and those who are most capable of Art, are always most fond of Nature.   On the contrary, people of the common level of understanding are principally delighted with the little niceties and fantastical operations of Art, and constantly think that finest which is the least natural."   Then follows the famous sarcasm on the eminent town gardener, who was prepared to furnish all sorts of imagery in evergreen, even to cutting family pieces of men, women, and children.

These noteworthy utterances by Pope and Addison come, it will be observed, in the years 1712, 1713, and Twickenham was completed before 1718.[3]   Kent did not return from his first visit to Italy till 1719, and his work on gardens comes later, his most important works falling probably between 1730 and 1748, the date of his death.

Bridgeman, though ahead of Kent in theoretical expression, was really his contemporary, for we find them mentioned as working together on some gardens, as Stowe, at the time when Brown was kitchen gardener there, and so probably after 1735.   Brown's (1715-1783) work begins during the last years of Kent's life.   Hence Pope and Addison antedated the work of the practical gardeners by some years.   The final and authoritative statement of Pope's principles did not come, however, till 1731, when the famous *Fourth Epistle* was published. Besides his scornful description of the formal garden he gave certain precepts, the underlying thought of which is that gardens should so be made as to conceal all traces of man's interference. This *Essay* marked a crisis in the theory of gardening, as Thom-

---

[1] Addison : Spectator, 477 (1712).
[2] Pope : The Guardian, 173 (1713).
[3] Letter to Jervas, Dec. 12, 1718.   Pope : Works, 4 : 494.

son's *Seasons* had marked the culmination of the interest in nature shown here and there in the poetry of the preceding years.

Two years before the publication of this *Essay* there had come from Allan Ramsay a eulogy of wild gardens.

> "Compar'd with prime cut plots and nice,
>   Where Nature has to Art resign'd
>   Till all looks mean, stiff, and confin'd."[1]

Among the early imitations of Pope's *Essay* is Mr. Bramston's *Man of Taste*, 1733, and Cawthorn's *Essay on Taste*, 1739. They are of value only as indicating the spread of the new ideas. Cawthorn's precepts, such as—

> " Examine nature with the eye of taste ;
>   Mark where she spreads the lawn, or pours the rill,
>   Falls in the vale, or breaks upon the hill ;
>   Plan as she plans,"

will illustrate the many weak expansions of Pope's rules.

The second step in landscape gardening seems to have been the *Ferme orné*. Here there was not merely a breaking of the line of demarkation between garden and park, but there was an endeavor to ornament the whole estate. One of the earliest attempts of this sort was by Mr. Southcote, on whom Mason's muse bestowed "no vulgar praise." But the most successful, as well as the most famous *Ferme orné*, was that of the poet Shenstone at Leasowes. Mason spoke of Shenstone as "one who knew how to harmonize his shade still softer than his song," and it is quite possible that his practical example at Leasowes helped on the return to nature as effectively as his poetry. As the first really successful experiment in landscape gardening Shenstone's place called forth much comment, and usually of an admiring sort. Dr. Johnson publishes nine of the poetical tributes to the place. Dodsley's description of Leasowes, usually bound with Shenstone's works, is the one that later stirred Sir Walter Scott's ambition to own a place.[2] The point to be noted here is that all

---

[1] Ramsay's Answer to the Foregoing (Epistle from Somerville).

[2] " I can trace, even to childhood, a pleasure derived from Dodsley's description of Shenstone's Leasowes ; and I envied the poet much more for the pleas-

tributes unite in eulogizing the skill with which the art of the gardener was hidden,

> " While Nature shines so gracefully revealed
> That she triumphant claims the total plan,
> And, with fresh pride, adopts the work of man."

In Shenstone's *The Progress of Taste* we have a full account of his absorption in the work of beautifying his estate according to the new principle. All was done for the sake of beauty. Nothing made the poet more indignant than to be asked the use of any of his improvements. In spite of the unnatural striving after natural effects, and the accumulation of historic and symbolic incongruities, we cannot fail to see that this estate illustrates a rapid advance in the appreciative regard for the beauty and freedom of nature. Shenstone's garden was in its prime between 1748 and 1756. His *Unconnected Thoughts on a Garden*, published in 1764, was a valuable contribution to the literature on the subject.[1] Two remarkable essays appeared in 1770 and in 1771. The first was *Observations on Modern Gardening*, by Whateley. It summed up in masterly fashion the principles and

ure of accomplishing the objects detailed in his friend's sketch of his grounds, than for the possession of pipe, crook, flock, and Phyllis to boot." Quoted by Hugh Miller. For full prose description of Leasowes and the neighboring place, Hagley, see Hugh Miller's Impressions of England and English People, pp. 147-169, 95-132. See also A Poet's Garden, by Goldsmith, for a description of Leasowes gone to decay. For an interesting supposed conversation between Shenstone and a utilitarian cockney visitor see Blackwood's, 14:262 (1823). For another early description see Letters on the Beauties of Hagley, Envil, and the Leasowes, by Joseph Heeley, 1777. See also poetical descriptions in Woodhouse's Poems and in Giles' Miscellanies. See also Mr. Wheatley in On Gardening (1770). He said that Leasowes was a perfect picture of the poet's mind. The influence and fame of this garden are indicated by the fact that the Marquis de Girardin at Ermenonville called his own place "The Leasowes of France." Anderson, in his Preface to Shenstone's Works, says that the planning of pleasure grounds in the manner of Leasowes "seems to require as great powers of mind as those which we admire in the descriptive poems of Thomson, or in the noble landscapes of Salvator Rosa, or the Poussins."

[1] See J. C. Loudon's Preface to H. Repton's Landscape Gardening. Downing in Landscape Gardening, p. 20, says that the term Landscape Gardening was first used in Shenstone's essay.

achievements of the new school.   The other was by Horace Walpole.   He had been at work on it, at intervals, for nine years when Whateley's essay appeared.   It is entitled *On Modern Gardening* and is one of his most brilliant productions.   Its denunciation of the formal garden is an admirable statement of the principles on which that garden was formed.   He gives unqualified praise to Bridgeman, Kent, and Brown.   In 1772 appeared the first portion of Mason's *English Garden*,' a long didactic poem in four books.   It is heterogeneous in character, but, in one way or another, contrives to sum up about all that had yet been said or thought on the garden.

Shenstone's garden was somewhat too ornate to be a true example of the school of Kent.   That school of Brown and his followers was really dominant till late in the century.   But along with this was growing up another school of which Leasowes was a sort of faint prophecy.   This is known as the Picturesque School. It had its origin in a natural revolt from the bareness and uniformity characteristic of much of the work of the Kent School. The dictum of the new school was that whatever looks well in a picture will look well in a landscape.   Kent's smooth lawns, and uniform curves and level surfaces, and clumps, and belts, did not compose well and so they were ruled out.   The forerunner of the new school was William Gilpin.   The record of his travels,[2] his attractive studies of wild scenery, his steady adoption of the painter's point of view, and his criticism of various places as unpicturesque, doubtless did much to stimulate the dislike of the tameness of Kent and Brown.   That Gilpin had no intention of throwing discredit on the existing school is evident from his high praise of Brown's work at Blenheim.   The same cannot be said of Knight and Price, the real champions of the picturesque.   They belong in 1794, and the Picturesque School goes down before the Gardenesque School in the hot controversy between Knight and Price on the one side and Humphrey Repton on the other.   There

---

[1] This poem appears to have been published in parts in 1772, 1777, 1779, 1782, but a note to Book 3 says that it was begun a few months after Gray's death in 1771.

[2] See the section on Travels.

was nothing too severe for Knight and Price to say of Kent and Brown.[1] Knight says that he became so weary of the extensive scene so dull and bare, of the flat, insipid, waving plains, of the uniform, eternal green, in gardening as then conducted, that he would have gladly welcomed back the old straight lines and clipped yews and formal terraces. He hates "shaven and shorn" scenery. He prefers it in its rough, undressed state. Mr. Price says in prose with almost equal heat what his friend has put into verse. The chief point of their controversy with Mr. Repton is on the closeness of the union of the arts of painting and gardening. Mr. Gilpin, Mr. Mason, Mr. Knight, and Mr. Price had all said, Study pictures of great artists if you wish to know how to manage your trees, your lights and shades, your colors, in a landscape. Repton said landscape gardening was an art by itself, and that the landscape might choose and refuse and combine details in a way not suited to a picture. Repton's system would carry us into the nineteenth century. It is sufficient to say that he combined and modified the principles that had been growing up through the century in such a way as to establish the beautiful parks and gardens in which England led the world.[2]

The picturesque garden had two offshoots that cannot be passed over. The idea of imitating a picture, when carried to an excess, led to frantic efforts to put cliffs, precipices, gnarled oaks, ruined, moss-grown fortresses, mouldering, ivy-hung abbeys, into every landscape. Frequent sage advice is given as to the best way to secure these effects. Richard Jago, a friend of Shenstone, urges the importance of appropriate sites—a cliff for a ruined castle, a well water'd vale for "the mouldering abbey's fretted windows."[3] Five years later Mr. Gilpin criticised Shuckburgh

[1] Richard Payne Knight: The Landscape.
Sir Uvedale Price: An Essay on the Picturesque.

[2] The influence and significance of the English Garden is well indicated in these words of Taine (Voyage en Italie):
"Aussi les jardins anglais, tels qu'on les importe chez nous à présent, indiquent l'avénement d'une autre race, la domination d'un autre goût, la règne d'une autre littérature, l'ascendant d'un autre esprit, plus compréhensif, plus solitaire, plus aisément fatigué, plus tourné vers les choses du dedans." Vol. I : 232.

[3] Edge Hill or the Rural Prospect Delineated and Moralized (1767). In this

because the ruins were not happily "fabricated," but he adds in exculpation, "It is not every man, who can build a house, that can execute a ruin." Then follows a long list of the mechanical difficulties, with the following conclusion, "When it is well done, we allow, that nothing can be more beautiful: but we see everywhere so many absurd attempts of this kind, that when we walk through a piece of improved ground; and hear of being carried next to *see the ruins*, if the master of the scene be with us, we dread the incounter." Mr. Mason deprecates building ruins but thinks a man to be congratulated, if on his grounds

> "one superior rock
> Bear on its brow the shivered fragment huge
> Of some old Norman fortress; happier far,
> Oh, then most happy, if thy vale below
> Wash, with the crystal coolness of its rills,
> Some mouldering abbey's ivy-vested wall."[1]

This search after ruins and their appropriate scenic accompaniments was a morbid and exaggerated development of the new love of the picturesque and wild in nature just as the sentimental melancholy phase of poetry was a morbid and exaggerated development of the new poetic turning to the wild and solitary. In the exaggerated form both phases were ephemeral, and it is interesting to observe that they were manifested at about the same time. Mr. Phelps gives 1740 to 1760 as the dates between which the sentimental melancholy spirit flourished in poetry. In 1767 we find rules for building the ruins so much desired. The custom must have antedated these rules, given as they are as if for something well established, by some years at least. And from the very nature of the case, the same mental impulse would show both its rise and decline more promptly in poetry than in buildings.[2]

poem Jago describes the country seats of fifty gentlemen. The most important are Farnborough, Packington, Shuckburgh, and Leasowes.

[1] The English Garden.

[2] Biese in commenting on the profusion of fantastic buildings, of temples dedicated to friendship and love and poetry and melancholy, finds them merely the appropriate and inevitable background of "die sentimentalen, in Thränen zerfliessenden Freundschaftsbündnisse" of the times. Die Entwickelung des Naturgefühls, p. 292.

The subject of oriental gardens was also much discussed in prose and verse. Sir William Chambers was the first important champion of the methods of Chinese gardens. He liked the "fancies and surprises" of Chinese effects and thought that Kent's plans made English gardens "no better than so many fields." His essay appeared in 1757.[1] Goldsmith's *Description of a Chinese Garden* came out in 1760. In 1772 came Sir William Chambers' *Dissertation on Oriental Gardens.* This brought out two replies from Mason in 1773 and 1774. The best practical illustration of this style of gardening was to be seen at Kew Gardens which Chambers remodeled. On the whole, however, oriental gardening was a fad that soon passed away without having exerted much influence. It is significant of the turning towards far countries, the romantic interest in the new and the remote, and is to be classed as a sign with the oriental and eastern Eclogues in the poetry of the period.

Incomplete and cursory as so short a study of so great a subject must be, the facts here presented seem to warrant the following statements :

The feeling toward nature in the period studied shows in gardening the same order of development, nearly the same dates, and the same phases as in poetry. There was first in both a pleased recognition of the supremacy of man, a rigid exclusiveness, a love of order, and symmetry, and of definite limits. Then came, in the early eighteenth century, a tentative turning from art to nature ; then an epoch-making statement in each art, Thomson's *Seasons* from 1726 to 1730, and Pope's *Epistle* in 1731. From this point on the development was in mass and variety rather than in the enunciation of new principles. The growing love for wild nature in the poetry, and the passion for the picturesque in gar-

[1] The rage for Chinese buildings began earlier than this for in The World March 27, 1755, is a plea by Marriott for an "anti-Chinese society." See also a similar letter in Feb. 1754. For a similar taste in furniture see a letter in March, 1753. In April, 1753, Coventry satirizes the Chinese bridges and buildings in gardens. Even so far back as Sir William Temple much had been said about Chinese gardens. For criticism of their artificiality see Walpole's On Modern Gardening. For a defense of the Chinese theory as an attempt to follow nature see Humboldt's Kosmos.

dening proceed side by side. At the end of the century all is ready in both arts for the splendid work of the new era. Throughout the century both have had curiously correspondent offshoots or temporary fads—sentimental melancholy in poetry, and the ruins, artificial and real, in gardening; foreign eclogues and studies of distant countries in the one art, and Chinese gardens in the other.

CHAPTER IV.

It is impossible to do more here than merely to sketch the possibilities in a " History of the Tour and the Guide Book," because the mass of material to be gone over is so great. Pinkerton's *Catalogue of Voyages and Travels*, published in 1814, gives over 4500 books. It is so elaborately tabulated that it is not easy to use, but it is possible to cull from its voluminous pages a fairly compendious list of such travels as were published in England in the eighteenth century. In this list there are about 360 books. Of these 360 books all but 84 are travels outside of Great Britain and Ireland. Their distribution through the century indicates a steady growth of interest in foreign lands, for nearly half of the accounts of travels in other countries belong in the last quarter of the century. The same pushing out of the romantic spirit in its curiosity to know the remote is shown by another interesting transfer of emphasis, half of the *Travels* before 1750 being devoted to Great Britain and Ireland, while after 1775, less than one-fifth of the whole number is given up to home explorations. But these foreign tours, however interesting as one note of Romanticism, are outside the present field of inquiry. They were undertaken usually with some definite purpose. Antiquities, curiosities, minerals; laws, manners, customs; utilitarian possibilities — these were the leading subjects of inquiry. In the titles such phrases as, " relating chiefly to the history, antiquities, and geography;" "remarks on Characters and Manners;" "chiefly relative to the knowledge of mankind, industry, literature, and natural history;" "with an account of the most memorable sieges;" "containing a great variety of geographical, topographical and political observations;" "containing specially a description of fortified towns;" "containing a Picture of the Country, the Manners, and the Actual Government," are of constant recurrence and serve to mark out the general scope of these works. There are, to be sure, in these books, many scattered descriptions of the natural scenes visited. This is especially true of the *Travels* in the last quarter of the century. But to study these descriptions, even superficially, would be too wide a work for the present limits. Furthermore, the accounts of the tours made in the United Kingdom will doubtless reveal the characteristics of the observations made in foreign lands.

One of the early books of English travel in the eighteenth century is Mr. Martin's *Description of the Western Islands of Scotland* (1704). It is this book that stirred Dr. Johnson to make his visit to the Hebrides, and it is from this that Mallet drew the details for his *Amyntor and Theodora*. In the Preface Martin says :

"Perhaps it is peculiar to those isles, that they have never been described till now by any man that was a native of the country, or had traveled them. . . . . "Descriptions of countries, without the natural histories of them, are now justly reckoned to be defective. This I had a particular regard to in the following descriptions, and have everywhere taken notice of the nature of the climate and soil, and of the remarkable cures performed by the natives merely by the use of simples."

This preliminary promise of first-hand observation, especially so far as nature is concerned, is hardly carried out. The book is a credulous, entertaining, unsifted narrative of whatever marvels came to his ears. His interest rested chiefly on strange cures made by the use of "simples." The *Description* has the negative importance of entirely ignoring nature. In its 120 pages there as not a word or phrase in recognition of the wild and beautiful scenery in these islands.

The same distinction holds of Brand's *Brief Description of Orkney, Zetland, Pightland-Firth, and Caithness* (1701). Brand was one of a commission sent by the General Assembly to inquire into religious matters in the northern islands, so it is not

strange that he bestows much attention on heathenish and popish
rites, charms, and superstitions. He is also much interested
in the prevailing diseases and the means of cure employed by
the natives. And he says much of their customs, manners, and
personal appearance. He describes the crops, the climate, the
favorite articles of food, but his eyes are holden to the charms of
scenery.

In 1715 appeared Alexander Pennecuik's *Description of
Tweeddale.* He was a physician and for thirty years his employ-
ment had obliged him to know and observe every corner of
Tweeddale. He found great pleasure in "herbalizing shady
groves and mountains," and the chief value of his work is
accordingly in its numerous botanical observations. Not a stray
sentence indicates pleasure in the beauty of the Lowland moun-
tains.

Except for the work of Brand, Martin, and Pennecuik, the
first half of the century shows but a meager list of travels.
Besides eight *Tours* published anonymously, Pinkerton records
only Gordon's *Itinerarium Septentrionale* (in Scotland and North-
ern England) in 1726, and Macky's *Journey through England* in
1732. In 1762 appeared Hamilton's *Letters from Antrim*, the
chief subject of which was announced to be "the Natural His-
tory of the Basaltes." Mr. Hamilton spoke occasionally of the
beautiful and picturesque appearance of the Irish coast, but he
professed himself an advocate of Mr. Locke's system of a dic-
tionary of pictures in preference to a dictionary of tedious
descriptions. From 1764 to 1769 Mr. Bushe added his contri-
bution to Irish *Travels*, the objects dwelt upon in his *Hiberna
Curiosa* being "Manners, observations on the state of Trade and
Agriculture, and Natural Curiosities."

Much of the work in *Travels* or *Tours* in the eighteenth cen-
tury is thrown into the form of familiar letters. By far the most
important of these tourists' letters from the present point of view
is Dr. Brown's description of Keswick in a letter to Lyttleton.
This letter was published in 1772, but its date is difficult to
determine. It was before 1766, for that is the year of the
author's death. Even this date puts it with *John Buncle* and Dr.

Dalton's *Descriptive Poem* as being one of the three earliest descriptions of the Lake Region.[1] Since it is so little known some unusually long extracts from it may be of value.

" But at Keswick, you will on one side of the lake, see a rich and beautiful landskip of cultivated fields. . . . On the opposite shore you will find rocks and cliffs of stupendous height, hanging broken over the lake in horrible grandeur, some of them a thousand feet high ; the woods climb up their steep and shaggy sides, where mortal foot never yet approached ; on these dreadful heights the eagles build their nests ; a variety of water-falls are seen pouring from their summits and , tumbling from rock to rock, in rude and terrible magnificence, while on all sides of this immense amphitheatre the lofty mountains rise around, piercing the clouds in shapes as spiry and fantastic as the very rocks of Dovedale. To this I must add the frequent and bold projection of the cliffs into the lake, forming noble bays and promontories ; in other parts they finely retire from it and often open in abrupt chasms or clefts, through which at hand you see rich and uncultivated vales, and, beyond these, at various dis-tance, mountain rising over mountain, among which, new pros-pects present themselves in mist, till the eye is lost in an agree-able perplexity,

> Where active fancy travels beyond sense
> And pictures things unseen —.

Were I to analyze the two places in their constituent principles, I should tell you that the full perfection of Keswick consists of three circumstances, beauty, horror, and immensity united ; . . . to give you a complete idea of these three perfections, as they are joined in Keswick, would require the united powers of

[1] I have been unable to find the exact date of this letter, but in all probabil-ity it antedates The Life of John Buncle and the Descriptive Poem by some years. It was probably before 1760, because at that time occurred the quarrel between Lyttleton and Brown. It seems also probable that it was before 1756, because at that time Dr. Brown took the living at Great Horkesley, near Colchester. The most natural period for the Letter is between 1748 and 1754, for at some time during that period, and apparently during the early part of it, Dr. Brown held the living of Morland, Westmoreland. (See Brown, Osbaldiston, Lyttle-ton in Nat. Dict. of Biog. and Memoir of Brown in British Poets.)

Claude, Salvator, and Poussin. The first should throw his deli-
cate sunshine over the cultivated fields, the scattered cots, the
groves, the lake and wooded islands. The second should dash
out the horror of rugged cliffs, the steeps, the hanging woods
and foaming waterfalls; while the grand pencil of Poussin
should crown the whole with the majesty of the impending
mountains.

"So much for what I would call the permanent beauties of this
astonishing scene. Were I not afraid of being tiresome I could
now dwell as long on its varying or accidental beauties. . . .
Sometimes a serene air and clear sky disclose the tops of the
highest hills; at others, you see the clouds involving their sum-
mits, resting on their sides or descending to their base, and roll-
ing among the valleys, as in a vast furnace; when the winds are
high, they roar among the cliffs and caverns like peals of thun-
der; then too the clouds are seen in vast bodies sweeping along
the hills in gloomy greatness, while the lake joins the tumult and
tosses like a sea; but in calm weather the whole scene becomes
new; the lake is a perfect mirror and the landscape in all its
beauty, islands, fields, woods, rocks and mountains, are seen
inverted and floating on its surface. I will now carry you to the
top of a cliff, where, if you dare approach the ridge, a new
scene of astonishment presents itself; where the valley, lake and
islands are seen lying at your feet; where this expanse of water
appears diminished to a little pool amidst the vast and immeas-
urable objects that surround it; for here the summits of more
distant hills appear beyond those you have already seen; and
rising behind each other in successive ranges and azure groups
of craggy and broken steeps, form an immense and awful pic-
ture, which can only be expressed by the image of a tempestuous
sea of mountains. Let me now conduct you down again to the
valley and conclude with one circumstance more, which is, that a
walk by still moonlight (at which time the distant waterfalls are
heard in all their variety of sound) among these enchanting dales,
opens such scenes of delicate beauty, repose and solemnity as
exceed all description."

Mr. Gilpin was evidently familiar with Dr. Brown's *Letter*, for

in his Cumberland *Tour* (pub. 1786) he justified his own prefer-
ence for Keswick by saying that this region had also been singled
out by Dr. Brown, " who was a man of taste and had seen every
part of this country." Certainly this *Letter from Keswick* in the
delight with which it dwells on the wild and terrible elements of
nature, in its detailed observation, in its artistic appreciation of
the accidental effects of atmospheric conditions, and in its sensi-
tiveness to the spirit of the place, comes very close to the mod-
ern enthusiasm for mountains. The details are sometimes
exaggerated and the author's rapture may seem over-stated, but
the genuineness of his feeling, and the reality of his knowledge
of mountains and lake, must remain unquestioned. The *Letter*
is one of the first, and the most considerable of the early contri-
butions to the literature of the Lakes.

The great period of English travels began in 1767 with
Arthur Young's *Six Weeks' Tour in the Southern Counties of
England and Wales*. In 1768 (June to November) he wrote his
Six Months' Tour in the North of England. His next important
work, *A Farmer's Tour through the East of England*, was pub-
lished in 1771. His *Tour in Ireland* appeared in 1779. The
professed design of these sketches was husbandry. Agriculture,
industry, population, farming experiments, prices, laws,—these
were the topics on which he wished to inform himself and others.
He had apparently no thought of describing the country through
which he passed. There is in this respect a significant difference
between the books of 1767–8 and that of 1779. In the first
two he kept the text rigorously free from all weakening admix-
ture of landscape, the descriptions, whether of picture galleries
or scenery, appearing modestly as footnotes. In the last
the descriptions are boldly incorporated into the text, and
form, what is more, a surprisingly large proportion of it. In
1767–8 he described such places as he happened to pass near. In
1779 he followed up one river and down another professedly in
search of " wild and romantic landscapes." In general charac-
ter the descriptions do not greatly vary in the three books. The
most numerous descriptions are of gentlemen's estates, perhaps
in courteous repayment of hospitalities received. These accounts

are always detailed and often tedious. Young apparently went about with the polite owner, sat in his seats, looked down his vistas, observed his temples,.and took notes thereon. Our chief interest in these passages is the testimony they bear to Young's own preference for estates where art had done the least and nature most. "The owner has had the good judgment merely to assist nature," or "merely to render natural beauties accessible " are characteristic words of praise. The best descriptions are not, however, of estates, but of grand natural scenes. It is views from Persfeld on the Why (Wye) ;[1] the wild country along the Tees : the English Lakes ; the waterfalls and wild glens near Powerscourt ; the mountains and lakes of Killarney, that really stir him. Such spots he describes with an enthusiasm that never flags. He is tediously minute. He cannot let a detail escape. And through all there is an eager, overflowing delight, a raptu-rous pleasure in wild scenery such as we find in no traveler before Young except Brown. He broods over a fine landscape. He is unwilling to lose one of its possible charms. At Derwentwater he rows all around the lake, around each island, stops to hunt up unseen waterfalls, climbs all crags that promise fine views. He is indefatigable. No peril stops him. He wonders why the people of Keswick do not at once cut paths to the fine views so that no one need miss. them. As he climbs Skiddaw he laughs with scorn as he mentally compares "the effects of a Louis' mag-nificence to the play of nature in the vale of Keswick." His exclamation. " How trifling the labors of art to the mere sport of nature !" certainly marks a rebound from conventional standards. The view of Winandermere from the heights on the eastern shore is, he thinks, "the most superlative view that nature can exhibit" or, if not, she is "more fertile in beauties" than his imagination can conceive. " To ride the eighteen miles from Bernard Castle to the falls of the Tees one could well afford," he says, "a journey of a thousand miles " He rides out to Haws Water. He makes a close study of Hulls Water. The whole region holds him with a fascination nowhere repeated till he finds

---

[1] Young explains that he cannot find any one to spell the names for him so he must spell them as they are pronounced.

himself, ten years later, among similar wild scenes in Ireland. Here, almost forgetting that he is a scientific farmer in search of information, he wanders along the picturesque banks of the Liffey, the Boyne, the Nore, the Boyle, visits Lake Ennel, Loch Earne, the lakes of Killarney, and writes descriptions in the manner of the most voluminous and ardent of modern sight-seers. Young's significance in this study rests not so much on any artistic excellence of expression as on his wide observation, his personal enthusiasm for nature, and his early date.

The next traveler of importance was Thomas Gray. The openness of Gray's mind to pleasure from the external world is hardly at all indicated in his poetry. In his prose we find it especially in the *Journal in the Lakes* in 1769. Thirty years before this, his *Journal in France* had given some hint of his taste for wild scenery, but at that time, though he expressed great pleasure in the " magnificent rudeness " of the Alps, he had not entirely broken away from the current conceptions and the current phraseology, as is shown by the sentence : " You here meet with all the beauties so savage and horrid a place can present you with."

Gray's published letters extend from 1739 to 1770. Scattered through these are occasional passages indicative of a genuine love of nature. In the midst of a humorous letter to Walpole (Sept. 1737) he speaks of " venerable beeches . . . . . . always dreaming out their old stories to the winds." After he came back from Scotland, in 1765, he wrote to Mr. Mason :

" I am returned from Scotland charmed with my expedition ; it is of the Highlands I speak ; the Lowlands are worth seeing once, but the mountains are ecstatic, and ought to be visited in pilgrimage once a year. None but these monstrous creatures of God know how to join so much beauty with so much horror. A fig for your poets, painters, gardeners, and clergymen, that have not been up among them ; their imagination can be made up of nothing but bowling-greens, flowering shrubs, horse-ponds, Fleet ditches, shell-grottoes, and Chinese rails."

So early as 1739 he expressed his dislike of formal gardens in his sarcastic description of the grounds at Versailles. The same feeling of irritation at the preponderance of art over nature recurs in his description of Warwick in 1754. That even the most natural garden did not satisfy Gray as did wild nature we see from Mason's lines written just after the death of Gray. He evidently had not approved of *The Garden* as a subject for a poem and Mason represents him as saying :

> " ' Why waste thy numbers on a trivial art,
>   That ill can mimic e'en the humblest charms
>   Of all-majestic Nature ?'   At the words
>   His eye would glisten, and his accents glow
>   With all the poet's frenzy.   ' Sovereign Queen !
>   Behold, and tremble, while thou view'st her state
>   Throned on the heights of Skiddaw ; call thy art
>   To build her such a throne ; that art will feel
>   How vain her best pretensions.   Trace her march
>   Amid the purple crags of Borrowdale,' " etc.

In general, however, the testimony of the letters is to a scientific rather than a poetic love of nature. There are many exact records of the weather, of the coming crops, of the blossoming of flowers. A single example may serve as typical. It is a record of observations made at Stoke Pogis in July 1754.

"Barley was in ear on the first day ; gray and white peas in bloom. The bean flowers were going off. Duke-cherries in plenty on the 5th ; hearts were also ripe. Green melons on the 6th, but watry and not sweet. Currants began to ripen on the 8th, and red gooseberries had changed color."

And so on with nearly a hundred more of these tabulated natural facts.

Of Gray as a traveler Sir James Mackintosh is quoted by Mitford as saying :

" Gray was the *first* discoverer of the natural beauties in England, and has marked out the course of every picturesque journey that can be made in it."

The dogmatic absoluteness of such a statement is its own ruin. We have already seen that Gray had at least three predecessors, Dalton, Amory, and Brown, in his recognition of the beauty of the Lake Region, and many a new tour was sought out by later lovers of the picturesque. But Gray's *Journal in the Lakes*, though not first, is certainly most important. Both in feeling and in spontaneity and adequacy of expression it shows a marked advance on his preceding work, and as literature it is distinctly in advance of what others had done.

The whole of this famous tour occupied but three weeks, and the trip in the Lakes but ten days. Gray was by no means so unwearied in sight-seeing as Young. He was " not fond of dirt," and he was fastidious about roads and inns. He did not go on an eager search for views. He did not climb Skiddaw, and he passed by Orrest-Head. He saw what he could see comfortably. His descriptions are quiet and controlled. They have none of the " dizzy raptures " of Brown and Young. There is no straining after epithets, no struggle to find expression adequate to the emotion. The following brief quotations may serve to indicate his style :

" The shining purity of the lake, just ruffled by the breeze, enough to show it is alive."

" The lake majestic in its calmness."

" Little shining torrents hurry down the rocks."

" The grass was covered with a hoar frost, which soon melted, and exhaled in a thin blueish smoke."

" In the evening walked alone down to the lake after sunset and saw the solemn colouring of night draw on, the last gleam of sunshine fading away on the hill-tops, the deep serene of the waters and the long shadows of the mountains thrown across them."

" At distance heard the murmur of many waterfalls not audible in the day-time. Wished for the moon, but she was *dark to me and silent, hid in her vacant interlunar cave.*"

The charm of Gray's descriptions lies in a certain bare perfection of phrase, in his direct, unadorned statement of beautiful facts. His words have a vital, penetrating quality, while his sense of form, his artistic reticence, keep his enthusiasm free from exclamatory extravagances.

Thomas Pennant's first tour in Scotland was made in 1769. The notes taken on this tour were put into shape and published in 1771. Dissatisfied with the result, he went again in 1772, and this *Second Tour in Scotland and the Hebrides* appeared in 1776. In the first tour his professed object was the study of Zoölogy. In the second he was assisted by two friends, one trained in Botany, and the other well up in Scotch customs and legends. But Pennant's interest was not confined to Zoölogy and Botany, to Manners and Customs. His curiosity was omniverous and insatiable. Everything was fish that came to his net, and his industry in note taking was prodigious. The two journeys occupied six months and it takes 570 folio pages to set down what he saw and heard.

In this mass of observations not more than ten pages, all told, have anything to do with the scenery through which he passed. Such descriptive passages as do occur are usually of torrents, rapid, rocky rivers, or the shores of lakes. The best of these are of the banks of the Nith, the falls of Cory-Lin in the Clyde, the Cascades at Moness, which he calls "an epitome of everything that can be admired in the curiosity of waterfalls," the falls and streams near Loch Maree, Ayrsgarth Force in the Ure, the little lake of Barrisdale on the Inverness coast, Coniston, and Derwentwater. He prides himself on being one of the first to describe Coniston. "The scenery about this lake, which is scarcely mentioned, is extremely noble. The east and west sides are bounded by high hills often wooded : but in general composed of grey rock, and coarse vegetation ; much juniper creeps along the surface ; and some beautiful hollies are finely intermixed. At the northwestern extremity the vast mountains called Coniston fells form a magnificent mass. In the midst is a great bosom retiring inward, which affords great quantities of fine slate."

He very often notes wide views, and he has an unfailing interest of a scientific, botanical sort in the forests through which they pass.

He never, however, notes any but the permanent details of a scene. There is not a hint that he saw the varying, evanescent atmospheric effects, so important an element in the beauty and sublimity of mountain scenery. He does admit that the "Highlands like other beauties, have their good and bad days," but there is nothing in his books to show that he knew them apart.

On the whole he shows a preference for a region of smooth, rich, arable land. On leaving the Highlands his comment is,

"The country continually improves; the mountains sink gradually into small hills; the land is highly cultivated, well planted, and well inhabited. I was struck with rapture at a sight so long new to me. Nothing can equal the contrast between the black, barren, dreary, glens of the morning ride and the soft scenes of the evening."

He dislikes the Borrowdale end of Derwentwater where "all the possible variety of Alpine scenery is exhibited, with all the horror of precipice, broken crag, or overhanging rock, or insulated pyramidal hills." He prefers the outlook towards Skiddaw. "But the opposite or northern view is in all respects a strong and beautiful contrast; Skiddaw shows its vast base, and bounding all that part of this vale, rises gently to a height that sinks the neighboring hills; opens a pleasing front, smooth and verdant, smiling over the country like a gentle, generous lord, while the fells of Barrowdale frown upon it like a hardened tyrant. Skiddaw is covered with grass to within half a mile of the summit; after which it becomes stony."

So far as nature is concerned, the passages cited show Pennant at his best. His descriptions are full, clear, painstaking, unimaginative. He is as impersonal and impartial, as conscientiously exact, in taking notes on a landscape as in recording the annual haul of fish in Scotch lakes. Beautiful scenes were to him an object of intellectual curiosity. They made no artistic or emotional appeal. "The visions of the hills and the souls of lonely places" were a strain upon him. He was glad to come forth into fertile valleys and pleasant corn lands.

All this is true, and Pennant shows much less of the new spirit than Brown, Amory, Young, and Gray. But his work was done independently of theirs, and in 1769. He must have been in the Lake District a month before Gray, and he penetrated into much wilder regions of Scotland than had before been described. That his instinctive shrinking from wild scenes should have been

so far overcome as it was, that he should have been often forced
into admiration, is of itself proof of the strength of the new
impulse.

The Rev. William Gilpin made many tours and gave full
accounts of them, but the accounts were not published till years
after the tours were made. His chief travels in their order are,

1. Tour in Norfolk, Cambridge, Suffolk, and Essex (1769;
account published 1809).

2. Tour along the River Wye (1770; pub. 1782).

3. Tour in Cumberland and Westmoreland (1772; pub.
1786).

4. Tour in North Wales (1773; pub. 1809).

5. Tour in Hampshire, Sussex and Kent (1774; pub. 1804).

6. Tour in the Highlands of Scotland (1776; pub. 1789.)

7. Tour in Western England (before 1778; pub. 1798).

Mr. Gilpin's point of view is clearly stated in the preface to
the first of these publications.

"The following little work proposes a new object of pursuit;
that of examining the face of a country by the rules of picturesque
beauty." He hopes that no one will consider his plan unduly
light and trivial for a clergyman. He is himself convinced that
to study the beauty of a country is as noble, in a way as useful,
as to study its agriculture.

By picturesque beauty Gilpin always means beauty that can be
put into a picture. He draws pictures of mountains to show
whether they have or have not a good sky-line. Some are too regu-
lar, some are grotesque, some look deformed. He seldom dwells
long on wide views because they are so difficult to make inter-
esting in a picture. The grandeur of Penmanmaur and Snowden
hardly makes up to him for their lack of picturesqueness. Pen-
manmaur "has no variety of line, but is one heavy lumpish
form." He starts up Snowden, but finding that it is merely "a
collection of mountains formed on the old gigantic plan of heap-
ing mountain on mountain," he does not go to the top,
but contents himself with quoting Pennant's description of the
view.

Gilpin's language is often borrowed from the art of painting.

He calls the steep banks of rivers "side screens;" the changing view before him as he floats down the river is a "front screen." He is always talking about foregrounds and backgrounds and perspective and composition. He says that Nature is "great in design and she is an admirable colourist, and harmonizes tints with infinite variety and beauty; but she is seldom so correct in composition as to produce a harmonious whole. Either the foreground or the background is disproportioned, or some awkward line runs through the piece; or a tree is ill placed, or a bank is formal; or something or other is not as it should be."

With his sense of form Gilpin has also an unusual sensitiveness to color, and to varieties of light and shade. The following description of a sunset is typical:

" The sun was now descending low, and cast the broad shades of evening athwart the landscape, while his beams, gleaming with yellow lustre through the valleys, spread over the inlightened summits of the mountains a thousand lovely tints—in sober harmony where some deep recess was faintly shadowed—in splendid hue where jutting knolls or promontories received fuller radiance of the diverging ray. The air was still. The lake, one vast expanse of crystal mirror. The mountain shadows, which sometimes give the water a deep, black hue (in many circumstances extremely picturesque) were softened here into a mild blue tint which swept over half the surface. The other half received the fair impression of every radiant form that glowed around. The inverted landscape was touched in fainter colours than the real one. Yet it was more than *laid in*. It was almost finished. What an admirable study for the pallet is such a scene as this ! "

"No one can paint a country properly," he says, "unless he has seen it in various lights." The local variations caused by the weather, the time of day, the time of year, "cannot be too much attended to by all lovers of landscape." "Every landscape is seen best under *some peculiar* illumination." He has always the painter's eye for fogs, mist, haze, soft coloring, atmosphere.

Gilpin studied nature according to the rules of art, because, as he said, these rules were drawn from nature. No man resented more quickly than he the transforming hand of man in natural scenes. If lands must be turned to agricultural uses, if fields must be marked off, he only wishes that it might be made as little apparent as possible. He hates "a multiplicity of glaring temples" in a landscape. He thinks most so-called adornments in private grounds are mere "expensive deformity," and he calls regular clipped hedges "objects of deformity." He apologizes for his severe strictures on several estates in the Cumberland region by saying that the grand natural scenes so filled his thought that he could not restrain his contempt for mere embellished, artificial ones. Such passages are an emphatic indication of the revolution in taste since the days of the formal garden. Here is a characteristic sentence written as they leave the Lakes:

"Here the hills grow smooth and lumpish, and the country at every step loses some of the wild strokes of nature and degenerates, if I may so speak, into cultivation."

Not infrequently Gilpin turns from the painter's study of the scene, and gives something of its poetical quality. In speaking of the appeal made by the Lake Country to the imagination he says,

"No tame country, however beautiful, however adorned, can distend the mind like this awful and majestic scenery."

Of Ulzwater on a perfectly serene day he says,

"So solemn and splendid a scene raises in the mind a sort of enthusiastic calm which spreads a mild complacence over the breast, a tranquil pause of mental operations which may be felt but not described."

And again in his *Essay on Picturesque Travel,*

"We are most delighted when some grand scene, though perhaps of incorrect composition, rising before the eyes, strikes us beyond the power of thought—when the *vox faucibus hacret* and every mental operation is suspended. In this pause of intellect, this *deliquum* of the soul, an enthusiastic sensation of pleasure overspreads it. We rather feel than survey the scene."

These last passages inevitably recall Wordsworth's analysis of his own emotions before a beautiful view when

"Thought was not ; in enjoyment it expired,"

or the better known lines in *Tintern Abbey.*

On the whole, Gilpin represents the new spirit more fully than any of the other early travelers. He notes the permanent and the evanescent. He observes color, form, and motion. The severely technical quality of his descriptions does not seriously interfere with the impression they give of pleasure in free, wild nature, and he again and again shows himself capable of an imaginative communion with nature.

In 1773, Mr. Hutchinson and his brother, an accomplished draughtsman, made a tour through the Lakes. In 1774, after the death of his brother, Mr. Hutchinson went over the ground again in order to verify his brother's incomplete sketches. The observations made in these two tours were published under the title *An Excursion to the Lakes in Westmoreland and Cumberland.* Hutchinson's dislike of the wild and desolate region of Stainmore has already been cited, but that quotation alone would give a most unfair impression of the book as a whole. His pleasure in nature is great. He cares especially for artistic effects of light and shade, and he often spends pages on the changing beauty of a landscape seen at sunset, or sunrise, or after a storm. A single passage may stand as illustrative of many similar ones in the book.

"At the foot of this vast range of hills three smaller mounts, of an exact conic form, running parallel, beautified the scene, being covered with verdure to their crowns; the nearest, called Dufton Pike, was shadowed by a passing cloud, save only the summit of its cone, which was touched by a beam which painted it with gold; the second pike was all enlightened and gave its verdure to the prospect as if mantled with velvet; the third stood shadowed, whilst all the range of hills behind were struck with sunshine, showing their cliffs, caverns, and dells in grotesque variety and giving the three pikes a picturesque projection on the landscape;—nature, as if delighted to charm the eye of man, at this time cast an accidental beauty over the scene; the small clouds which chequered the sky, as they passed along, spread their flitting shadows on the distant mountains and seemed to marble them; a beauty which I do not recollect has struck any painter, and which has not been described even by the bold hand of the immortal Poussin."

Mr. Hutchinson had evidently read many of the books treating especially of the beauty of nature. He quotes the whole of Dr. Brown's *Letter* and much of Mr. Dalton's *Poem.* He also quotes freely from Thomson's *Seasons*, Mason's *Garden*, and Pennant's account of Derwentwater. He was familiar with the earlier landscape painting, for he frequently compares pleasing scenes to the work of Claude or Poussin. Some of the most effective descriptions are of the road from Keswick to Ambleside, "the finest ride in the north of England ;" of the cataract near Ambleside. probably Stock Gill Force ; of the ascent of Skiddaw and of a thunderstorm seen from its summit ; of Derwentwater from various points of view, and of a moonlight row upon the lake. They are too long to quote, but they all show faithful and minute observation, artistic appreciation of beauties of form and color, and, occasionally, a lively sense of the deeper significance of the places visited.

The most important English tours were made between 1768 and 1778. Pennant, Gray, Young, Gilpin, and Hutchinson made during this ten years sixteen rather extended journeys, of which they gave full accounts. Besides these we have Dr. Johnson's *A Journey to the Hebrides* (1773 ; pub. 1775), Boswell's *Journal of a Tour to the Hebrides* (1773 ; pub. 1786), and Bray's *Tour Into Derbyshire* (1777). In Boswell's *Journey* there is not the slightest indication of any interest in the scenery through which they passed, and the general impression given by Boswell is that Johnson's indifference was equal to his own. For instance, Boswell wonders at the outset if a man who has known "the felicity of London life" can fail to find any narrower existence "insipid or irksome." He quotes Dr. Johnson as saying at Portree that he "longed to be again in civilized life." He records his famous sayings, "By seeing London I have seen as much of life as the world can show," and "Who *can* like the Highlands?" This is not quite fair to Johnson, because in his own account of the Scotch tour and in his letters there are a few passages that indicate close observation, and even enjoyment, of the wild scenes about him. The finest passage is a description of a storm :

"The night came on while we had yet a great part of the way to go, though not so dark but that we could discern the cataracts which poured down the hills on one side, and fell into one general channel that ran with great violence on the other. The wind was loud, the rain was heavy, and the whistling of the blast, the fall of the shower, the rush of the cataracts, and the roar of the torrent, made a nobler chorus of the rough music of Nature than it had ever been my chance to hear before."

But Johnson's attitude towards the external world was, on the whole, the typical classical one, and is well illustrated by his reply to Mr. Thrale's attempt to win his admiration of a fine prospect.

"Never heed such nonsense ; a blade of grass is always a blade of grass, whether in one country or another.   Let us, if we *do* talk, talk about something ; men and women are my subjects of inquiry."

Mr. Bray's *Tour* has a full map and is written somewhat in the guide-book style. Industries, architecture, history, family chronicles, anecdotes, inscriptions, fill up its 135 closely printed folio pages. There is comparatively little about the scenes through which he passed. In describing the various estates which he visited pages are given to house-furnishings for a single paragraph on the grounds. But these seldom go unnoticed. He dislikes the formal garden. He objects to the regular cascades at Matlock.   He thinks that the conceits in the waterworks at Chatsworth might have been deemed wonderful when they were made, "but those who have contemplated the waterfalls which nature exhibits in this country . . . will receive little pleasure from seeing a temporary stream falling down a flight of steps, spouted out of the mouths of dolphins or dragons, or squirted from the leaves of a copper tree." The most extended description is of the gardens at Stowe, which he praises because, though laid out in the formal style, their regularity has been broken up and disguised. Mr. Bray also shows a liking for wild and romantic scenery. He frequently mentions wide views, and condemns Compton Wyngate because it has no prospect, of which, he adds, "our ancestors appear to have scarce

ever thought." The spots he enjoyed most are Matlock High
Tor, and wild places on the Dore and the Derwent, Aysgarth
Force in the Eure, and rocky Gordale. He noted especially
waterfalls and rivers. Of the Derwent at Matlock he says:

"It is a most romantic and beautiful ride. The river is some-
times hid behind trees, sometimes it glides smooth and calm,
sometimes a distant fall is heard; here it tumbles over a ledge of
rocks stretching quite across, there it rushes over rude fragments,
torn by storms from the impending masses. Each side, but par-
ticularly the farther one, is bordered by lofty rocks, generally
clothed with wood, in the most picturesque manner."

Passages such as this, though perhaps not very effective, show
an attention arrested by the beauties of nature. There is a close-
ness of detail indicating first-hand observation, and the prevailing
tone shows that Mr. Bray justly claims for himself "a taste for
nature in her genuine simplicity."

Of the *Travels* after 1778, numerous as they are, few need
special mention, because almost no really new elements appear in
them. A few new tours are sketched out, as to the Isle of Wight
and the Isle of Man. But in general the same old ground is
gone over, the preference still being accorded to Scotland, Wales,
and the English Lakes. In 1796, but three years before Words-
worth went to Dove Cottage, there appeared four new *Tours* to
the Lakes by Rudworth, Walker, Houseman, and Hutchinson.
In 1794–5 there were five *Tours* in Wales. Of a few of these
books perhaps some mention should be made.

The Rev. Mr. Shaw's *Tour* (1788) in the west of England is
significant for two reasons. It is one of the first books to make
literary associations prominent in the description. He says that
Woodstock is classic ground because Chaucer lived there; Horton
is sacred because of Milton; Beaconsfield, because of Waller;
Windsor Forest, because of Pope; and Stoke Pogis, because of
"the sublime and the pathetic Gray." The second point of sig-
nificance is Mr. Shaw's evident irritation at the apparently over-
weening attention to mountains. He says that if people could
forget Skiddaw and Ben Lomond for a little while they might
be able to see the rich beauty of the champaign country about

Malvern Hills. Mr. Shaw goes back to the "crowds and bustle" of London with great regret because, he says, no matter what society you find there, nothing can make up for the pensive enjoyments of a feeling mind in a picturesque country.

Hassel's *Tour of the Isle of Wight* (1790) is in the style of Gilpin's work. The general knowledge of the Lake Country and the general admiration of it is shown by his comparisons. A certain spot has "all the appearance of a Westmoreland scene." Certain noble hills "rise with all the majesty of the Skiddaw mountains." Hassel's purpose is a search for the picturesque. He especially notes rich effects of color, and the varying lights of sunrise and sunset. He sees nature in a succession of pictures, but his language is free from the technicalities of Gilpin.

Robertson's *Tour in the Isle of Man* (1794) has little effective description, but it is noteworthy as one of the first books of travel to be infected by the sentimental melancholy of the romancers. His Manxmen "recline by some romantic stream" in the true pensive spirit. He visits churchyards and solitary places. He pores over the mazy stream, he watches the rooks, he listens to the sighing evening breeze, very much like one of Mrs. Brooke's lovelorn heroes. Occasionally he has some expressions of deeper import, as when he says that Nature not only charms the eye "but purifies and ennobles the soul." "The mind is filled with divine enthusiasm." He is, however, perhaps adequately characterized by the word "romantic," which he uses until it becomes almost unbearable.

Of *Travels* in general we may say that the transfer of emphasis from man to nature is strongly marked. The love of nature as shown in *Travels* is later in development than it is in poetry, but when the new feeling does find expression it sounds no uncertain note, and by the end of the century has reached a statement as bold and unqualified as that which is found in the poetry itself.

CHAPTER V.

FICTION.

The great achievement of the eighteenth century was in the
development of fiction.   The famous names here are, of course,
Richardson, Fielding, Smollett, and Sterne.   After them, and also
to a less degree, contemporary with them, are many writers of
fiction the quality of whose work has consigned them to the
list of "The Neglected, the Disdained, the Forgotten," and
in most cases it would be a literary misfortune if by any chance
they should fall into the fourth class, "The Resuscitated," As lit-
erature they are almost unreadable.   It is only from the histori-
cal point of view that they can arouse any real interest.   For the
present purpose I do not pretend to have read all the works of
fiction written in the eighteenth century.   The forty-three men-
tioned here were selected because by their dates they represent the
century as a whole, and because they represent also the various
kinds of fiction.   I shall first speak of these briefly in chrono-
logical order, and then indicate such general statements as may
seem the legitimate outcome of the facts presented.   The one
point to be considered is the use made of external nature in the
novel or romance.

The *Sir Roger de Coverley* papers (Addison and Steele, 1712)
are continuous narratives marked by some at least of the charac-
teristics of the coming English novel.   Many of these papers pur-
port to be written from the country and Will Wimble complains
that they "begin to smell confoundedly of woods and meadows."
After a time the author finds himself growing short of subjects in
the country and returns to town as the true "field of game for
sportsmen of his species."   Though written from the country the
papers have nothing about country scenes except frequent phrases
such as, "We then took a walk in the fields," and one brief

description of "a solemn walk of elms," unless, indeed, we might add the pleasure the author took in his friend's poultry yard. The stress is all on country people.

Robinson Crusoe (Defoe, 1719), the first great example of the *voyage imaginaire*, necessarily regards nature from the point of view of immediate utility. The whole interest of the book rests on the mechanical ingenuity whereby man subdues nature. There are few if any passages where Robinson Crusoe is represented as being in any way sensitive to the beauty or charm of nature.

In *Pamela* (Richardson, 1740) there is much talk about the value of travel in Great Britain and on the continent, but there is not a word about the scenery of the places visited. Pamela sums up her impressions of travel in England in one sentence. "These excursions have given me infinite delight and pleasure, and enlarged my notions of the wealth and power of the kingdom." (Vol. 3, p. 304.) When Lord B. and Pamela are spending their honeymoon in their Kentish house they plan certain improvements such as cutting a vista through the coppice ; they train the vines around the windows because they love the mingled odors of woodbines and jessamines ; and they listen for two hours at a stretch to the "responsive songs of two warbling nightingales" (2:163). Earlier in their career, during a walk in the garden, the fragrance from a bank of flowers inspires Lord B. to sing a typical eighteenth century song of which this is one stanza :

> "The purple violet, damask rose,
> Each, to delight your senses, blows.
> The lilies ope as you appear ;
> And all the beauties of the year
> > Diffuse their odours at your feet,
> > Who give to ev'ry flower its sweet."

There is not a hint in the book of any feeling towards nature except such as is characteristic of the pseudo-classical poetry.

In *Joseph Andrews* (Fielding, 1742) there are four brief passages in which nature is touched upon. Two of these are evidently meant as satires on the ordinary descriptions of sunrise. The first one is as follows :

"Aurora now began to show her blooming cheeks over the hills, whilst ten millions of feathered songsters, in jocund chorus, repeated odes a thousand times sweeter than those of our laureate" (p. 43. Cf. p. 219). The longest description is of a vale with a winding rivulet, many trees, and soil "spread with a verdure which no paint could imitate," the whole place being such as "might have raised romantic ideas in older minds than those of Joseph and Fanny" (p. 226).

In *Jonathan Wild* (Fielding, 1743) there are no references to the world of nature.

In *David Simple* (Sarah Fielding, 1744) the search of the hero for a true friend is so complicated and absorbing an occupation that there is no room for observation of the external world.

In *Clarissa Harlowe* (Richardson, 1748) there is one simile drawn from nature (2:478), one mention of the "variegated prospects" from Hampstead Heath (3:198) and one reference to an overgrown ivy so thick as to be a shelter from the rain (1:394).

In *Roderick Random* (Smollett, 1748) there are no references to nature.

Of the eight passages referring to nature in *Tom Jones* (Fielding, 1749) two are satirical of the conventional descriptions and similitudes of the day.

"Aurora now first opened her casement, *Anglicè*, the day began to break" (2: 9).

"As in the month of June, the damask rose, which chance hath planted among the lilies, with their candid hues mixes his vermilion; or, as some playful heifer in the pleasant month of May diffuses her odoriferous breath over the flowery meadows; or as, in the blooming month of April, the gentle, constant dove, perched on some fair bough, sits meditating on her mate," so sits Sophia, "looking a hundred charms, and breathing as many sweets, her thoughts being fixed on her Tommy" (2: 61).

A third passage, also satirical, is,

"And now the moon began to put forth her silver light, as the poets call it (though she looked at that time more like a piece of copper)" (2: 172). There is one appreciative reference to the attractive scenery of Devon and Dorset. The description of Mr.

Allworthy's estate which owed "less to art than to nature," is modern in tone and marks the break already made with the formal garden (1 : 12).   In another passage there is an expression of pleasure in a wide prospect, seen by moonlight, for "the solemn light which the moon casts on all objects is beyond expression beautiful, especially to an imagination which is desirous of cultivating melancholy ideas" (1:422).   The other passages are of no significance.

Peter Wilkins (Robert Paltock, 1750) is the first and most famous of the successors of *Robinson Crusoe*. The scene of Peter's trials and successes is laid in Africa and the southern islands. There is but one brief passage in which there is even the slightest indication that the author thought of nature from any but the utilitarian point of view.

Pompey the Little (Coventry, 1751) is a romance ostensibly relating with serio-comic minuteness the life and adventures of a lapdog much in the manner of the *Novele picaresco* of Mendozo and Aleman, but really dealing in thinly disguised social satire. It makes no use of nature, unless we may count poor Mr. Rhymer who looks at the moon and quotes Milton to the extravagant amusement of a group of dandies who observe him.

In *Peregrine Pickle* (Smollett, 1751) Peregrine sings one of the conventional songs to Emilia, beginning,

> " Thy charms divinely bright appear
> And add new splendor to the year."

This is the only use of nature in the book. The eighteen months of travel in France and Holland do not suggest a single phrase about the scenery of those countries.

Mrs. Lennox's *The Female Quixote* (1752) is a record of the absurd and futile attempts of a beautiful maiden unfortunately brought up on " the languishing love romances of the Calprenedos and the Scuderis" to make over the practical world about her according to the laws of love and chivalry. Almost all her adventures occur in the country, but there are only two references to the outdoor world. Of the estate of the marquis it is said:

" The most laborious endeavours of art had been expended to

make it appear like the beautiful product of wild uncultivated nature."

In another passage the heroine is said to lead her unhappy friend into the garden, "supposing a person whose uneasiness proceeded from love would be pleased with the sight of groves and streams."

In *Ferdinand Count Fathom* (Smollett, 1753) there is merely a conventional description of a furious storm.

In *Sir Charles Grandison* (Richardson, 1753) there are two interesting passages concerning the estate of Sir Charles. It was his aim not "to force and distort nature, but to help it as he finds it, without letting art be seen in his works, where he can possibly avoid it (2: 276). A part of the estate was evidently laid out according to the ideas of Kent and Brown, but the orchard "with its regular semicircle rows of pears, apples, cherries, plums and apricots, arranged according to the season of flowering," belonged to the days of Sir Thomas, when symmetry and regularity ruled (4:238). In this novel also is Richardson's frequently quoted description of Savoy, "equally noted for its poverty and rocky mountains. . . . one of the worst countries under heaven " (3:138–142).

We have now passed the middle of the century and there has not been in the works of fiction mentioned a single passage indicating any close observation or love of nature, and hardly a passage showing any knowledge of nature except as found in parks and gardens. But in 1756–66 there appeared a fantastic novel by Thomas Amory called *The Life of John Buncle*, which is notable in the present study because nearly all the adventures whereby the hero gains and loses his seven Socinian wives occur among the mountains of Westmoreland and Cumberland. We have but to compare the book with Mrs. Ward's *Robert Elsmere* to see how extravagantly unreal are most of Amory's descriptions. They often contain marvels equal to those of *Vathek*. The mountains are made as lofty and dangerous as the most inaccessible Alps, and they are so heaped in together that progress from one valley to another would be out of the question were it not for convenient caves and natural tunnels by which the venturesome hero makes his way from vale to vale.   But in the midst of these absurdities and impossiblities, there are occasional passages of effective description, and of real appreciation of wild mountain scenery.   It is an entirely new note in fiction and it followed close upon the poem by Dr. Dalton, which was probably the first poetical tribute to the scenery of the Lakes.   Mr. Amory aptly describes mountain tarns as pools of " black, standing, unfathomable water." (Vol. 1, p. 290.)   He frequently gives enthusiastic descriptions of the views from mountain tops.   In one passage he says :

" I climbed up to the top by a steep, craggy way.   This was very difficult and dangerous, but I had an enchanting prospect when I gained the summit of the hill. . . . . The vast hills had a fine effect in the view" (2: 122; cf. 1: 167).

Of Westmoreland he says :

" The Vale of Keswick and Lake of Derwentwater, in Cumberland, are thought by those who have been there to be the finest point of view in England, and extremely beautiful they are, far more so than Dr. Dalton has been able to make them appear in his descriptive poem ; or than the Doctor's brother, Mr. Dalton, has painted them in his fine drawings ; and yet they are inferior in charms to the vale, the lake, the brooks, the shaded sides of the surrounding mountains, and the tuneful falls of water to which we came in Westmoreland.   In all the world, I believe, there is not a more glorious scene to be seen in the fine time of the year " (3: 93).   And, again, " Westmoreland is the most beautiful and romantic solitude in the world " (3: 151). The first volume of Amory's book appeared in 1756. The other volumes written at intervals thereafter, were published in 1766. The best passages are in the third volume, but at the latest they must have been written three years before Gray made his tour to the lakes. It would be interesting to know whether Gray had read *John Buncle*, as Amory had Dalton's poem.   At any rate Amory's novel shows how early the Lake District was visited by lovers of the beautiful, for he not only describes it himself, but he speaks as if there were already a good deal of discussion as to the rival charms of Keswick and Westmoreland.

In *Rasselas* (Dr. Johnson, 1759) the scenery of the Happy Valley is briefly described. Since it was a spot where "all the diversities of the world were brought together, the blessings of nature were collected, and its evils were extracted and excluded," it would be in vain to look for first-hand description. We have merely an impossible combination of millennial details. After leaving the Happy Valley Imlac wanders through the world, but his only impression from nature is a feeling of repulsion at the "barren uniformity" of the ocean. When he tried to be a poet he did, to be sure, turn to nature. He "ranged mountains and deserts for images and similitudes" in true classical style. He studied trees and flowers, he wandered along rivulets, and sometimes he watched the clouds, for "to a poet nothing can be useless." Dr. Johnson's use of nature in *Rasselas* is tasteless and insipid.

Sterne's one allusion to nature in *Tristram Shandy* (1759–67) is too characteristic to be omitted. It occurs in the description of a journey.

"There is nothing more terrible to travel-writers than a large rich plain, especially if it is without great rivers or bridges ; and presents nothing to the eye but one unvaried picture of plenty ; for after they have once told you that it is delicious or delightful (as the case may happen); that the soil was grateful and that nature pours out all her abundance, etc., they have then a large plain upon their hands which they know not what to do with and which is of little or no use to them but to carry them to the next town."

In *Almoran and Hamet* (Hawkesworth, 1761), an Oriental Tale, there is no use of nature except in a few far fetched similes, and one or two phrases about the lengthening evening shadows.

In *Sir Launcelot Greaves* (Smollett, 1762) there is no reference to nature except in a sarcastic allusion to poets who cannot talk of a beautiful girl without "blending the lily and the rose and bringing in a parcel of similes of cowslips, carnations, pinks, and daisies."

Mrs. Brooke's *The History of Lady Julia Mandeville* (1763)

has a hero and a heroine who rejoice in "a genuine taste for elegant nature," and their letters contain some descriptive passages evidently intended to combine vividness and elegance. The gardens and parks behind the house are "romantic beyond the wantonness of imagination," and the whole adjoining country has "every charm of lovely unadorned nature." Beyond the house there is "an avenue of the tallest trees which lets in the prospect of a fruitful valley, bounded at a distance by a mountain, down the sides of which rushes a foaming cascade, which spreads into a thousand meandering streams in the vale below." In the woods are rustic temples "in the most elegant style of simplicity." At the close of a walk they come to a grotto "wildly lovely, its entrance almost hidden by the vines that flaunt over its top," and there they find an opportune repast with servants in attendance. The motherly care with which Mrs. Brooke preserves her delicately bred characters from roughness or fatigue or hunger interferes somewhat with her attempts to represent "simple, unadorned nature," and in spite of her protests against "the gloomy haunts of London" she never quite gets out into the free country. Her raptures have a forced, made-up air. The exclamatory ecstacy of such passages as the following is certainly open to suspicion :

"What a divine morning ! how lovely is the face of nature! The blue serene of Italy with the lovely verdure of England ! But behold a more charming object than nature herself ! The sweet, the young, the blooming Lady Julia!"

There is a more genuine ring to Lady Wilmot's protest,

"The finest landscape is a dreary wild without people."

Most of the action in Mrs. Brooke's second novel, *Emily Montague*, is laid in Canada, which country Mrs. Brooke had visited. The book represents her enjoyment of the strange scenes about her. The beauty of the river Montmorenci more than repays Miss Arabella Fermor for the fatigues of a voyage across the Atlantic. The hero finds that the streams and mountains of England seem petty when he is in the presence of the majesty and sublimity of the western world. The descriptions are perhaps over elaborate, but they are not ineffective, and they show much closer knowledge of natural phenomena and more real interest in them than do the tamer passages in the preceding novel.

In the famous *Castle of Otranto* (Walpole, 1764) there is no use whatever of nature.

In Brooke's *Fool of Quality* (1766) the sky is fitly spoken of as "a stupendous expanse sumptuously furnished with a profusion of planets." Certainly no other sort of sky would have presumed to bend down over Mr. Brooke's stupendous little prig of a hero. The chief use of nature, however, is in similes for Harry's countenance which is "like sunshine on a dark day," or a "lake on a summer's evening showing heaven in its bosom," or, if bathed in tears as it frequently was, "like the sun in a shower."

The charm of *The Vicar of Wakefield* (Goldsmith, 1766) rests upon its sweetness and purity, its quaint humor, and its quality of fresh, open-air wholesomeness. Its use of nature is of the most casual, unemphasized sort. There are not in the whole work twenty-five lines concerning the country scenes in which all the action takes place. And yet these simple, direct phrases have a magical power of suggestion. The seat under the hawthorn where the family drank their tea and watched the sunset, the dinner in the hayfield, the brief description of the little farm, have in them the power of reality and do more to give a free, out of-doors atmosphere to the story than all Mrs. Brooke's panegyrics. But here, as in Goldsmith's other works, the stress is on the characters, and the little, truthful pictures of nature seem almost accidental.

In Sterne's *Sentimental Journey* (1768) there is no use of external nature.

Of Mackenzie's *Man of Feeling* (1771) the same may be said unless, indeed, we except one reference to a scene "not unlike Salvator's back-grounds."

Smollett's *Humphrey Clinker* (1771) is the last of his novels and the only one in which there is effective use of nature. Smollett was born and brought up in the valley of the Leven; and he spent some months there before the final trip to Italy for his health. He was in Leghorn about a year before he died and during this year he wrote *Humphrey Clinker*. It recounts the travels of Matthew Bramble in search of health. The love of nature comes out chiefly in the letters supposed to be written from Scotland. He speaks with pleasure of the "huge dusky mountains of the West Highlands, piled one over another," and of Loch Lomond, that "surprising body of pure, transparent water, unfathomably deep in many places" with its green, wooded islands. "I have seen the Lago di Gardi," he exclaims, " Albano, De Vico, Bolsena, and Geneva, and, upon my honor, I prefer Loch Lomond to them all; a preference which is certainly owing to the verdant islands that seem to float upon its surface, affording the most enchanting objects of repose to the excursive view. Nor are the banks destitute of beauties, which even partake of the sublime. On this side they display a sweet variety of woodland, cornfield, and pasture, with several agreeable villas emerging as it were out of the lake, till at some distance the prospect terminates in huge mountains, covered with heath, which being in the bloom, affords a very rich covering of purple. Everything here is romantic beyond imagination (p. 261).

"Above the house is a romantic glen or cleft of a mountain covered with hanging woods, having at bottom a stream of fine water that forms a number of cascades in its descent to form the Leven; so that the scene is quite enchanting . . . . This country is amazingly wild, especially towards the mountains, which are heaped upon the backs of one another, making a most stupendous appearance of savage nature, with hardly any signs of cultivation, or even of population. All is sublimity, silence, and solitude" (p. 263–265).

In the country of Ossian they find especial delight:

"These are the lonely hills of Morven, where Fingal and his heroes enjoyed the same pastime. I feel an enthusiastic pleasure when I survey the brown heath that Ossian was wont to tread; and hear the wind whistle through the bending grass . . . . The poems of Ossian are in every mouth."

Smollett's love for the Leven, that "charming stream . . . . transparent, pastoral, delightful," is further evidenced by his *Ode to the Leven*, a single stanza of which may be quoted here :

> " Pure stream in whose transparent wave
> My youthful limbs I wont to lave;
> No torrents stain thy limpid source,
> No rocks impede thy dimpling course,
> That sweetly warbles o'er its bed,
> With white round polished pebbles spread" (p. 262).

Smollett has one character who labored under αλροφοβια, or *horror of green fields*, but that was manifestly not his own case. Though he completely ignored nature in his other books, *Humphrey Clinker* is ample proof of his sensitiveness to nature and his descriptive power. It needed a touch of homesickness and the vivifying force of early associations to bring the feeling to the surface, but as soon as it found expression there was revealed a closeness of observation and a genuineness of affection for nature in her milder forms not found in any novel before *Humphrey Clinker*. The nearest approach to it is in the fantastic work of Amory.

In Clara Reeve's *Old English Baron* (1777) there is one brief conventional passage about the morning serenade of the birds and the fragrance of the woodbine (p. 27).

In *Julia de Roubigné* (1777) Mackenzie makes more use of nature than he had in *The Man of Feeling*. Julia and Savillon are both represented as finding pleasure in the beautiful country around them. In one letter Julia says,

" Methinks I should hate to have been born in a town; when I say my native brook, or my native hill, I talk of friends of whom the remembrance warms my heart." In the serenity of nature she finds calmness after spiritual tumult. Belville, the home of Julia, is described as "a venerable pile, the remains of ancient Gothic magnificence." The most attractive part of the estate was "a wild and rocky dell, where tasteless wealth had never warred on nature, nor even elegance refined or embellished her beauties. The walks are only worn by the tread of shepherds and the banks only smoothed by the feeding of their flocks." There is great regret expressed when the new owner of Belville cuts down the trees, and puts in modern adornments "which they call Chinese." In this novel Mackenzie shows a real though narrow appreciation of free, unsubdued nature.

In Fanny Burney's *Evelina* (1778) the only touch of nature is a criticism of Vauxhall Gardens as being too formal and regular. In *Cecilia* (1782) there is no use of nature.

William Beckford's *Vathek* (1784) is an extravaganza where there is no pretense of representing nature as it is. A single quotation will give the general tone. It is a description of a high mountain:

" Upon it grew a hundred thickets of eglantine and other fragrant shrubs, a hundred arbours of roses, jessamines and honeysuckle, as many clumps of orange trees, cedar, and citron whose branches interwoven with the palm, the pomegranate, and the vine, presented every luxury that could regale the eye or the taste. The ground was strewed with violets, harebells, and pansies, in the midst of which sprang forth tufts of jonquils, hyacinths, and carnations, with every other perfume that impregnates the air."

In Dr. Moore's *Zeluco* (1789) neither the hero himself, that " finished model of depravity," nor any of the characters associated with him, show any knowledge of the existence of any world outside their own intrigues and counter-intrigues.

Mrs. Inchbald's *A Simple Story* (1791) is a study of true and false education. There is in it no word concerning nature. The same may be said of her *Nature and Art*, published in 1796.

Godwin's story, *Caleb Williams* (1794), has one brief, conventional description of a sunrise. This ignoring of nature seems the more surprising in Godwin since his next novel, published ten years later, *Fleetwood, or the New Man of Feeling*, is full of the wild scenery of Wales and is really the study of a character made sensitive by early and constant communion with nature. But this novel would carry us into the next century.

Another novel of some repute towards the close of the century is Robert Bage's *Hemsprong, or Man as He is Not* (1796). It was read chiefly for its political bias towards the popular democratical doctrines. The scene is laid chiefly in the country and there are occasional pleasant bits of description. They are unimportant, but the book cannot be dismissed without a reference to the hero who was compelled, by lack of funds, to seek a country retreat, and who fortified his failing resolution to leave the beloved city by quoting Thomson's *Seasons*.

The two authors who first made extensive use of nature in fiction are Mrs. Charlotte Smith and Mrs. Ann Radcliffe.

Mrs. Smith shows in her novels and poems a really ardent enjoyment, though seldom a close knowledge of nature. She indulges in long and animated descriptions of places of which she has only vaguely heard and the result is sometimes as amazing as the scenes in *Vathek*. In *The Old Manor House* (1793), her best work, a part of the scene is laid in the northern United States and Canada. Here is her idea of spring in that region:

"The forest in only a few hours after the severest weather, which had buried the whole country in snow, burst into bloom, and presented, beneath the tulip tree and the magnolia, a more brilliant variety of flowers than art can collect in the most cultivated European garden."

"The following is a description of Canada on the banks of the St. Lawrence, "a very few days" after the severest winter weather:

"On the opposite side of the river lay an extensive savannah, alive with cattle and coloured with such a variety of swamp plants that their colour, even at that distance, detracted something from the vivid green of the new-sprung grass . . . . The acclivity on which the tents stood sinking very suddenly on the left, there gave place to a cyprus swamp . . . . while the rocks rising suddenly and sharply were clothed with wood of various species; the evergreen oak, the scarlet oak, the tulip tree and magnolia, seemed bound together by festoons of flowers, some resembling the convolvuleses of our garden, and others the various sorts of clematis with vegenias and the Virginia creeper . . . . beneath these fragrant wreaths that wound about the trees, tufts of rhododendrons, and azalia, of andromedas and calmias, grew in the luxuriant beauty; and strawberries already ripening, or even ripe, peeped forth among the rich vegetation of grass and flowers."

Mrs. Smith's imagination certainly had other laws than the

dull ones imposed by the facts of the case. She could hardly have mixed up zones and seasons and flowers and fruits more successfully if she had tried. But the notable point here is that there was in her mind an instinctive and inevitable dwelling upon the scenery of the country through which she led her hero. The English scenes are much better. The following passage shows well her emotional openness to the influence of nature.

"Just as he arrived at the water, from the deep gloom of the tall firs through which he passed, the moon appeared behind the opposite coppices, and threw her long line of trembling radiance on the water. It was a cold but clear evening, and, though early in November, the trees were not yet entirely stripped of their discoloured leaves; a low wind sounded hollow through the firs and stone pines over his head, and then faintly sighed among the reeds that crowded into the water; no other sound was heard but, at distant intervals, the cry of the wild fowl concealed among them, or the dull murmur of the current, which was now low. Orlando had hardly ever felt himself so impressed with those feelings which inspire poetic effusions: Nature appeared to pause and to ask the turbulent and troubled heart of man, whether his silly pursuits were worth the toil he undertook for them. Peace and tranquillity seemed here to have retired to a transient abode; and Orlando as slowly he traversed the narrow path over ground made hollow by the roots of these old trees, stepped as lightly as if he feared to disturb them. Insensibly he began to compare this scene, the scene he everyday saw of rural beauty and rural content with those into which his destiny was about to lead him."

Mrs. Barbauld says that Mrs. Smith was one of the first to introduce description of scenery into fiction. That she had predecessors we have already seen, but it is true that she laid much more stress on nature than had any other novelist except Mrs. Radcliffe. Mrs. Smith has frequent descriptions that are not needed for the progress of the plot or the development of the characters, but are written purely for their own sake. She also often uses nature as dramatic background and she represents her hero as deeply influenced by nature. Mrs. Smith's poems further attest her love of nature. In one poem she says,

> " Farewell, Aruna! on whose varied shore
> My early vows were paid to Nature's shrine."

In another she addresses the South Downs,

> " Ah, hills beloved, where once a happy child,
> Your beechen shades, your turfs, your flowers among,
> I wove your bluebells into garlands wild."

Mrs. Smith's life was a most unhappy one, and she found her real comfort in nature.

Mrs. Radcliffe's *Romance of a Forest*—(1791) appeared two years before *The Old Manor House*, and *The Mysteries of Udolpho* (1794) one year after. In these novels by Mrs. Radcliffe the romantic landscape was presented in its complete form. Except in the most rapid parts of the story there is greater stress on the scenery than on the characters. Emily, Adeline, and Clara seldom indulge in an emotion without first describing the dell or glen or forest glade, to which they have wandered. They are never too deeply agitated to observe the glories of sunrise and sunset. A wide view can sooth any grief. This susceptibility of the heroines to nature is represented as one of their greatest charms. Mrs. Radcliffe had never seen most of the scenes she described. She had never been in France, Italy, or Switzerland. The landscapes she gives us do not bear the stamp of reality. They are ideal compositions but they are never merely an inventory nor are they impossible combinations. Though not exactly true, they can be read with pleasure because the details are blended into harmonious and lovely pictures which seem to have caught the actual spirit of the places described. She delighted in all kinds of nature, peaceful or wild, but her especial pleasure was in those phases of nature ignored by the classicists. Mountains, the ocean, the phenomena of the sky, and deep forests are chiefly dwelt upon in her descriptions. Her love of the ocean is really a new element in the general attitude towards nature. Painting, poetry, and fiction had up to this time practically ignored the ocean, but Mrs. Radcliffe in frequent passages shows that her own feeling was that of Adeline, of whom she says,

"Of all the grand objects which nature had exhibited the

ocean supplied her with the most sublime admiration.   She loved
to wander alone by its shore."   It is, however, in the representation
of forest scenes that Mrs. Radcliffe's most effective work is done.
The wild and terrifying influence of the dark woods that cover
the Appenines, all the dim and shadowy loveliness, all the mys-
tery and suggestiveness of the romantic forest about the ruined
abbey reappear in her descriptions.   Her feeling towards moun-
tains is one of almost extravagant delight in their vastness, their
wildness, their remoteness, and inaccessibility.   She is deeply
sensitive to all the "goings on" in the sky.   She catches with
accuracy the most ethereal, delicate, evanescent effects.   It is
especially mystery and remoteness that she loves, hence night,
moonlight, and stars attract her.   Closely connected with her
pleasure in the sky is her artistic openness to all aërial transfor-
mations.   In her wide views over land and sea, in vistas caught
through forest glades, in pictures of twilight, or dawn, of sunrise,
or sunset, she seldom fails to note the quick shiftings of color
and form, the interplay of light and shade, the dimness, the trans-
parence , the luminosity, resulting from atmospheric changes.

She looked upon nature not only, as she said of one of her own
characters, "with the eye of an artist, but with the raptures of a
poet."   The effect of nature on man in soothing his grief, modi-
fying his passions, and elevating his character is everywhere
insisted upon.   As Adeline's eyes "wandered through the roman-
tic glades that opened into the forest her heart was gladdened."
Through the melancholy boughs the evening twilight which still
coloured the air, " diffused a solemnity that vibrated in thrilling
sensations upon the hearts of the travellers. . . .   The
tranquillity of the scene, which autumn had touched with her
sweetest tints, softened her mind to a tender kind of melancholy."

The Alps " filled her mind with sublime emotions."   The
solitary grandeur of these scenes both "assisted and soothed
the melancholy of her heart." . . .   The stillness and total
seclusion of the scene, the stupendous mountains, the gloomy
grandeur of the woods, "diffuse a sacred enthusiasm over the
mind and awaken sensations truly sublime." . . .   Such a
scene "fills the soul with emotions of indescribable awe, and

seems to lift it to a nobler nature." . . . "It was in the tranquil observation of beautiful nature" that Clara's mind recovered its tone. . . . The moonlight on the sea seemed to "diffuse peace." . . . Twilight sometimes "inspires the mind with pensive tenderness," sometimes "exalts it to sublime mediations." The Alps inspire reflections that "soften and elevate the heart and fill it with the certainty of a present God." Such expressions were repeated with an insistence that becomes monotonous. There is, indeed, an element of sameness in all the descriptions, an effect the more tiresome because they are so numerous. So large a descriptive element would hardly be admitted in a novel today unless justified by some remarkable power of word painting. Mrs. Radcliffe's descriptions would doubtless invite the modern reader, at least after a steady progress through four or five volumes, to do some judicious skipping. But thought of as in her own day, Mrs. Radcliffe must always rank as a discoverer, so new and fresh was this element she brought into fiction. As is usual with discoverers she overworked her idea. She was not a great genius. She was often weakly sentimental. But she had a genuine and most ardent love of nature, and, when at her best, had exceptional descriptive power. Her fame and her influence on succeeding literature rest on these characteristics.

In *Fiction*, as in *Travels* and *Poetry* and *Gardening*, there is the transfer of interest from what man does or is to the powers of untrammeled nature. The new spirit here, as in *Travels*, is late in finding adequate expression. We can hardly put any real beginnings of it earlier than *John Buncle* (1756-66). Even after that, development is spasmodic and slow. In most of the novels and romances we find the romantic impulse to see strange lands, but men and manners absorb the attention of the travelers. Mrs. Radcliffe's fugitives in *The Romance of the Forest*, the travelers in *The Mysteries of Udolpho*, and Mrs. Brooke's soldier in *Emily Montague* are really the first to make much of the scenery through which they pass.

In general we may say that novels had little to do with nature, and romances much. This may account for the lack of reality in the descriptions. There is nothing in any work of fiction at all correspondent to the temperate, truthful, clear-cut work of Cowper and Burns. There is practically nothing of the bald realism of John Scott, whose poetry was written rather in the scientific temper with which most travels were undertaken. Nor, on the other hand, is there anything of the visionary, mystical power of Blake. The best use of nature in fiction is more akin to the emotionalism of Beattie. Really, except for Mrs. Radcliffe, and she came late in the century, fiction contributed less to bring about the new attitude towards nature than did any other form of art expression, except, perhaps, landscape painting.

CHAPTER VI.

LANDSCAPE PAINTING.

Two serious difficulties present themselves in any attempted study of the development of English landscape painting up to 1800. One difficulty is that most of the pictures are practically inaccessible, many of them being known only by name and the more famous ones being scattered through various private and public galleries. The second difficulty in tracing any progress or development is that the pictures are usually undated. As a rule the most that can be known is that such and such a picture belongs in the earlier or later portion of the artist's productive period. Furthermore, any adequate study would require close knowledge of artistic technicalities and mechanical processes, for much of the development is along the line of improved paper, better pigments, new methods of work.

A recognition of these difficulties confines the following brief sketch to very narrow lines. But fortunately the objective point in the present study renders first-hand and technical knowledge less imperative than it would otherwise be. It is not so much the artist's method or his degree of success that is here of interest. It is rather what his tastes led him to wish to do, what subjects he thought worthy of serious study, what conception of nature guided his work. Such information may be fairly gleaned from biographies, letters, historical accounts, and critical essays.[1]

[1] In this sketch the following works have been used :
Adolph Siret : Dictionnaire Historique des Peintres.
Spooner : Dictionary of Painters.
Champlin and Perkins : Cyclopedia of Painters and Paintings.
Bryan : Dictionary of Painters and Engravers.
Cunningham : British Painters.
Brydall : Art in Scotland.
Redgrave : Water Colour Painting in England.

Up to 1725 English painting is almost entirely concerned with portraits and occasional historical pictures. Even a landscape background is of rare occurrence. The same spirit prevails throughout the eighteenth century; the predominating interest is in such aspects of painting as have especially to do with man. But along with this interest in portraits and historical representations, there was growing up an interest in landscape for its own sake; and in the pictures where the human element still ruled there was a change from the portrait of the noble lord or lady, to pictures of humble life in rustic surroundings. It is this twofold change that is to be briefly indicated here.[1]

Though Gainsborough and Wilson are usually counted the founders of the modern English school of landscape painting, we find indications that before their day some essays had been made towards the representation of nature. Francis Place (d. 1728) is casually mentioned as having painted "a few landscapes" for his own amusement. Samuel Scott, whose work comes after 1725, was called the best marine painter of his time. Two fine examples of his work are *Westminster Bridge, 1745*, and *London Bridge, 1745*. George Lambert (1710–1765) is said by Bryan to be "the first English painter who treated landscape with a pleasing and picturesque effect." John Wooton (d. 1765) painted chiefly racehorses and hunting scenes. In 1727 he illustrated Gay's *Fables*. He also painted "excellent landscapes"

[1] Biese in Die Entwickelung des Naturgefühls, pp. 209–248, gives a brief résumé of the development of landscape painting in Germany. He calls Rubens and his school the first to make the painting of nature an independent branch of art, while Ruysdael (1681) is the one in whom "die ganze Poesie der Natur" finds expression. His chapter closes with these words: "Alle diese grossen Niederländer eilen weit der Poesie ihrer Zeit voraus; Gebirge und Meer finden im Wort erst 100 Jahre später ihre begeisterten Schilderer, und ein in sich stimmungsvoll, abgeschlossenes, lyrisches Landschaftsbild wird erst am Ende des achtzehnten Jahrhunderts in der deutschen Dichtung geboren." In England, it will be observed, the love of nature finds earlier and more abundant expression in poetry than in painting, and its completest expression in Wordsworth's poetry precedes its complete expression in the great English landscape painters of the early 19th century. See also for brief résumé of "Landschaftsmalerei" as an indication mainly of the increasing knowledge of distant lands new forms of vegetation, etc., Humboldt, Kosmos, Vol. 2, pp. 47–58.

in the Italian style. The Smiths of Chichester were brothers who attained much local celebrity by the landscapes they painted of the scenery in their own neighborhood. Their work comes after 1735. Of more importance is Paul Sandby (1725–1809), a talented artist who at eighteen went as a draughtsman with the Duke of Cumberland through the Scotch Highlands, and who was so deeply impressed with the beautiful scenery that he brought back many drawings of it. Nine years later he made seventy drawings of the scenery about Windsor. He also traveled in North and South Wales and made many drawings of the picturesque scenery there. He is called " the first to infuse nature into topographical drawings."[1] An Irish painter of this period was John Butts (d. 1764), the talented pupil of a mediocre artist named Rogers, who is called the father of landscape art in Ireland. Butts's early landscapes were " impressive copies from the wild scenes which abound in the county of Cork, and the romantic views that abound on the margin of Black Water." Brydall says that James Norris was " probably the first to create, or at least to minister to the taste for landscape painting in the Scottish metropolis." Alexander Runciman (1736–1785) began to paint landscapes when he was but twelve years old. " Other artists," it was said, " talked meat and drink, but Runciman talked landscape." He exhibited landscapes in 1755, but finding that no one would buy his pictures he turned, in 1750, to historical paintings. One of Runciman's most romantic undertakings was the decoration of the hall at Pennycuik with paintings representing the poems of Ossian.

From this brief summary of landscape art in Great Britain before 1755 it will be seen that, late and feeble as were these beginnings, they are yet significant of the coming treatment of nature in art. There is an effort to represent landscape, an evident enjoyment of it, some first-hand study, and some pleasure in the wilder aspects of the external world.

---

[1] Scott, in his Essay on Painting, speaks of "Smith's delightful spots " and 'Sandby's pleasant fields." In the same Essay he proposes hay-fields and hop-grounds as new subjects of landscape, acknowledging that he is indebted for the idea to Walpole.

The period before 1755 may properly be called the period of inception. The rest of the century is the period of establishment, at the very beginning of which stand Gainsborough and Wilson.

Richard Wilson (1713–1782) intended to be a portrait painter and went to Italy to study under Zuccarelli. While there he sketched a landscape in "an idle hour" and was straightway persuaded by Zuccarelli and Vernet that he had found his true work. His success was almost immediate. In 1755 he returned to England and in 1760 exhibited the "Niobe" which established his reputation as a landscape painter. For the representation of nature he had a twofold preparation, his youth in Wales and his years of study in Italy. "He had long," says Allan Cunningham, "been insensibly storing his mind with the beauties of natural scenery, and the picturesque mountains and glens of his native Wales had been to him an academy when he was unconscious of their influence." In Italy he was led by his extravagant admiration of Claude to study such landscape effects as Claude had produced. His appreciation of nature was doubtless, as Cunningham says, greatly strengthened by his early surroundings, but it was the years in Italy that determined his choice of artistic themes. He always preferred scenes of classic fame. The four pictures in the Vernon Gallery, "The Ruined Temple," "Ruins in Italy," "Hadrian's Villa," and "Lake Avernus," are fine characteristic specimens of his work. But though his pictures are foreign in subject and manner of treatment, and though he did sometimes introduce "gods, goddesses and ideal beings" into his landscapes, he was nevertheless the first of English artists to show the possibilities of landscape art. He loved his work passionately and became so devoted to it that he lost all interest in men or in animals except as they "composed well" in his landscapes. He did not copy other painters, but depended on nature for his inspiration. While he counted painting "facsimiles of scenes" mere "unpoetic drudgery," he was always true to the general spirit of the landscape. Cunningham says that he caught the very "hue and character of Italian scenery." "He observed Nature in all her appearances," says Fuseli, "and had a characteristic touch for all her forms." There was, moreover, a grandeur and sublimity of conception, a depth and tenderness of poetic feeling about Wilson's pictures such as is not found in English landscapes again before Girtin. Cunningham sums up his work in the following words: " Wilson had a poet's feeling and a poet's eye, selected his scenes with judgment and spread them out in beauty and in all the fresh luxury of nature. He did for landscape what Reynolds did for faces—with equal genius, but far different fortune."

Sir George Beaumont, himself an amateur artist of no small ability, said that Wilson's genius had the qualities of Gray's poem *The Bard*, while Gainsborough was more akin to *The Elegy*.

The point of this remark so far as Gainsborough (1727–1788) is concerned must be simply that he was distinctively the painter of rural England. His love of nature was early shown. Before he was twelve it was his delight to spend his mornings in the woods of Suffolk sketching from streams, trees, cattle, sheep, and peasants. From fourteen to eighteen he was in a London academy studying portrait painting, but though he made that his business, "landscape had his heart." "Madam Nature, not man, was his sole study," says Thickesse speaking of later days at Ipswich. He said himself that to be well-read in the volume of nature was all the learning he wished. He rebelled against the doctrine of the schools. He said that landscape could be studied only from nature herself and felt with Hogarth that the canvas should not be "thrust between the student and the sky—tradition between him and God." So far as earlier artists influenced him at all it was the Dutch and Flemish schools whose methods he studied. He gave especial attention to Wynants and Ruysdael. His earlier pictures show " close adherence to local scenery and minute and careful finishing," as for instance the " young oak painted leaf for leaf." Reynolds speaks of his " portrait like representation " of nature, and adds: " If Gainsborough did not look at nature with a poet's eye it must be acknowledged that he saw her with the eye of a painter, and gave a faithful if not a poetical representation of what he had before him." To this

view of the fidelity of Gainsborough's English landscapes all
agree, but the lack of poetry in his pictures is certainly denied
by one as well able to judge as Reynolds. Constable, one of the
best early English landscape painters said of Gainsborough's
landscapes; "They are soothing, tender, and affecting. The
stillness of noon, the depths of twilight, and the dews and pearls
of the morning are all to be found on the canvases of this most
benevolent and kind-hearted man. On looking at them we find
tears in our eyes, and know not what brings them. The lonely
haunts of the solitary shepherd,—the return of the rustic with
his bill and bundle of wood,—the darksome lane or dell,—the
sweet little cottage girl at the spring with her pitcher, were the
things which he delighted to paint, and which he painted with
exquisite refinement, yet not a refinement beyond nature." " He
was first," says Thornbury, " to show us that there was poetry in
English rustic life."

It seems fortunate for English landscape art that two men so
unlike in education, temperament, and taste as Wilson and
Gainsborough should have come at the formative period of that
art. One brought in the Dutch, the other the Italian influence,
yet each was too strong an individuality to be a mere copyist.
The one painted with poetic comprehension, and even with a
touch of sublimity, the sunny skies, clear air, bright lakes and
ruined temples of classic lands. The other painted with genuine
tenderness and affection the lovely scenes of rural England.
Both loved nature passionately, both strove to express this love in
their pictures. Whatever the imperfections of their work from
an artistic point of view, from the point of view of a growing
taste for nature the landscapes of these artists are of the greatest
importance. They show that shortly after the middle of the cen-
tury the new spirit had entered the realms of art as it had entered
other realms of thought and emotion. The transfer of interest
from man to nature is in many of the pictures of Wilson and
Gainsborough distinctly marked.

Contemporary with Wilson and Gainsborough were many
artists of less genius and subsequent fame, some of whom must
be mentioned here because they show the different phases taken

on by the growing love of nature.   Of *genre* painters only those need be mentioned who depicted rustic people in country surroundings.   Of these the chief are David Allan and George Morland.   David Allan's (1744–1796) best work is his set of illustrations of *The Gentle Shepherd.*   He went to the Pentland Hills and studied both the places and the people he wished to represent.   "He visited," says Cunningham, "every hill, dale, tree, stream, and cottage, which could be admitted into the landscape of the poet.   .   .   .   Glaid's farm house, the Monk's burn, the Linn, the Washing Green, Habbie's How, New Hall House, and that little breast-deep basin in the burn, called Peggie's pool, were all carefully drawn."   It was Allan's endeavor to do in painting what Ramsay had done half a century before in poetry, and though 'his pictures are far from expressing the brightness and beauty of the poem, they fairly take rank as important attempts to represent native landscapes from careful, first-hand observation.

George Morland's (1764–1804) very early pictures were copies from Dutch originals, mainly tavern interiors, but he afterwards painted some admirable scenes from the Isle of Wight which he loved to visit.   In general his landscapes were of inland scenes and of the most confined, homely sort.   The "barn-yard, the piggery, and the cow-house" were his favorite subjects.   He never idealized his rustics or their surroundings.   His merit was absolute fidelity to fact, and he made no poetic selection of the facts to be represented.   He was literally a copyist from nature. His pictures of country life and scenery had the relentless realism of Crabbe's poetry, and it is interesting to note that Crabbe's *Village* came out in 1783, when Morland was painting his most disagreeably truthful pictures of English country life.

Of the painters who after 1760 devoted themselves chiefly to landscape we find a number who show an interest in the mountainous regions of Wales and the Lake District similar to that shown in Poetry, Fiction, and Travels.   One of the most excellent pictures of Joseph Wright of Derby (1734–1797) who was reckoned almost equal in power to Wilson, was "The Head of Ulleswater."   Edward Dayes (1760–1804) also made many studies of Keswick Lake, Windermere, and the neighboring scenes. Mr. Gilpin in the Preface to his book on Cumberland (pub. 1786) says that description seems useless since there are prints "so accurate and beautiful" as those of Mr. Farrington representing Lodore, Skiddaw, Derwentwater, and other places. That there were earlier studies we know from Amory's statement in *John Buncle* that Cumberland scenery was far more beautiful than Dr. Dalton's brother's drawings would seem to indicate. Late in the century came William Havell (1782–1841), who began to paint mountain scenes while still a mere boy. He studied in Wales and then for two years in Westmoreland. Of far greater genius than any of these is Thomas Girtin (1775–1802) of whom Ruskin says : " He is often as impressive to me as nature herself ; nor do I doubt that Turner owed more to his teaching and companionship than to his own genius in the first years of his life." Poynter says that Girtin was "the first who successfully attempted to represent in water colors the grandeur and sublimity of mountain scenery, and to imitate the bold contrasts of light and shadow, of gloom and sunshine which occur in nature." He made excursions into " the most paintable parts of England and Wales, and even extending his excursions to Scotland." He painted views from Scotland, Wales, the Lake District and Devonshire. John Crome (1769–1821), founder of the Norwich School, and famous for his studies of foliage, is another of the artists who studied nature in the Lake District.

The interest in wild scenery is largely confined to northern England, but, as we have seen, Wales is not neglected. And along with Girtin's studies of Scotland are George Barret's views (1795) of Yorkshire and Loch Lomond. Another painter of mountains is Charles Fox (1749–1809). He is interesting as the first recorded artist to visit Norway, Sweden, and Russia, for the purpose of representing the wild scenery of those countries. The interest in mountains and lakes was so well established by the end of the century that when Constable made a tour of Westmoreland and found nothing to his mind but turned rather to cultivated scenery, his preference was counted something rather novel.

Other phases of interest in nature manifest themselves. The

romantic interest in the remote combined with the interest in nature shows in such pictures as those of South Sea Island scenery by John Webber, who went with Cook on one of his voyages (1780); or Thomas Hearne's water-color sketches of "the lovely scenery of the West Indies" (1768–71); or Alexander's drawings of Chinese scenery (1792-8); or the Russian scenes already noted, by Fox, or the Italian scenes painted for Mr. Beckford by John R. Cozens (1742-1799).

Among the artists who painted English scenes are some who are noted for specific excellencies, as Francis Nicholson (1753-1844) who studied especially waterfalls and rapid streams. Abraham Pether (1756-1812) devoted himself so exclusively to moonlight and evening that he was known as "moonlight Pether." J. Ibbetson was highly praised in his own day for his truth to English scenes. A critical review by "Anthony Pasquin" of the pictures exhibited in 1795 speaks of Ibbetson in terms that show what had at that time come to be recognized as some of the desirable qualities in an excellent piece of landscape work, namely first-hand observation, truth to such nature as the artist himself knew, and individuality of presentation. "Anthony Pasquin" says,

"When many of our present race of landscape painters wish to make a *study*, they do it by their firesides; they take an old perished copy of Wynants, Ruysdael, or Hobbima, or a damaged copy from some eminent artist, and *compose* by stealing a tree from one, a dock-leaf from another, and a waterfall from a third. By this means we have Flemish landscapes peopled with English figures, and the same unvaried scenes served up *ad infinitum*. Very different is the conduct of Mr. Ibbetson. His views are taken from nature; and in his pictures we see our own country as in a mirror, painted in a style peculiarly his own."

The landscape painters of the eighteenth century evinced little interest in what Bakhuysen called "sea-scapes." Though several artists are marked as marine painters, a closer examination shows in most cases that the pictures designated as marine correspond well with Young's *Sea Pieces*. For instance, the forty pictures ascribed to Dominic Serres (*circa* 1765) are all of naval engagements in honor of English prowess, and done in his official capacity as "Marine Painter to the King." An artist who exhibited about 1770, John Cleveley, had been a dock-hand, and he painted his sea-views *con amore* but without much technical skill. Nicholas Pocock first exhibited in 1782. He had been brought up at sea and did his first work as an artist while still commanding a vessel. He devoted himself chiefly to naval actions. A more gifted artist was Richard Wright of the Isle of Man. In 1764 and 1766 he took the prizes offered by the Society of Arts for the best marine pictures. "The Fishery," engraved by Woollett, is his best known work. The great period of English landscape art does not come till some years after 1798, the limit of this study. But Turner was born in 1775, and Constable in 1776, so that they did much of their studying, and practically fixed their ideals of work under such influences as the eighteenth century brought.

In general we may note with regard to landscape painting that from the beginning to the end of the century the pendulum has taken its usual swing. It has traversed the arc from a predominating interest in man to a predominating interest in nature. From having landscape as an unimportant background, man has become an unimportant detail in landscape. But the love of nature in art is later in its beginnings than in poetry, and comes to its final maturity some years later than does the poetry. The characteristic work of Coleridge, Scott, and Wordsworth was practically done before that of Constable, Turner, Copley Fielding, and David Cox.

The chief foreign influences were Dutch and Italian. Claude, the Poussins, and Salvator Rosa were the artists most studied The atmospheric effects, the wide landscapes, and the ruined temples of Claude were especially attractive to the artists of the time, and he was assiduously copied. On the whole, painting was less original and freed itself more slowly from masters than any other form in which the love of nature found expression.

The general phases of interest as shown in the painting are similar to those in the poetry. The awakened curiosity of the age finds expression in the many pictures of foreign scenes. The delight in rustic life is well represented by Morland and Allan

on its homely realistic side, and by Gainsborough on its refined
side. There are frequent attempts to represent the evanescent
beauties of sunrise and sunset, of twilight, and moonlight. There
is much enthusiasm for wild scenery. No one characteristic of
the painting is more marked than its devotion to mountains and
lakes, especially those of northern England. There is a strong
personal delight in nature for her own sake, and sometimes not
merely a sensuous pleasure in color and form, but a deeper poetic
conception of the significance and power of nature.

CHAPTER VII.

GENERAL SUMMARY.

During the period from Waller to Pope the general feeling towards nature was one of indifference. The whole emphasis

Feeling toward nature in early 18th century compared with feeling in early 19th century was on man in his higher social relations, and only such parts of nature as were easily subordinated to man were looked upon with pleasure. The facts of nature were little known. They were stated in terms merely imitative and conventional. The new feeling towards nature, as exemplified in the early nineteenth century poets, especially Wordsworth, on the contrary, is marked by full and first-hand observation, by a rich, sensuous delight in form, color, sound, and motion; by a strong preference for the wilder, freer forms of nature's life, by an enthusiasm for nature passionate in its intensity, by a recognition of the divine life in nature, and finally by a consciousness of the interpenetration of that life and the life of man. At the beginning of the eighteenth century, in poetry, travels, fiction, painting, and gardens, it was the classical feeling toward nature that predominated. By the end of the century the new feeling had found abundant, varied, and original statement. The change is a great one. From Pope to Wordsworth, from Le Notre to Repton, from Kneller to Turner, from Richardson to Mrs. Radcliffe, from Brand to Gilpin, the pendulum swings. Whether men painted pictures or made gardens, or went on journeys, or told tales of love and adventure, or wrote poems, the new spirit was at work within them, sending them forth into the world of nature and bidding them bear witness to her power and loveliness.

Early manifestations of the new spirit did not, however, find exactly contemporaneous expression in these various art-forms.

Thomson's *Seasons* and Pope's *Fourth Epistle* are in 1726-31. Gainsborough and Wilson do not bring out their work until after 1755. Thomas Amory's *John Buncle* is in 1756–66, and Brown's *Keswick Letter* comes within the same period. Thus the decisive beginnings of the new spirit in painting, fiction, and travels are about contemporary, but are thirty years behind poetry and gardening. Furthermore, the time between the decisive beginnings and the final full expression is greatly varied. In poetry it is seventy-three years, in gardening about sixty-five, in painting about fifty, in fiction not over twenty-five, and in travels only about fifteen years.

The dates of development of love of nature in different art forms

In spite of these variations in date there seems to be in each art the same general order of development. First there is a dim period of tentative, unconscious, or apologetic indications of a new spirit. Then some original mind seizes upon the new idea and gives it consistency and at least partially adequate expression. After this there follows a period of less vigorous but widespread and varied efforts to find a statement for some portions of the new thought. Then a master mind seems to feel all these diffused, struggling, half-expressed conceptions and sums them up in the final perfect form. In the poetry of nature these stages are clearly marked in the work before Thomson, in Thomson, in the period from Thomson to Wordsworth, and in Wordsworth. In painting are Wilson and Gainsborough on the one hand and Turner on the other. In gardening, travels, and fiction we find the periods marked respectively by Kent and Repton, Brown and Gilpin, Amory and Mrs. Radcliffe. In these three art-forms, especially in the last two, we do not find the period of development ending in the work of consummate genius. We go rather from a meager statement to a statement that is full, many-sided, enthusiastic. The progress is in the love of nature rather than in the power of adequate, final expression. The development in gardening is more in the nature of a series of experiments open to wide discussion, and the final outcome takes the form given it by the man whose study of past failures and successes has led him to

General order of development

the surest comprehension of the artistic and mechanical laws involved. A glance at the accompanying table will make the general statement clear, the main point being that in at least five of the ways in which men express their ideas it is possible to trace the growth of a complete change of attitude towards nature. The poets who helped to bring about this change have already been studied in detail, but some further general statements may not be out of place here.

As a rule, such significant poetry of nature as appeared during the transition period was the work of men who had spent much of their youth in the country or in country villages: **During the transition period the significant poetry of nature the early work of men brought up in the country** it was practically their earliest poetic venture, and usually the work of their youth; and, in most cases where there was an extended literary career, the poetry of nature speedily gave way to work of a didactic or dramatic sort, in which nature played but a small part. To any such general statement there would be of course important exceptions. Blake, for instance, was a town-bred poet. So was Collins, and his *Ode to Evening* is not his earliest work. Cowper was town-bred. He was old when he began to write, and his poetry of nature is his latest rather than his earliest work. But, taken as a whole, the poetry of nature during the eighteenth century bears out the statement as made. It is well illustrated by Armstrong, who was born and who apparently spent his youth in Castleton, a little village in the wildest part of the mountainous country around the Derbyshire peaks, wrote his *Winter* before he was fifteen, went to Edinburgh and then to London to study, and wrote as the work of his mature years a didactic poem on the *Art of Preserving Health*. Or by Dyer, who was brought up in South Wales, wrote *Grongar Hill* and *The Country Walk* at twenty-five, went up to London, and wrote as his mature work *The Ruins of Rome* and *The Fleece*. Or by Thomson, who lived until he was fifteen in Southdean, a little hamlet at the foot of the Cheviot Hills, the last of whose *Seasons* appeared when he was thirty and whose later work was a succession of dreary tragedies. Or by Akenside, who, though brought up in Newcastle-on-Tyne, made

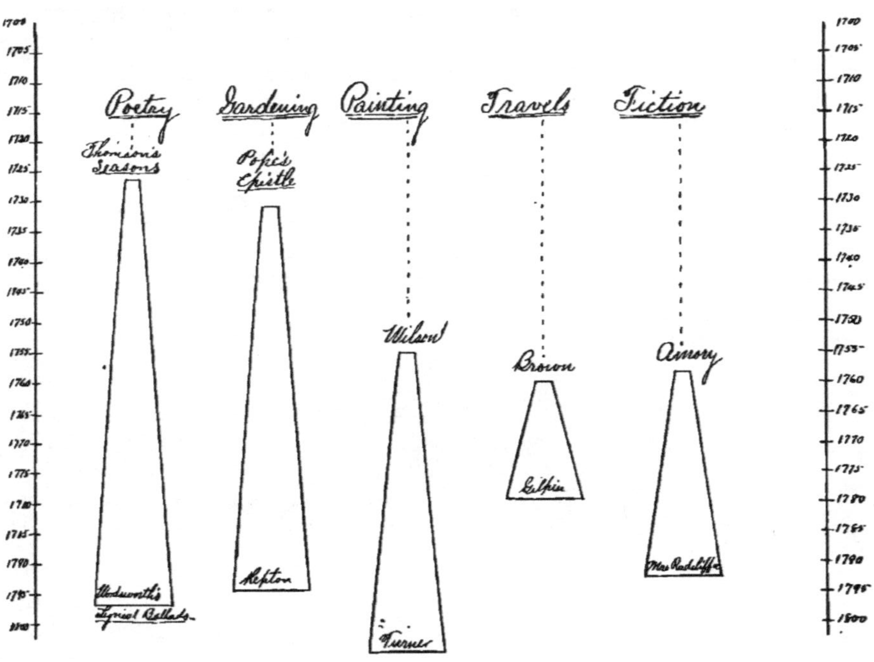

1700
1705
1710
1715
1720
1725
1730
1735
1740
1745
1750
1755
1760
1765
1770
1775
1780
1785
1790
1795
1800
Poetry
Gardening
Painting
Travels
Fiction
Thomson's Seasons
Pope's Epistle
Wilson
Brown
Amory
Wordsworth's Lyrical Ballads
Repton
Turner
Gilpin
Mrs Radcliffe

frequent visits to the country during his youth, wrote *The Pleasures of the Imagination* at seventeen during one of these visits, and in his after life wrote much prose and poetry in which there is no hint of the early enthusiasm. Allan Ramsay lived in a secluded spot among the Pentland Hills until he was fifteen, and his earliest important poem, *The Gentle Shepherd*, is really a memory picture. William Pattison spent his youth at Appleby, a village on the Eden, in Westmoreland, where he wrote his earliest poems. Mickle spent his youth at Langholme on the Esk, and his first important poem, *Pollio*, written at eighteen, was in memory of his life there. Bruce was brought up at Kinneswood, a village on Lochleven, and his early poetry had much to do with the scenery about that place. Beattie spent his youth at Lawrenckirk, and Fordoun on the east coast of Scotland, and *The Minstrel*, his first important poem, is a record of his early life. It would certainly be a mis-reading of these facts to infer that to write well of nature the poet must have been brought up in the country. Genius has the rare gift of seeing a very little and straightway knowing a great deal. It would be equally wrong to infer that poets write of nature when they are young and give it up when they put away childish things. The import of these facts in this period seems to be merely that there was a genuine and widespread love of nature on the part of many isolated poets, who, by the circumstances of their lives, knew nature better than they did literature, but that this love was not sufficiently robust in individual cases to withstand the cramping influences of city life and literary coteries. The developing tradition was carried on not so much by the persistent influence of a few as by the constant springing up of the same spirit in many minds.

In a transition period the predominant spirit is self-conscious, authoritative, and full of maxims drawn from its own successes. The new spirit comes in, as it were, by chance. It **Self-conscious statements** is but slightly theoretic, following instinct rather than well-defined principles. In its first stages it is apologetic rather than aggressive. These characteristics, on the whole, mark the love of nature in the early eighteenth century poetry. There are, however, occasional indications that some poets, at least, not only wrote according to new canons of taste, but were distinctly conscious of their revolt from the old. So early as 1709 Ambrose Philips in the Preface to his *Pastorals* justified his choice of country themes by pointing out the pleasing effect of natural scenes on the mind. John Gay's enunciation of a creed, though meant as a satire, was so just a condemnation of existing poetic conventions, and so apt a prophecy of one phase of the new spirit that it really deserves to rank among revolutionary statements of theory. Allan Ramsay's Preface to *The Evergreens* is equally emphatic in its scorn of classical limitations, and it was meant in downright earnest. The thought of the *Preface* finds expression several times in his poems as well. Dyer gives utterance to a similar scorn of Parnassus in *The Country Walk*. Shenstone, in his *Prefatory Essay on Elegy*, shows a timid but perfectly clear recognition of the fact that he is breaking away from poetical canons. Mason in the Preface to *Elfrida* says that he has introduced descriptions with a purpose of rendering the drama more pleasing. Whitehead's *Enthusiast* with its elaborate statement of both sides of the case in man *versus* nature is an important indication of the clearness with which the points of the controversy were at that time recognized. The strongest and most detailed statement of a creed came about four years later in Joseph Warton's *Essay on Pope* (1756). Nothing else so clear, direct, and full appeared before the Prefaces of Wordsworth. After Warton it is not so necessary to indicate all self-conscious statements. It will suffice briefly to indicate Langhorne's statement of his purpose in writing, Goldsmith's vigorous attacks on falseness and affectation in poetry, Beattie's Wordsworthian Preface to *The Minstrel*, John Scott's criticism on existing poetry and his statement of his own aim in the Preface to his *Amœbœan Eclogues*, Crabbe's expressed determination to treat of nature as it really is, Cowper's pleasure in the fact that his knowledge and inspiration come straight from nature and his persistent reiteration of his belief in the superiority of the country over the city, and finally Burns's many critical remarks on the essential qualities of descriptive poetry.

The characteristics of the poetry of nature that was growing up during the eighteenth century have been already indicated in one way and another, but it seems necessary here to gather them up into general statements. The easiest and clearest way will be to make a somewhat detailed summary of such traits of this poetry as seem to foreshadow the later treatment of nature, especially as exemplified in Wordsworth. In the comparison I keep mainly to Wordsworth both for the sake of simplicity, and because, though in romantic periods each poet works out his own salvation along original and self-determined lines, yet Wordsworth more nearly than any other poet expresses the variety and complexity of interest in the new feeling towards nature.

Wordsworth the best representative of the new feeling towards nature

Wordsworth said that a part of his endowment as a poet was a peculiar openness to sense impressions, and that this endowment was cultivated by his environment in youth until the real facts of nature were reported to him with fullness and accuracy. In his wholesale condemnation of the period between *Paradise Lost* and *The Seasons* the chief count in the indictment is the absence of new images drawn from nature. Full, accurate, first-hand knowledge of nature is then with Wordsworth a *sine qua non*, a basis on which interpretation must rest. During the eighteenth century no one man had Wordsworth's inevitable ear or practiced eye, but the whole impression made is that men were at last out of doors, looking and listening for themselves. Each man sees many facts not before noted, and collectively the poetry of the period presents a great body of natural phenomena of all sorts. Poets, artists, travelers, writers of fiction, unite to swell the stock of facts about the external world. Dorothy Wordsworth's *Journals* show with what delight she and her brother dwelt upon the baldest statement of the actual facts of nature. Gray in his *Letters*, John Scott in his *Eclogues*, show this same pleasure in simply cataloguing the lovely facts of the outdoor world. Lady Winchelsea, Gay, Thomson, Dyer, Cowper, Burns, all the landscape painters

Variety and extent of knowledge of nature during the transition period

from Wilson to Girtin, Mrs. Smith and Mrs. Radcliffe, but are leaders of the many who were striving to make report of what they found in waters and skies, in field, mountain, and plain. The wide range of these facts is astonishing. The knowledge of the poet is no longer confined to parks and gardens, to the mild and lovely aspects of nature. His aroused curiosity pushes him out into new realms of inquiry. All kinds of nature, animate and inanimate, wild and tame, remote and close at hand, attract interested attention.

The mere mass and variety of this accumulated knowledge is sufficiently significant in its bearing on the development of a new

Accuracy and delicacy of observation

taste for nature, but a further general question arises as to the accuracy and delicacy of the observation. There certainly was none of the scientific spirit that would feel the charm of bare exactness, and there was hardly any of Wordsworth's feeling that to misrepresent a fact of nature would be sacrilege. Facts were, indeed, often noted in a loose, careless way, as if of slight importance. But taken as a whole the observation bears the mark of the eye on the object. From Lady Winchelsea to Bowles every poet who has been esteemed noteworthy in the study of nature gives the impression that he speaks from personal knowledge, and no poetry can make that impression unless it is in its main lines true. Delicacy of observation is another matter.

What the eighteenth century poets did was to give truthful expression to very many natural facts of a kind fairly obvious to an age well versed in the lore of field and wood; but new to an age just emerged from the gates of a park. It is observation of this abundant, truthful, obvious sort that we find in Ambrose Philips, Gay, Ramsay, Shenstone, John Scott, and largely this even in Thomson. The commonest facts of nature, the blue sky, wild flowers on a rocky ledge, rough little streams, were a wonder and a delight. Discrimination comes after general and obvious facts have been accepted and assimilated. It is inevitable, even setting aside their different temperaments, that Cowper should have more of it than Thomson. The strange thing is that in the early stages of the poetry of nature we should find any observation so close and delicate as that in the study of night by Lady Winchelsea, of burns and mountain pools by Allan Ramsay, of winter skies and ice-burdened streams by Armstrong ; or as that in Thomson's sunset after rain, Dyer's wide views and homely bits of country life, Collins's evening, Gray's sky-lark and song-thrush, Thomas Warton's opening spring, Logan's cuckoo, and Scott's trees.

The fullness and accuracy of the eighteenth century study of nature may be further seen by a brief analysis of the sense impressions most frequently noted.

Wordsworth is said to have been physically deficient in the sense of smell, hence the noticeable absence of odors in his poems may be accounted for. But it is doubtless true of **Odors** all poetry that fragrances are more scantily recorded than are other facts, and there is seldom much closeness of observation so as to discriminate between various sorts of sweet odors. For this reason such slight study of odors as we find in the transition poetry is the more to be dwelt upon. There are certainly not infrequent observations showing close knowledge. J. Philips notes the faint sweetness of cowslips; Relph speaks of the odor of the "fresh primrose on the furst of May;" Dyer and Shenstone of the fragrance of brakes; Dyer of sweet-smelling honeysuckles; Shenstone, Thomas Warton, and Cowper of the fragrant woodbine; J. Philips and Mickle of scented orchards ; Cowper calls attention to the odor of limes and the fresh smell of turf; Lady Winchelsea speaks of the "aromatic pain" from the odor of a jonquil, the "potent fragrance" of which is recognized also by Thomson. Two odors frequently mentioned are of "the perfuming flowery bean" celebrated first by John Philips, then by Gay, Thomson, Savage, Shenstone, and Joseph Warton; and the fragrance of hay noted by Thomson, Gay, Ramsay, Savage, Potter, Relph, Thomas Warton, and Mickle. When homely, unusual odors, like that of the bean, are noticed there is often exceptional vividness of statement. What took rank in the poet's mind as his own discovery brought out a natural freshness of phrase. One other fact frequently noted is that odors are strongest at morning or evening or after a rain. These specific references are of real importance in showing new powers of perception, but it must be admitted that in general the use of odors was of the conventional sort, referring rather vaguely to sweet breezes blowing over flowery fields.

The sensitiveness to sound so often remarked in Wordsworth's poems is a characteristic of the poetry of nature throughout the century before Wordsworth. The music of nature was a source of widespread delight. The "pleasant noise of waters," for instance, receives some notice from nearly every poet in the list, while in travels and fiction some of the most effective passages are on the sounds of rapid streams and waterfalls. In poetry the old words "warbling," "tinkling," and "murmuring," are still much used, but Ramsay's rill that "makes a singin din," Thomson's roused-up river that "thunders" through the rocks, Mallet's river with its "sounding sweep," Collins's "brawling springs," and Cowper's "chiming rills" are a few of the phrases that mark a more individual and personal way of listening One of Wordsworth's often quoted lines on sound has to do with the greater distinctness of the song of mountain streams by night. Mr. Heard gives this passage as an instance of Wordsworth's peculiarly close observation. But the clearness with which falling or running water is heard at night had been noted at least six times in the literature before Wordsworth. Lady Winchelsea mentioned it in her *Revery*. Beattie speaks of waterfalls heard from afar amid the lonely night, and again of the quiet evening when naught but the torrent is heard on the hill. The lines in John Brown's *Rhapsody* have already been quoted, as also his *Letter* in which he notes the variety of sounds from distant waterfalls as one of the attractions of a walk at night. And Gray also speaks of the murmur of many waterfalls not audible in the day time. Several other authors as Dyer and Mallet have practically the same idea when they mention the unusual clearness of the sound of falling water in a breathless noon, or in the depths of a silent forest.

The sounds made by winds are also often and particularly noted. They sigh through reeds, they make a remote and hollow

Sounds

Sounds from water

noise in "wintery pines," they murmur through the poplars,
they rustle lightly over "deep embattled ears of corn," they join
in concert with woods and waters, or they sweep
Sounds from in mighty harmonies through ancient forests.
winds The whispering breezes, and dying gales of the
classical poetry do not often occur. Brown in his
Letter shows how deeply he was impressed by the roaring of the
winds through the mountains, and the one passage in which Dr.
Johnson showed any appreciation of wild nature is a description
of the combined sounds of streams and wind on a stormy night
in Scotland. A characteristic passage is Thomson's fine descrip-
tion of thunder among the mountains. Wordsworth, from the
peculiar delicacy of his perceptions and perhaps from his con-
templative nature, was deeply sensitive to the silences in the world
about him. There is some though but little indication of a
similar pleasure in preceding poetry. One of the best passages
is Thomson's description of the boding silence before a storm.
This has, however, much less of the real Wordsworthian spirit
than has Brown's conception of the silence that spoke from the
starry vault, the shadowy cliffs, the motionless goves, and the
faint mirror of the placid lake.

Of sounds from animate nature the emphasis is of course on
birds. But the feathered choir of the classical period has been
resolved into distinct species, each with a voice of
Songs of its own. The nightingale is not supplanted but
birds she is no longer a monopolist in the realms of the
muses. In this transition poetry the cuckoo takes
an interesting place. Wordsworth's address to the bird as "the
darling of the spring" gives the association of ideas found in
most of the early poems. The cuckoo is the harbinger of spring.
Armstrong and A. Philips have the loud note of the cuckoo as
one of the first hints of the opening year, and Thomson's sym-
phony of spring is introduced by "the first note the hollow
cuckoo sings." Mendez says it is "the cuckoo that announceth
spring," and Gray speaks of the cuckoo's note as part of "the
untaught harmony of spring." The peculiarity of the cuckoo's
note is also often mentioned. Other birds have many notes,

says John Cunningham, " the cuckoo has but two." Logan, as Wordsworth after him, records the fact that the bird is usually unseen, and both speak of the schoolboy's surprise as the strange cry falls on his ear. The lark, the nightingale, and the linnet are frequently mentioned, but usually in terms somewhat conventional. They had been in poetry so long that a distinct effort would have been needed to think of them under new phrases. To be released from the captivity of a stock diction and conventional sentiment they waited for Shelley and Keats and Wordsworth. It is in observations on birds not counted poetical property that we find fresh and exact expression. A mark of the new spirit is the pleasure in such sounds as the call of the curlew, the boom of the bittern, the chattering of magpies, the caw of rooks, the piping of quails, the scream of jays, the clang of sea-mews, the shrill clamor of cranes, the shriek of the gull, the whistle of plovers, the whir of the partridge. To hear such sounds the poet must wander over moors, by sedgy lakes, along rough shores, far enough from trim parks. To bring such sounds into poetry marked a great revolution in taste from the days of the lorn nightingale and the plaintive turtle. As a whole we may say that the treatment of sound in eighteenth century poetry is abundant, accurate, and often very effective.

The process of passing from general to specific statements as a result of increased knowledge shows itself again in the use of color. The universal paint of the classical school has been resolved into some of its constituent elements. These are not many, however, and there is not much nice discrimination into shades and tints. The colors most often observed are green, blue, yellow or gold, purple, red or crimson, and brown, the order given being the order of their frequency. Purple is used less frequently than in the classical poetry and usually has some real artistic significance. Yellow, a comparatively new word, is used often of harvests, of trees in autumn, of moonlight, and of various sunlight effects. Dyer gave early prominence to the word as an epithet applied to nature. Brown is applied in somewhat the conventional manner to streams and shadows. Thomson,

Dyer, Savage, and Cowper made the most effective use of color, and it is important to observe that their advance consisted not so much in seeing many more colors than had been seen before, as in discovering color in many more objects than formerly. They did not merely see that " all above is blue and all below is green." They saw the blue heavens, but they saw, too, the blue of " sky dyed plumbs," of mists, of distant hills, of streams and bays, of ice-films, of the halcyon's wing, of curling smoke, of the lightning flash. The endive, the lavender, the lilac, the violet, the harebell, the heath-flower, are singled out as blue. And Dyer speaks of the blue color of the poplars, and Dalton of blue slate roofs. Not merely the general green of a summer landscape is commented upon, but there are closer observations concerning the varying shades of green as the trees are massed together. The russet tints brought out in green tree tops at sunset, the funereal green of yews, the yellow-green in a sunset sky, the yellow tinge in green grass almost ready for the scythe, the glossy green of the holly, the deep green of box, the contrasting green of elm, oak, and maple, are some typical observations.

The use of color, however, seems, on the whole, in spite of its abundance and picturesqueness, hardly so varied and individual as the use of sound.

A division into colors and sounds leaves many sorts of observation unnoted, and frequently these are of great importance as indicating close knowledge; but they have been so often commented upon in the study from author to author that even a suggestive recapitulation is hardly needed here. Enough has been called to mind to show that there was much knowledge of the external world, and that much of this knowledge was reported in words so direct and truthful that they must have come from personal experience.

In the classical period we have seen that only the milder forms of nature were cared for. Wordsworth was, on the other hand, essentially the poet of mountains, lakes, and streams. It will be of interest to note the attitude of the transition poetry toward the various kinds of nature. And first we may sum up the evidences of mountain enthusiasm.

In the first fifty years of the century we have only the expressions of pleasure in climbing mountains or hills by J. Philips, Gay, and Dyer; the various descriptive references in Ramsay and in Mallet; and Paul Sandby's sketches in the Highlands. Ramsay and Mallet show a consciousness of mountains, and evidently regard them as noticeable and picturesque elements of a scene, and Dyer is of distinct importance because of his lingering pleasure in the beautiful views opening up before him as he climbs the mountain, and especially because of his poetic comprehension of mountain solitudes. But it is during the next twenty-five years that we find the most adequate eighteenth century treatment of mountains. During this period Brown, Pennant, Young, Gray, and Gilpin visited Scotland, Wales and the English Lakes, and wrote of mountains with an enthusiasm hardly equaled in the succeeding century. In fiction were Amory's eulogy of Westmoreland, and his exaggerated pictures of Cumberland, and Smollett's description of the country round Loch Leven. In painting, Dalton, Sandby, Butts, and Wright were studying mountain scenery in northern England, Wales, and Ireland. In poetry we have Coventry's address to Vaughan on mountain climbing; Dalton's apostrophe to Skiddaw; Brown's rhapsody on the mountains and lakes of Westmoreland; the mountain scenery in Gray's *Bard* and the poems of *Ossian;* the many descriptive references in Dyer's *Fleece*, Jago's *Edge Hill*, Mickle's *Almada Hill* and *May Day*, and Scott's *Amwell;* and Beattie's study of the influence of mountains on a poetic mind. During the last twenty-five years of the century there is, in poetry, a curious apparent cessation of mountain interest. The most highly poetic minds, Blake, Cowper, and Burns, have none of it. Crabbe does not touch upon mountains. Lesser poets, except Bowles at the very end of the century, are equally silent. This is not, however, true of fiction, travels, and painting. During this period Fox is studying mountain scenery in Russia; Farrington, Dayes, Crome, Havell, and Girtin are in the Lake District; Havell and Girtin also travel in Wales for purposes of study; and Barret is in Scotland. Mountain scenery is a large element in Mrs. Radcliffe's Romances. And there is a band of travelers going over the country already described. Thus the interest in mountains, practically dropped in poetry, was carried on in romances, accounts of travel, and pictures, until in the next century it reached its highest expression in Wordsworth.

Many lovers of nature and of poetry have commented with surprise on the slow development of the poetic appreciation of mountains. It is, perhaps, even more strange that **The ocean** English poetry should have been still slower in its discovery of the ocean. It is as if English poets from Dryden to Byron had all lived inland. Even in Wordsworth, in spite of some wonderful lines, there is no treatment of the ocean at all comparable to his study of mountains. In the classical age the ocean was a dreary waste. In the transition poetry we do not find much more knowledge or appreciation. The one quality of the ocean that receives anything like adequate expression is its boundlessness. Characteristic lines are by John G. Cooper.

> " In unconfined perspective send thy gaze
> Disdaining limit o'er the green expanse
> Of ocean."

Armstrong says that the "floating wilderness"

> " Scorns our miles and calls Geography
> A shallow prier."

Mickle looks upon the awful solitude of ocean and his imagination is stirred by

> " the last dim wave in boundless space
> Involved and lost."

These are the best lines I have found. The chief expressions of pleasure in the ocean are Gay's mild delight in a sunset across the sea, and subsequent moonlight effects, and Beattie's pleasing dread as he seeks the shore to listen to the wide-weltering waves. We find in Cowper's letters a more appreciative passage on the ocean than occurs in any of the poetry. The most sincere ocean enthusiasm is in Mrs. Radcliffe's Romances. Travelers, even those who went along the coast of Wales and among the Scottish

Islands or to the Isle of Wight, say little of the sea. The ocean was, in fact, much such a burden as Sterne's plain. When the poet had once said that it was big and awful his stock of impressions was exhausted. In painting, the ocean was not entirely ignored, but in this province, too, there was meagerness of conception and expression. The ocean waited for Turner and Byron and Shelley.

One of the interesting characteristics of the love of nature in the eighteenth century is a delight in wide views. What had in the classical period "tired the travelling eye," with **Wide views** the dawning of the new spirit gave satisfaction. It was in accord with the mental revolt against close boundaries of any sort. From the day when John Philips ventured to express some pleasure in the view from a hill, and Gay climbed Cotton Hill to raise his mind nearer heaven, and Dyer spent days in studying with an artist's eye the colors and forms of the view from Grongar Hill, to the time when Beattie eagerly climbed the rugged steeps of Scottish mountains so that he might see the morning mists rolling and tumbling over the rough hills beneath him, do we find this pronounced delight in wide views. Even poets who show no great love for mountains, as Thomson, Mallet, Collins, the Wartons, Langhorne, Mickle, and John Scott, and even poets of confessedly tame scenery as Cowper, love "green heights" and extended prospects. To the expression of this feeling Amory and Mrs. Radcliffe, Brown, Young, and Pennant make large contributions. This feeling shows itself also in gardening. The cutting down of tall hedges, the opening up of vistas, were a result of the change of taste and a contribution to it. With this development of the new spirit the artists, and Gilpin, working as he did from the artist's point of view, had little to do. Wide views seemed to be outside their province.

We have seen that during the classical poetry the skies in favor were cloudless and that of all sky phenomena the rainbow excited most attention. In the transition poetry **The sky** we find much of this love of fair summer skies and expressed sometimes with a new freshness as when Dyer wishes nothing above his head but "the roof

on which the gods do tread," or when Ramsay looks with joy
upon "the lift's unclouded blue," or when the clear gladness of
heaven shines down from the lovely skies of Blake. But on the
whole, references to the serene day-time sky are conventional.
It is another illustration of the fact that such aspects of nature
as were already known and had come to be spoken of after a set
fashion were slow to be emancipated into a new phraseology.
Better work is done in describing what Coleridge calls the
"goings-on" of the sky. Thomson knew the sky in all its phases.
Parnell describes well the airy tumult of clouds after a storm.
Mallet has one or two rather effective studies of a stormy sky.
One of Beattie's best descriptions is of a shifting cloudy sky
on a windy autumn day, and he has other effective cloud studies.
But taken in the mass the material is scanty and not of great
value. It was Wordsworth and Shelley who first gave adequate
expression to the mysterious and varied charm of the day-time
sky.

The love of the night sky and of night itself is first found in
Lady Winchelsea, and for close observation and delicate feeling
there is nothing better throughout the century.
There is, however, much use of night, moonlight,
and stars in a new and appreciative fashion. In

Night

Gay's *Dione* there are several attractive little moon-
light pictures. Parnell was impressed by the depth, the serenity
and the silence of a starry sky on a clear night. Coventry observes
how fast the moon travels through light clouds as if bent on a
journey, while in clear weather she sits steady empress of the
skies. Joseph Warton notes the shining of hills and streams
under the light of a full moon. Mickle has some beautiful lines
on both moon and stars as they rise from behind certain favorite
hills. He walks much at night and loves to watch the trembling
line of light from the moon as it shines across the lake, or the
soft effect of the yellow moonlight sleeping on the hills. Beattie
stays out all night to watch the aspects of the sky till the dawn of
day. Morning and evening twilight are less often spoken of.
There is certainly nothing else in the century to compare with
Collins's *Evening*. Sunset and sunrise are often described, but

nowhere with more general effectiveness than in Thomson, or with more minute color study than in Savage.

Closely connected with the knowledge of the sky is the new feeling towards storms.   In the classical poetry they had been ignored or used as similes for disaster.   But one of the first evidences of a new spirit was in the appre-

Storms

ciative description of winter storms, as in Riccaltoun, Armstrong, and Thomson.   The early descriptions and the multiplicity of storms in Thomson and Mallet give at first the impression that this element held a larger place in poetry than it really did.   Ramsay has some good lines on winter storms. There is an admirable stanza in Collins's *Ode to Liberty*, and another in Thomas Warton's *Grave of King Arthur*.   In Beattie's *Minstrel*, and in several of Burns's poems there are expressions of delight in the fierce play of the elements, but that exhausts the list of notable passages.   It is only in Beattie that we find any of the modern sense of kinship between the tumult of life and nature's fierce conflicts, and the imaginative force of a passage like that in *The Excursion* where the Wanderer longs to be a spirit and so mingle with primal energies in their mightiest activities, or the lyric passion of a cry like that in Shelley's apostrophe to the West Wind, are not even hinted at.

The most pronounced change came with reference to these grander, wilder aspects of nature.   We have still to note the treatment of the gentle pleasant things of nature as birds, flowers, trees.

There was, through the classical period, abundant delight, in a general way, in meadows bursting into bloom, and in bright flowers in the garden.   The use of the words "flowery," "adorned," "decked," "enameled," etc.,

Flowers

usually had reference to fields of flowers thought of in a vague, pleasant way.   The changes that come during the transition poetry are a resolving of the general into the specific, a concentration of attention on English flowers, and a greatly increased knowledge of individual flowers.   The rose and the lily often give place to homely flowers as the blossoms of peas and beans, the bramble rose, butter flowers, clover, heath-bells, crowfoot, the tangled vetch, the mandrake, the thistle. The increased minuteness of observation shows itself in such studies of garden flowers as we find in Thomson and Cowper. A feeling of personal relationship towards flowers finds its highest and sweetest expression in Burns's *Daisy*.

In the classical poetry trees in general are an important part of the stock in trade. The new feeling shows itself in a growing

Trees
tendency to think of trees as individuals. In a landscape trees are mentioned by name. The thin leav'd ash, whispering poplars, the glossy rind'd beech, venerable oaks tossing giant arms, waving elms, quivering aspens, murmuring pines, hoary willows, sycamores green, tawny, or scarlet, according to the season, white-blossomed hawthorn, deep green hollies, elders with silver blossoms, stand out from the mass and are known for their own qualities. Minute observation is indicated by the descriptive phrases used. The color of the trunk, the spread of the branches, the changing hue of the leaves, the kind of blossoms, are severally noted. Two special studies of trees are by Lady Winchelsea and Dr. Dalton, and are of early date. Dyer and Cowper give the best studies of trees seen in a mass, and yet individually noted. While there is not a touch of the deep forest in this poetry, there are many lines describing woodland effects. Thomson, Potter, and Cowper find especial pleasure in the lovely interplay of light and shade in a pathway overhung by woven branches. The brown shadows and the softened light in a deeply wooded nook are observed. Gentle streams sing happily under a cooling covert of green boughs. The quiet of the woods is broken only by the plash of waters, the rustle of boughs, the whisper of leaves, the hum of insects, the song of birds, sounds from distant flocks and herds, or the stroke of the woodman's axe. Trees also form an important part of every general landscape. But no poet has given so much of the real forest feeling as Mrs. Radcliffe. Of travelers Young has most to say about trees but his observations are largely scientific and utilitarian. On the whole we may say that trees are given abundant and discriminating attention, but that this attention seldom penetrates beyond external, artistic

qualities. Personal friendship for trees such as we find in Lowell, for instance, has hardly yet reached expression.

Birds have already been discussed under sound, but it remains here to state that the habits of birds, their manner of flight, their

Birds

nests, the trees they choose, their ways of protecting their young, were all topics on which much was known. Of minor poets, the best who knew birds well, are Jago, Potter, and Bruce. Gray adds some perfect touches. Best of all for accurate description and real understanding are Thomson, Cowper, and Burns. The prominent place of the cuckoo has already been spoken of. The red-breast and the thrush with " speckly breast " rank not far behind in interest. The red-breast found early honor in Armstrong's *Winter*, and then in Thomson's, and is one of the pleasing elements in Cowper's *Winter Walk*. On the whole, birds of the lakes and streams seem to be better known than birds of the tree and copse.

One phase of the literary treatment of birds is a recognition of their rights as free, living beings. This feeling, not towards

Recognition of the rights of animals

birds alone but towards all animals, is one of the marks of the new spirit. There is even in Lady Winchelsea's *Revery* a slight hint of the conception that animals would not suffer if man had not proved himself a tyrant, and Gay carries out the same thought in one of his *Fables*. Thomson's protests against killing animals for food are the first strong statements of the new feeling. Shenstone, in *Rural Elegance* and *The Dying Kid*, shows some sympathetic regard for animals. Jago and Potter and Langhorne protested vigorously against cruelty to birds. Beattie had the strongest possible dislike towards so-called English sports. The feeling of close fellowship and almost human love towards animals, so marked in Wordsworth and Coleridge, did not find expression in the transition poetry until Burns and Cowper gave it full statement.

Throughout the poetry of the eighteenth century we have observed a turning from the general to the specific. There is likewise a similar tendency to localization. The classical poetry of nature belonged to no special spot, hardly to any special country. The poetry of Wordsworth and of Walter Scott was, on the other hand, eminently local. They celebrated the mountains and islands and streams of the region they **Localization** knew. Wordsworth complained that before his day no one had sung of British mountains. It is interesting to note the growth of this passion for certain spots definitely pointed out and named, certain natural scenes known and loved as a person might be. A brief survey of the mountains and streams thus celebrated in eighteenth century poetry will serve as illustrative. After Dyer's *Grongar Hill* come other mountains of Wales. The hoary heights of huge Plynlymmon ; the wide, aërial side of Cader-ydris; the craggy summits of cold Snowdon, king of mountains ; Clyder's cloud enveloped head ; Caer-caraduc and others are spoken of with evident pleasure and not a little artistic perception. In Scotland the Hills of Cheviot, the Pentland Hills, the mountains in the Ossian country, and those around Lochleven, are chief. In England we have the scarry side of Braids, Dafset's ridgy mountain, Edge-Hill, Almada Hill, Derwent's naked peaks, huge Breaden, blue-topp'd Wrekin, giant Skiddaw, the solemn wall of Malvern, the Cambrian Hills, the Hills of Ilmington, and others. The spirit of localization in its application to mountains does not often go beyond calling the mountain by its own name, and using some phrase showing that this mountain is known as separate from the general mass. In its application to streams the feeling is more detailed in expression. Ramsay's streams and pools are closely localized. Dyer celebrates not only Towy's flood, but the Vaga, the Ryddal, the Iftwith, the Clevedoc, the Lune, and especially the Usk. Dr. Dalton traces the course of the Borrowdale Beck from Lodore Falls to the lake. Langhorne follows the track of the Bela through solitary meads, and then through the rough realms of Stainmore. He also celebrates his joy as a child in the river Eden. Smollett, on his sick bed, writes an ode to Leven Water. Bruce sings of the Po, the Queech, the Severn, and especially of his youthful delight in the Gairney. Mickle writes of the Forth, the Annan, the Ewes, and the Wauchope, but dwells with most zest on his early love of the Esk. Of peculiar interest is Akenside's apostrophe to the Wansbeck. Hamilton, Langhorne and Logan wrote of the Yarrow, Cowper of the Ouse, Burns of the Ayr, the Doon, the Nith, the Afton, the Devon, and many another Scotch stream, while Bowles wrote of the Itchin, the Tweed, the Cherwell, and the Wansbeck. A map might be made on which should be represented only the mountains and streams spoken of with some particularity, with something more than a mere mention, in English poetry between 1650 and 1720, and a similar map of the period from 1720 to 1795. A comparison of the two would be an interesting commentary on the growth of knowledge and interest in British scenes.

All that has been so far presented goes to show that in the antithesis between town and country the balance of favor swung round during the eighteenth century to the country. Usually the preference is implicit, and is to be inferred from the change of theme, but occasionally the antithesis is sharply stated, as, to take types, in Thomson, the Wartons, and Cowper. It is Thomson who first gives adequate statement of the transfer of sovereignty from the "fine lady muses of Richmond Hill" to "the muses of the simple country." It is his hatred of the noisome town, his delight in fields and woods untouched by man, that established the new canon of taste. In the Wartons, twenty years later, the breach between the city and the country is almost an impassable gulf. Combined with the love of nature in her external forms there is that spirit of romantic melancholy by virtue of which the poet regards nature as a refuge from the tormenting complexities that beset the life of men in communities. There is usually a touch, sometimes more than a touch, of morbidness in the passionate eagerness to escape not only from the city into nature, but from man and all traces of his dominion into a solitude free from all human suggestiveness. Forty years after the Wartons, Cowper's famous epigram, " God made the country and man made the town," summed the matter up according to the new view. Cowper is as emphatic in his preferences as his predecessors, and much more detailed and minute in his expression. With him there is no vague generalizing, no morbid or passionate over-statement. His love of the country is a fundamental fact not only in his physical, but also and even especially in his moral and spiritual life. It is a fixed principle, quiet, rational, inevitable. The anti-classical side of the city and country antithesis receives in Cowper's poetry its most decisive and most reasonable eighteenth century statement. We hardly find anything so conclusive in fiction or in travels. There is an occasional expression of regret at going back to towns after a trip through the mountains and lakes, but as a rule the preference for the country is left to be inferred from the general tenor. of the traveler's writings. Mrs. Brooke protests much against London, and declares her preference for nature unadorned. Mackenzie's Julia rejoices over her country birth and education, and Mrs. Radcliffe reiterates the desirability of living far from towns and as close as possible to the influence of nature. Cowper, however, remains as having given the final, emphatic statement.

Through all this detailed study and wide knowledge of nature there runs an undercurrent of personal enthusiasm which is quite

Personal enthusiasm for nature a separate thing from the knowledge of nature, but which led to that knowledge and was fed by it. Sometimes we are left to infer this enthusiasm from results, but oftener it finds clear statement. There is frequent expression of such "unspeakable joy" as Ambrose Philips felt when he gazed on a little country home, or of Ramsay's "heartsome joy" on a bright spring morning

> "to see the rising plants,
> And hear the birds chirm o'er their pleasin' rants,"

or of Hamilton's rapturous joy as he lies on the flowering-turf, his soul "commercing with the sky." In many passages Thomson expresses his passionate delight in the music, the color, the fragrances of the outdoor world. Dyer's joys run high as he lies on the mountain-turf. Shenstone says that the beauties of nature alone bear perpetual sway, and he thinks with scorn of a soul so narrow that it cannot relish nature's calm delights. Joseph Warton cannot find words to express the ecstasy with which he looks on nature. John Langhorne's only wish is that he may enjoy the blessings nature gives to those who love her, and says that her charm alone is unfading. Beattie says that the man who goes to nature has rapture ever new. Cowper thinks that any man who turns away from nature starves deservedly. Burns says that he looked upon nature with boundless joy. This feeling of exhilaration, of rapturous delight, is pervasive. It is often inadequate, or vague, or extravagant in statement, but the delight is unfeigned, the enthusiasm real, and in poet after poet it demanded expression. That it seldom found the perfect statement only means that art is long and that much thinking and feeling in an age as in an individual must go before the final art-form.

Much of this delight in nature is in kind though not in degree like that which Wordsworth in *Tintern Abbey* calls his second period of love for nature, the time when **God in nature** the colors and forms of the external world were a sufficiently engrossing pleasure, and he felt no need of " a remoter charm by thought supplied." But Wordsworth quickly passed from this stage of pleasure to another. In his best descriptions, as in *The Yew Trees*, he gives a few external details, and then at once penetrates to the inner spirit of the scene. He is like a portrait painter who represents the features with truth and simplicity but makes the face live because he has divined the qualities of soul behind it. Now whatever philosophical tenets Wordsworth held he certainly thought of this soul of nature, whether of nature as a whole, or in special parts, as in some way a manifestation of divinity. In other words he saw God immanent in nature. The classical conception also saw God in nature, but as the remote Architect, Artificer, Lawgiver. The universe was dead, cold, inert matter. For the difficulty with which it was made to serve men's needs the defenders of Omnipotence felt apologetic explanations necessary. We have seen that during the eighteenth century there came a great and joyous awakening to the external charm of the world. Are there also indications that the divine life in nature was felt?

Throughout the eighteenth century the usual thought of God in relation to nature is the classical one. He is the author and

controller; of the universe; but there are some poems or passages
or separate lines that seem to indicate a new conception. Lady
Winchelsea recognizes a curious correspondence between nature
and her own heart, and says that in the quiet of a beautiful night
she feels the presence of something too high for syllables to
speak. There is a similar feeling in Hamilton's description of a
silent grove. In the *Nocturnal Revery* and in *Contemplation* the
idea of divinity is not explicitly stated, but in Parnell's *Hymn* the
song of praise is professedly to the Source of all Nature, because
through nature the divine spirit had spoken peace to the poet's
troubled heart. The incessant and ever-present creative activity
of God is clearly set forth in Thomson's *Hymn*. Each ray of
sunshine, every blossoming flower of spring, every leaping
stream, every rolling orb, performs its function as a direct
expression of divine energy. And some lines give a further sug-
gestion of divine immanence. The rolling year is full of God.
The seasons are but the varied God. The beauty of God walks
forth in the flushing spring. Such expressions as these mark a
half-involuntary poetic seizing of the new idea of nature as the
bodily presence of which God was the soul, but they do not
indicate Thomson's leading ideas. Mallet, imitative of Thomson
in this as in other respects, usually speaks of God as the Creator,
but in one passage touches on the full stream of universal Good-
ness that is ever-flowing through earth, air, and sea, and on the
ceaseless song of praise going up from the great community of
nature's sons. Boyse in his *Deity* thinks of God as an Almighty
Architect, but has a few lines in which he represents all nature as
being momently derived from God. Young has a significant
line when he says that night is the " felt presence of the Deity."
The theme of Akenside's poem is to show the response which
the imaginative mind finds in nature, and this response is, he
says, the voice of the divine spirit. His conception is usually,
to be sure, that the divine spirit speaks through the forms of
nature, rather than that the form and the spirit have an essential
union. Yet sometimes he speaks more clearly the new thought.
He says that the man who loves nature holds daily converse with
God himself. The beauty of nature flows directly from God.

The order in nature is sacred. The influence whereby nature soothes and cheers and elevates man is really a divine influence. This is the fullest recognition of an in-dwelling God until we reach Cowper. In his poetry we find a clear statement of belief,

> "There lives and works
> A soul in all things, and that soul is God,"

but the point is not one on which he dwells. These passages certainly foreshadow Wordsworth's conception of God in nature, but they are comparatively feeble and unimaginative in expression. There is nothing so Wordsworthian in Thomson's sonorous lines or in Akenside's ample statement as there is the feeling that penetrates the brief words of Lady Winchelsea and Parnell. Compared to these even Cowper seems cold and intellectual.

Wordsworth did not, however, lay special stress on his belief that the spirit he felt in nature was divine. He rather took that for granted, or allowed it to be implied in the passionate fullness and intensity of his expressions of gratitude to that spirit for gifts of mind and heart. This sense of indebtedness to nature found no place in the classical poetry. But in the transition period it receives surprisingly full and varied expression. Sometimes it takes the form of personal gratitude for special gifts; sometimes it is a general statement of what man owes to nature. A brief review of the more significant passages will serve to show the characteristics of this feeling towards nature.

Sense of personal indebtedness to nature

To begin with, nature gives peace. This is the gift most often spoken of. Even John Philips said that nature calmed his mind. Ambrose Philips liked the songs of birds because they brought him into a mood of "sweet and gentle composure." Lady Winchelsea enjoyed the night because its influence disposed her heart to silent musings and made her conscious of a "sedate content." Parnell had long vainly sought contentment until at last his heart received the message of peace through the voices of nature. Hamilton said that all the passions in the troubled breast of man could be calmed by the quiet of a grove. Thomson finds in

Peace

nature a power that can "serene his soul" and "harmonize his heart." Dyer finds peace and quiet in "the meads and mountain-heads." Mallet follows Thomson in thought and phrase when he represents that nature has power to "serene the soul." Akenside says that the spirit of nature lulls man's passions to a divine repose. Cooper says that a contemplation of the order and regularity in nature's life will induce a like harmonious action in the human heart, and that the fiercest passions of horror and revenge can be soothed by nature. Joseph Warton says that all nature conspires to sooth and harmonize the mind. William Whitehead speaks of the "philosophic calmness" that comes to man from nature. Beattie's hermit found in nature a power that could subdue the wildest passions and give "profound repose." Bruce found in nature "harmony of mind." Bowles felt a "soothing charm" that brought "solace to his heart" and "bore him on serene." So, too, was it with Cowper. Nature gave him heart-consoling joys, and brought peace and quiet into his life. This power of nature to sooth the mind of man and to modify his passions receives full expression also in Mrs. Radcliffe's romances.

Nature gives not only peace and rest to man. She gives him joy. The sense of ecstasy and rapture in this joy has already been indicated in the passages expressive

Joy of personal enthusiasm for nature. Sometimes it was a joy rising out of the delight of agreeable physical sensations, as when Lady Winchelsea felt in the odor of the jonquil a pleasure so keen that it was pain, or when Langhorne sank down oppressed by the boundless charms of field and wood, or such joy as Gray's convalescent knew when he went out again into nature. But here a more spiritual joy is referred to. It is rather the disturbing joy of elevated thoughts of which Wordsworth speaks. This uplift of soul in the presence of nature is felt by Parnell when he seeks to give expression to the great chorus of thanksgiving to God from all existences. Lady Winchelsea and John Langhorne felt it when nature gave them "thoughts too high to be express't." Akenside felt it, and in a truly Wordsworthian sense, when he said that in the presence of nature the intellect is charmed into a suspension of its graver cares, while love and joy alone possess the soul. Burns finds that nature exalts, enraptures him, making him conscious of an elevation of soul. And, finally, in Gilpin, we find, though awkwardly expressed, an exact statement of the enthusiastic calm, the visionary joy, with which Wordsworth looked on nature.

A third gift of nature is poetical inspiration, and that, too, in the sense in which Wordsworth believed that nature set him apart for poetry and assisted him in his develop-**Inspiration** ment. Akenside's apostrophe to the Wansbeck along whose banks he wandered in childhood, "led in silence by some powerful hand unseen," his assertion that these influences fixed the color of his life for every future year, his thought of nature's "tender discipline" when skies and streams and groves conspire to guide the predestined sons of Fancy, are strikingly Wordsworthian. Langhorne says that in his lonely youth "the woodland genius" came and touched him with the holy flame of poetry. To the Genius of Westmoreland he ascribes the sacred fire within his breast. The whole theme of Beattie's *Minstrel* is, as has been pointed out, the effect of nature on a poetically sensitive mind.

Nature also gives a wisdom such as books and schools cannot give. The earliest expression of this thought is in Pattison's comparison of the deep wisdom drawn **Wisdom** from nature and the superficial knowledge of the schools. Gay in the contest between the Shepherd who knew nature and the Philosopher who knew cities and books determined that nature without the schools can make men wise. Langhorne says that "fair Philosophy," like Poetry, must be sought for in nature. There is, however, no other eigtheenth century statement of this idea so complete as Cowper's eulogy of the wisdom of the heart that nature gives.

Nature is also considered as inspiring to morality and virtue. Gay, in a fable already quoted from, says that nature can make men "moral" and "good," if they will learn her lessons. Thomson meditates on nature because thence he hopes to learn lessons of morality. Mallet says that nature inspires the soul with "virtuous raptures" and prompts man to forsake sin-born vanities and low pursuits. Akenside's chief theme is

Incitements to virtue the power of nature to lead men from petty interests and hurried, sordid lives into a beneficent and ordered activity of the soul. Cooper ascribes to "every natural scene a moral power." John Langhorne says that the sweet sensations of nature, move the "springs of virtue's love," and have a "moral use." and that religion, fled from books, can be found in nature whence we first drew both our knowledge and our virtue. Beattie says that the charms of nature work "the soul's eternal health." They inspire love and gentleness. They incite to high living. and the man who neglects them can hardly hope to be forgiven. A pervading thought in Cowper's poems is his moral and spiritual indebtedness to nature.

Wordsworth not infrequently indicates his belief that the spirit of nature consciously blesses man. This idea is sometimes found in the transition poetry, as in Hamilton's *Contemplation*, and especially in Akenside and Cowper who represent nature as making the happiness of man "her dear and only aim."

So far we have discussed the knowledge of nature and the feeling towards it rather than its use in literature. That this knowledge was abundant and varied, that this feeling was

Literary use of nature enthusiastic and often deeply reverential, may, perhaps, pass without further question. But a different problem presents itself when we ask what literary use the eighteenth century poet made of nature. It must be conceded at the outset that many references to natural facts are not literary at all. In Mallet's *Excursion*, for instance, his journey through stellar spaces renders frequent mention of the sky and stars inevitable, but the references might as well be to macadamized roads. His purpose is merely to get from one point of vantage to another. Such brief, cold, unpicturesque use of details for purposes of transition are really non-literary. In any tabular statement of an author's work some discount must be made to allow for this mechanical use of nature, and in certain authors, as notably Mallet and Young, the discount is large. Another non-literary use of nature is in the catalogue or summary. John Scott gives the extreme example of this unorganized accumulation of details. The instinct of the artist is wanting. The poet does not even attempt to make nature a part of a well-fused literary product. He is encumbered by his material. He crowds his canvas. His full and realistic presentation is without artistic reservations. His record is prompted simply by interest in the separate facts. No literary purpose determines his selection or rejection of detail. A recognized theme, unity, proportion, are absent. Such summaries may be of the highest importance as showing the abundance and exactness of the author's knowledge of nature, and separate phrases may have real literary quality, but the passage as a whole is no more literary than an inventory.

When, however, a purpose is apparent in the use of nature, when there is discrimination under the dominance of a central idea, then, however crude and feeble the actual result, there is at least an attempt to use nature in a literary way.

This dominating purpose may be merely description for its own sake, an attempt to present aspects of nature in successive, isolated, artistically composed pictures, each complete in itself and having its parts organically related. Such description is entirely objective. Its aim is the reproduction of sights and sounds by which nature under given conditions appeals to the senses. When highly elaborated its obvious danger is that there will be, in spite of the most artistic management, a certain vagueness and heaviness of effect. There are, nevertheless, very beautiful examples of pure detailed description dissociated from any purpose except that of making a picture in words, in both Thomson and Cowper, and here and there less successful examples in other writers.

A more subtle use of nature is when the poet assembles his details in order to reproduce not a scene or an aspect of nature, but the typical impression they have made on his mind. Lady Winchelsea tells many facts about night, but her purpose is not the description of a single night; it is the reproduction of the loving delight and tender awe awakened in her own heart by many soft summer nights. The purpose of Parnell's descriptive details is the reproduction of the mood of spiritual content induced by certain scenes. Passages such as these are often more or less detailed summaries, but they have literary quality because the motif produces unity of effect.

Again, the facts and descriptions may be adduced in support of a theory, as in Young's *Night Thoughts*, Akenside's *Pleasures of the Imagination*, Shenstone's *Progress of. Taste*, Beattie's *Minstrel*, and Cowper's *Task*. Here. too, an organizing purpose is discernible, though there is the greatest possible difference in the various ways of using the material for the given purpose ; Young's facts for instance, being used in a cold, argumentative fashion, while Beattie's and Cowper's are suffused with emotion.

Another use of nature is based on the poet's perception of the analogies between external nature and human life or character. One outcome of this sense for analogies is in abundant similitudes, a literary use of nature common in all languages, at all periods. In the pseudo-classical poetry of England we have seen that the similitudes were conventional and superficial. In a period of intimate knowledge and love of the outer world there is stress on the truth and beauty of the picture from nature as well as on the human fact symbolized, and the analogy is subtly and sympathetically conceived. Wordsworth's

> "A violet by a mossy stone
> Half hidden from the eye"

is perfect in itself as a picture of nature, and it is exquisitely apt in describing Lucy. He discovered in nature that which in its inner significance was truly a counterpart of the human idea. With regard to the similitudes of the transition poetry I have noted two interesting facts. In the first place, in proportion to the whole use of nature the use of nature in similitudes is very much less in the transition than in the classical poetry. In the second place, in no other way of using nature was the changed conception of the outer world so slow to manifest itself. Stock similes persisted even in authors who, in other respects, gave clear evidence of the new spirit. It was apparently easier to be original and individual in a new realm, than to break away from the established conventions of an accepted literary form. As another outcome of the recognized correspondence between nature and life the facts of nature become, as it were, an allegory of human experience. From Dyer on there is a strain of pensive, gently didactic moralizing drawn from the poet's observation of nature. A river, however beautiful in itself because of its varying motion, its shifting colors, its varied banks, its progress to the sea, is transformed in the poet's mind into a symbol of the vicissitudes and the final goal of life. Of the more obvious analogies of this sort we find many examples, but of the highly imaginative use of nature whereby the external fact, however truly and beautifully perceived, seems hardly thought of except as a symbol of the hidden things of the spirit and of the life to come we find almost no examples outside of Blake.

The use of nature in connection with man's joys or sorrows may be lyrical or it may be dramatic in tone. Under the lyrical use of nature may be classed the numerous passages in which the poet dwells upon his youth and the early joy he had in forest stream and field. The homesick longing, the genuine human feeling, and the marks of local fidelity to fact make this use of nature usually excellent. It often takes the form of an apostrophe to some specific river or grove or hill. This autobiographic use of nature is well exemplified in Thomson, Akenside, Beattie, Langhorne, Mickle, Bruce, and Cowper. Again, the poet recounts with lyrical fervor his debt to nature. He gives thanks for content, joy, peace, serenity, or he implores nature to appease the longings of his sick heart, to restore his soul to health. In either case there is a mingling of human emotions and details from nature. Such passages may easily be feebly hysterical, but sometimes as in Dyer, Beattie, Akenside, Langhorne, and Cowper, they are marked by genuine beauty and pathos as well as by directness of vision. Perhaps the best examples of scenes thus indissolubly connected with phases of spiritual experience are Bowles's sonnets, and unquestionably the highest purely lyrical use of nature is in Burns's songs.

Nature is used dramatically when it is made the appropriate background or accompaniment of human life. This use of nature may be merely to intensify the reader's impression by certain effects of harmony or contrast. Night, for instance, is considered the appropriate setting for reflections on man's mortality, as in Young and Parnell. A certain sort of scenery becomes the conventionally fit background for romantic aspirations and dejections, as in all the sentimental melancholy poets. But oftener nature is not merely a background. It is mingled with the thought and action. This is true of most of the reflective, moralizing poetry, and is true in a more dramatic sense in such pastorals as Ramsay's and Gay's where it is impossible to think of the people and their doings apart from the nature about them. A similar dramatic use of nature is to be seen in Gray, in Collins, in Ossian, and, in a briefer form, in the Ballads. It is, however, in romantic fiction that this use of nature is most abundant during the eighteenth century. As background, as accompaniment, and further, even as a force contributing to the progress of the story by its determining influence on mood and character, external nature plays an important part. This background, indeed, sometimes becomes unduly important, almost usurping the place of the picture, as in Mrs. Radcliffe's romances.

Nature may, finally, be regarded not only as making a sensuous appeal to man, or as entering in some way into relationship with him, but as having an independent and separate existence. The poet who thus conceives of nature gives little detailed external description ; nor does he think of a scene in its human connotations, but he goes through facts and perceives the spirit of the scene, the essential qualities that make it what it is. Of such use of nature we find few eighteenth century examples. It demands not only Wordsworth's wise passiveness of mood, and clarity of vision, and depth of feeling, but likewise the power to speak the inevitable word.

The detailed study of a barren field in its most barren aspect would be inexcusably dull and dreary from any but the historical point of view. The moment that point of view is adopted interest begins. The study of literature as a growth, an evolution, gives a new significance to periods of transition. The pleasure of the biologist in the lower forms of life is paralleled by the delight of the student of literature in tracing out the first vague, ineffective attempts to express ideas that are afterwards regnant.

The final effect of the present study is one of surprise to find how completely the ideas of the early nineteenth century poetry of nature were represented in the germ in the eighteenth century. The whole impression is that before the work of such men as Wordsworth, Coleridge, and Scott there was a great stir of getting ready. The love of nature was awake in the hearts of men. Their eyes were open to her beauty. Their ears drank in her harmonies. Their spirits were conscious of· her higher gifts. Before Wordsworth most of his characteristic thoughts on nature had received fairly explicit statement.

We note also the vitality of the impulse toward nature as indicated by the many directions in which it pushed out and demanded expression. With little self-conscious direction, and independently of each other apparently, the various arts were irresistibly impelled to some sort of expression of the new interest in the external world. Nor can we ignore the fact that behind all forms of art expression there must have been the great impulsive force of a love of nature active in the hearts of the mute inglorious many.

When at the end of such a period of preparation the great poet comes, he is great by virtue of his power to penetrate beneath literary conventions and to give free, vigorous, adequate expression to the struggling, half-articulate thoughts and feelings of his own age. He is not an inexplicable, isolated phenomenon. He has his natural place in the development. The profound significance of the work that marks an epoch in thought is that it not only directs the future, but it sums up the past.

BIBLIOGRAPHICAL INDEX.

COLLECTIONS.

British Novelists, An Edition with Essays and Lives: Ed. Anne Letitia Barbauld. 50 vols. London, 1810.

British Poets, Less-Known: Ed. C. C. Clarke. 3 vols. Edinburgh, 1868.

British Poets, Works of the: Ed. Thomas Park. 42 vols. *Supplement*, 6 vols. London, 1805–8.

British Poets: Ed. Robert Anderson. 13 vols. Edinburgh, 1794.

Collection of Poems by Several Hands: Ed. R. Dodsley. 6 vols. London, 1755–1758. *Supplement:* Ed. Pearch. 4 vols. 1783.

Collection of Voyages and Travels in All Parts of the World: Ed. Pinkerton, John. 17 vols. London, 1809.

English Poets, Later: Ed. Robert Southey. 3 vols. London, 1807.

English Poets, The Works of: Ed. Dr. Samuel Johnson. 63 vols. London, 1779–1781.

English Poets from Chaucer to Cowper: Ed. Alexander Chalmers. 21 vols. London, 1810.

Fugitive Poets, Classical Arrangement of: Ed. John Bell. 8 vols. London, 1789.

TEXTS AND BOOKS OF REFERENCE.

Addison, Joseph : *Works.* 6 vols. Bohn Ed., London, 1892.

Akenside, Mark: *Poetical Works.* Ed. Dyce. London, 1885.

Amory, Thomas : *Life of John Buncle.* 3 vols. London, 1825.

Armstrong, John : *Poems.* Park's *British Poets*, Vol. 34.

Bage Robert: *Hemsprong.* Mrs. Barbauld's *British Novelists.*

Beattie, James : *Poetical Works.* Aldine Ed., London.

Beckford, William : *Vathek.*

Biese, Alfred : *Die Entwickelung des Naturgefühls im Mittelalter und der Neuzeit.* Leipzig, 1892.

Blackmore, Richard : *Poems.* Dr. Johnson's *English Poets*, Vol. 23.

Blair, Robert: *Poems.* Chalmers' *English Poets*, Vol. 15.

Blake, William: *Works.* Eds. Ellis and Yeats. 3 vols., London, 1893.

Blomfield, Reginald and Thomas, Inigo : *The Formal Garden.* London, 1892.

Blümner, Hugo : *Die Farbenbezeichnungen bei den Römischen Dichtern.* Berlin, 1895.

Boswell, James : *Life of Dr. Johnson.* Ed. Birkbeck Hill. 6 vols. Oxford, 1887.

Bowles, William Lisle: *Poetical Works.* Ed. C. C. Clarke. Edinburgh, 1868.

Boyse, Samuel: *Poems.* Chalmers' *English Poets,* Vol. 14.

Bramstan, James: *Poems.* Bell's *Fugitive Poets.* Vol. 3.

Brand, J.: *Brief Description of Orkney, Zetland,* etc. Pinkerton's *Collection.* Vol. 3.

Brooke, Henry: *The Fool of Quality.* 3 vols., New York. 1860.

Brooke, Mrs.: *History of Lady Julia Mandeville.* Mrs. Barbauld's *British Novelists. The History of Emily Montagu.* 4 vols., London, 1769.

Brooke, Stopford A. *Theology in the English Poets.* London, 1891.

Broome, William: *Poems.* Dr. Johnson's *English Poets,* Vol. 43.

Brown, Dr. John: *Poems.* Anderson's *British Poets,* Vol. 10. *Description of Keswick.* Bell's *Fugitive Poets.* Vol. 2, Notes.

Bruce, Michael: *Poems.* Anderson's *British Poets,* Vol. 11, Pt. 1.

Browne, Isaac Hankins: Bell's *Fugitive Poets.*

Bryan, Michael: *Dictionary of Painters and Engravers,* London, 1884.

Brydall, Robert: *Art in Scotland.* London, 1859.

Buckingham, Duke of: *Poems.* Dr. Johnson's *English Poets,* Vol. 25.

Burroughs, John: *Fresh Fields.* Boston, 1885.

Burnet, Thomas: *The Sacred Theory of the Earth.* 2 vols. London, 1759.

Burney, Francis: *Evelina.* London, 1892. *Cecilia.* 2 vols. London, 1890.

Burns, Robert: *Works.* Ed. William Scott Douglas. London, 1891.

Butler, Samuel: *Poems.* Dr. Johnson's *English Poets,* Vols. 6 and 7.

Cawthorne, James: *Poems.* Bell's *Fugitive Poets,* Vol. 3.

Chambers, Sir William: *Dissertation on Oriental Gardens.* London, 1744.

Champlin and Perkins: *Cyclopedia of Painters and Painting.* New York, 1892.

Chapman, George: *Homer's Iliad and Odyssey.* Ed. R. H. Shepherd. London, 1885.

Chaucer, Geoffrey: *Poetical Works.* 6 vols. Aldine Ed., London, 1883.

Collins, William: *Poetical Works.* Ed. M. M. Thomas. Aldine Ed., London.

Congreve, William: *Poems.* Dr. Johnson's *English Poets,* Vol. 29.

Cooper, J. G.: *Poems.* Chalmers' *English Poets.,* Vol. 15.

Coventry, Francis: *Poems.* Dodsley's *Collection,* Vol. 4. *Pompey the Little.* Mrs. Barbauld's *British Novelists,* Vol. 23.

Cowley, Abraham: *Poems.* Dr. Johnson's *English Poets,* Vols. 1 and 2.

Cowper, William: *Poetical Works.* Ed. William Benham. New York, 1889.

Crabbe, George: *Poetical Works.* 8 vols. London, 1851.

Croxall, Samuel: *Poems.* Southey's *Later English Poets,* Vol. 2.

Cunningham, Allen: *British Painters.* London, 1879.

Dalton, Dr. John: *Poems.* Bell's *Fugitive Poems,* Vol. 2.

Defoe, Daniel: *The Life and Strange, Surprising Adventures of Robinson Crusoe.* Ed. G. A. Aitken, London, 1895.

Denham, John: *Poems.* Dr. Johnson's *English Poets,* Vol. 9.

Dodsley, Robert: *Poems.* Chalmers' *English Poets,* Vol. 15.

Downing, A. J.: *Landscape Gardening and Rural Architecture.* New York, 1860.

Dryden, John: *Works.* 9 vols. Eds. Scott and Saintsbury. Edinburgh, 1882.

Duck, Stephen: *Poems.* Southey's *Later English Poets*, Vol. 2.

Dyer, John: *Poems.* Dr. Johnson's *English Poets*, Vol. 53.

Etherege, Sir George: *Plays and Poems.* London, 1888.

Evelyn, John: *The Diary of John Evelyn from 1641 to 1705-6.* Ed. William Bray. London, 1890.

Falconer, William: *Poetical Works.* Aldine ed., London, 1882.

Famous Parks and Gardens of the World. London, 1880.

Fenton, Elijah: *Poems.* Chalmers' *English Poets*, Vol. 10.

Fielding, Henry: *Works.* 10 vols. Ed. Leslie Stephen. London, 1882.

Fielding, Sarah: *The Adventures of David Simple.* 2 vols. London, 1741.

Fischer, Ch. A.: *Drei Studien zur Englischen Literaturgeschichte.* Gotha, 1892.

Garth, Sir Samuel: *Poems.* Dr. Johnson's *English Poets*, Vol. 20.

Gay, John: *Poems.* Dr. Johnson's *English Poets*, Vols. 41 and 42.

Gilpin, William: *Essays on Picturesque Beauty.* London, 1808.

Gosse, Edmund: *Seventeenth Century Studies.* London, 1885. *From Shakespeare to Pope.* New York, 1885. *A History of Eighteenth Century Literature.* New York, 1891.

Gray, Thomas: *Works.* Ed. Edmund Gosse. 4 vols. New York, 1890.

Graeme, James: *Poems.* Anderson's *British Poets*, Vol 11, Part 1.

Grainger, James: *Poems.* Chalmers' *English Poets*, Vol. 14.

Green, Matthew Paris: Chalmers' *English Poets*, Vol. 15.

Halifax, Earl of: *Poems.* Dr. Johnson's *English Poets*, Vol. 12.

Hamilton, Rev. Wm.: *Letters from Antrim.* Pinkerton's Collection, Vol. 3.

Hassel, J.: *Tour to the Isle of Wight.* Pinkerton's *Collection*, Vol. 2.

Hawkesworth, John: *Almoran and Hamet.* Mrs. Barbauld's *British Novelists.*

Hill, Aaron: *Poems.* Anderson's *British Poets*, Vol. 8.

Howell, James: *Epistolæ Ho-Elianæ.* London, 1737.

Hughes, John: *Poems.* Dr. Johnson's *English Poets*, Vol. 22.

Humboldt, Alexander Von: *Kosmos.* 4 vols. Stuttgart, 1890.

Hutchinson, W.: *An Excursion to the Lakes in Westmoreland and Cumberland.* London, 1776.

Inchbald, Mrs.: *A Simple Story.* Mrs. Barbauld's *British Novelists.*

Jago, Richard: *Poems.* Anderson's *British Poets*, Vol. 11.

Jencks, J. W.: *Rural Poetry.* Boston, 1856.

Jenyns, Soame: *Poems.* Bell's *Fugitive Poets*, Vol. 1.

Johnson, Samuel: *Works.* 9 vols. Oxford English Classics, 1825.

King, William: *Poems.* Dr. Johnson's *English Poets*, Vol. 20.

Langhorne, John: *Poems. British Poets*, Vol. 11.

Laprade, Victor de: *La Sentiment de la Nature chez les Modernes.* Paris, 1870.

Lecky, W. E. H.: *History of England in the Eighteenth Century.* 8 vols. New York, 1882.

Lee, Vernon: *Euphorion.* Boston, 1885.

Lennox, Mrs.: *The Female Quixote*. Mrs. Barbauld's *British Novelists*.
Logan, John: *British Poets*, Vol. 11.
Loudon, J. C.: *Encyclopædia of Gardening*. London, 1871.
Lyttleton, Lord: *Poems*. Dr. Johnson's *English Poets*, Vol. 56.
Mackenzie, Henry: *The Man of Feeling. Julia de Roubiqué*. Mrs. Barbauld's *British Novelists*.
Macpherson, James: *Poems of Ossian*. Ed. Dr. Blair. Tauchnitz Ed. Leipzig, 1847.
McLaughlin, Edward T.: *Studies in Mediæval Life and Literature*. New York, 1894.
Mallet, David: *Poems*. Dr. Johnson's *English Poets*, Vol. 53.
Marriott, Mr.: *Poems*. Dodsley's *Supplement*, Vol. 4.
Martin, Mr.: *Description of the Western Islands of Scotland*. Pinkerton's *Collection*, Vol. 3.
Marvell, Andrew: *Works*. 4 vols. Ed. Grosart. Fuller Worthies' Library, 1875.
Mason, William: *Poems*. London, 1764. *The English Garden*. Jencks's *Rural Poetry*.
Mendez, Moses: *The Seasons*. Bell's *Fugitive Poets*, Vol 6.
Mickle, Wm. J.: *Poems*. Park's *British Poets*, Vol. 34.
Miller, Hugh: *Impressions of England and its People*. London, 1847.
Milton, John: *Poetical Works*. 3 vols. Ed. Masson. New York, 1894.
Moore, Dr.: *Zeluco*. Mrs. Barbauld's *British Novelists*.
Montagu, Lady Mary Wortley: *Letters and Works*. 2 vols. London, 1887.
Paltock, Robert: *The Life and Adventures of Peter Wilkins*. 2 vols. London, 1884.
Parnell, Thomas: *Poetical Works*, London, 1890.
Pattison, William: *Poems*. Anderson's *British Poets*.
Pennant, Thomas: *Tours in Scotland*. Pinkerton's *Collection*, Vol. 3.
Pennecuik, Alexander: *Works in Prose and Verse*. Leith, 1815.
Percy, Bishop: *Reliques of Ancient English Poetry*. 3 vols. Ed. H. B. Wheatley, London, 1891.
Perry, T. S.: *English Literature in the Eighteenth Century*. New York, 1883.
Petrarca, Francesco: *Lettere Famigliari*. 5 vols. Florence, 1863.
Phelps, W. L.: *The Beginnings of the English Romantic Movement*. Boston, 1893.
Philips, Ambrose: Dr. Johnson's *English Poets*, Vol. 14.
Philips, John: Dr. Johnson's *English Poets*, Vol. 21.
Pitt, Christopher: *Poems*. Dr. Johnson's *English Poets*, Vol. 43.
Pope, Alexander: *Works*. 10 vols. Eds. Edwin and Courthope. London 1671.
Potter, R.: *Poems*. Bell's *Fugitive Poets*, vol. 6.
Price, Sir Uvedale: *An Essay on the Picturesque*. London, 1794.
Prior, Matthew: Dr. Johnson's *English Poets*, Vols. 30, 31.

Radcliffe, Mrs.: *Romance of a Forest*. 3 vols. London, 1803. *Mysteries of Udolpho*. 4 vols. London, 1803.

Ramsay, Allan: *Poems*. 2 vols. Paisley, 1877.

Redgrave, Gilbert: *Water-color Painting in England*. New York, 1892.

Reeve, Cora: *Old English Baron*. Mrs. Barbauld's *British Novelists*, Vol. 21.

Repton, Humphrey: *Landscape Gardening and Landscape Architecture*. Ed. J. C. Loudon. London, 1840.

Richardson, Samuel: *Works*. Ed. Leslie Stephen. 12 vols. London, 1883.

Robertson, David: *Tour Through the Isle of Man*. Pinkerton's *Collection*, Vol. 2.

Roscommon, Earl of: *Poems*. Dr. Johnson's *English Poets*, Vol. 10.

Rowe, Nicholas: *Poems*. Dr. Johnson's *English Poets*, Vol. 26.

Ruskin, John: *Modern Painters*, 2 vols. Bantwood Ed., London, 1891.

Savage, Richard: Dr. Johnson's *English Poets*, Vol. 45.

Scott, John: *Poems*. Anderson's *British Poets*, Vol. 11, Part 2.

Shadwell, Thomas: *Dramatic Works*. 2 vols. London, 1820.

Shaw, Rev. Mr.: *Tour to the West of England*. Pinkerton's *Collection*, Vol. 2.

Shairp, J. C.: *On the Poetic Interpretation of Nature*. Boston, 1890.

Shenstone, William: *Poems*. Dr. Johnson's *English Poets*, Vol. 52. *Unconnected Thoughts on Landscape Gardening* in *Works*. 3 vols. London, 1764–69.

Siret, Adolph: *Dictionnaire Historique des Peintres*. Bruxelles, 1848.

Smart, Christopher: *Poems*. Chalmers' *English Poets*, Vol. 16. *Song to David*. Clarke's *Less Known British Poets*, Vol. 3.

Smith, Mrs. Charlotte: *The Old Manor House*.

Smollett, Tobias: *Works*, 6 vols. London, 1890.

Somerville, William: *Poems*. Dr. Johnson's *English Poets*, Vol. 47.

Spooner, Shearjashub: *Dictionary of Painters*. New York, 1853.

Spratt, Thomas: *Poems*. Dr. Johnson's *English Poets*, Vol. 9.

Stephen, Leslie: *English Thought in the Eighteenth Century*. 2 vols. London, 1887.

Stepney, George: *Poems*. Dr. Johnson's *English Poets*.

Sterne, Laurence: *Works*. Ed. James P. Browne. 2 vols. London, 1885.

Symonds, J. A.: *Essays Speculative and Suggestive*. London, 1893.

Swift, Jonathan: *Poems*. Dr. Johnson's *English Poets*, Vols. 39 and 40.

Taine, H. A.: *Voyage en Italie*. Paris, 1893.

Temple, Sir William: *Works*. 2 vols. Ed. Jonathan Swift. London, 1831.

Thompson, William: *Poems*. Anderson's *British Poets*, Vol. 10.

Thomson, James: *Poetical Works*. 2 vols. Aldine ed. London, 1867.

Tickell, Thomas: *Poems*. Dr. Johnson's *English Poets*, Vol. 26.

Veitch, John: *The Feeling for Nature in Scottish Poetry*. 2 vols. Edinburgh, 1887.

Waller, Edmund: *Poems*. Dr. Johnson's *English Poets*, Vol. 8.

Walpole, Horace: *Works*. 5 vols. London, 1789.

Warton, Joseph: *Poems.* Clarke's *Less Known British Poets*, Vol. 3. Dodsley's *Collection*, Vol. 3. *An Essay on the Genius and Writings of Pope.* 2 vols. London, 1806.

Warton, Thomas: *Poems.* Anderson's *British Poets*, Vol. 11, Part 2.

Watts, Isaac: *Poems.* Dr. Johnson's *English Poets*, Vol. 46.

Whateley, Thomas: *Observations on Modern Gardening.* London, 1798.

Whitehead, William: Anderson's *British Poets*, Vol. 11, Part. 2.

Winchelsea, Lady (Anne Finch): *Miscellany Poems on Several Occasions. Written by a Lady.* 1713.

Wordsworth, William: *Poetical Works.* New York, 1889.

Yalden, Thomas: *Poems.* Dr. Johnson's *English Poets*, Vol. 10.

Young, Arthur: *Tour in Ireland.* Pinkerton's *Collection*, Vol. 3. *Tour through Southern Counties.* London, 1772. *Tour in Ireland*, 2 vols. London, 1780. *A Farmer's Tour.* 4 vols. London, 1771.

Young, Edward: *Poems.* Dr. Johnson's *English Poets*, Vols. 50, 51, 52.

GENERAL INDEX.